Communicative Styles
of Japanese and Americans

Communicative Styles
of Japanese and Americans
Images and Realities

Dean C. Barnlund
San Francisco State University

Wadsworth Publishing Company
Belmont, California
A Division of Wadsworth, Inc.

COMMUNICATIONS EDITOR: Kristine M. Clerkin
EDITORIAL ASSISTANT: Melissa Harris
PRODUCTION EDITOR: Gary Mcdonald
PRINT BUYER: Karen Hunt
DESIGNER: MaryEllen Podgorski
COPY EDITOR: Pat Tompkins
COMPOSITOR: Better Graphics, Inc.
COVER: MaryEllen Podgorski

Printed in the United States of America   19

1 2 3 4 5 6 7 8 9 10---92 91 90 89 88

LIBRARY OF CONGRESS CATALOGING-IN-PUBLICATION DATA

Barnlund, Dean C.
    Communicative styles of Japanese and Americans : images and realities /
Dean C. Barnlund.
        p.   cm.
    Bibliography: p.
    Includes index.
    ISBN 0-534-09372-8
    1. Intercultural communication. 2. Communication—Social aspects—
United States. 3. Communication—Social aspects—Japan. 4. Interpersonal
relations.   I. Title.
HM258.B365 1989
303.4'82—dc 19
                                                              88-3954
                                                                CIP

O brave new world,
That has such people in't!

SHAKESPEARE, *THE TEMPEST*

Contents

Prologue   xi

CHAPTER 1   **Images of the Twentieth Century**   1

Twentieth-Century Images: Literature   2
Twentieth-Century Images: The Fine Arts   6
Twentieth-Century Images: The Popular Arts   8
Twentieth-Century Images: Philosophy   9
Twentieth-Century Images: Behavioral Sciences   11
Images or Realities?   12
Are Human Relations at a Point of Crisis?   14

CHAPTER 2   **The Changing Context
of Communication**   15

The Silent Revolution   16
The First Cities   17
The New Supercities: Product of the
Population Explosion   18
The Social Consequences of Urbanization   20

The Social Ordering of Urban Life   22
The New Social Reality   27
Cultures: The Mediating Factor   31
Personal Relations: Japan and the United States   32
From Conjecture to Fact   33

CHAPTER 3   **Exploring Social Space:
Japan and the United States**   35

Similar Features of Two Societies   35
Cultural Profile: The United States   37
Cultural Profile: Japan   38
Interpersonal Profiles: Japan and the United States   39
The Parameters of Inquiry   44
The Instrument: Dimensions of
Interpersonal Relations   46
The Sample: Japanese and Americans   48
The Qualitative-Quantitative Dilemma:
A Final Note   50

CHAPTER 4   **A World of Strangers**   53

Urban Indifference   55
Engagements with Strangers   56
Strangership: The Cultural Variable   62
Japanese and American Profiles   68
Strangership: The First Stage of Intimacy   70

CHAPTER 5   **Profiles of Intimacy**   73

Forms of Attachment   74
The Acquaintance Inventory   76
Parameters of Partners   77
Choosing Companions: Seven Key Characteristics   79
Highlights of the Findings   85
The Interact Scale   86
Encounters with Close Companions: Three Profiles   92
Permutations   93

CHAPTER 6   **Intimacy: Its Verbal Dimension**   97

Communicating Through Words   98
Symbol and Self   101
Verbal Disclosure: Steps Toward Intimacy   104
Design of the Verbal Communication Scale   109
What We Talk About: Japanese and Americans   110
Cultural Convergence and Divergence   118

CHAPTER 7   **Intimacy: Its Nonverbal Dimensions**   121

Limits of Language   122
The Nonverbal Code   123
Some Preliminary Considerations of
Nonverbal Communication   125
Physical Style of Communicating in Japan   127
Physical Style of Communicating in the
United States   130
Cultural Contradictions   131
Design of the Physical Communication Scale   132
The Silent Languages: Overall Cultural Profiles   134
Extrapolation: What the Findings Suggest   143

CHAPTER 8   **Commitment, Conflict, Integration**   147

Ties That Bind: Interpersonal Commitment   147
Culture and Commitment: Japan and the
United States   150
The Accommodation Scale   151
Intimacy: The Challenge of Differences   153
The Difference Scale   158
The Consequences of Intimacy: Ego Incorporation   160
The Affiliation Scale   164
Ego Boundaries: Japanese and American   166
Reconsidering Cultural Images   167

CHAPTER 9   **The Vital Connection:**
             Images and Realities 169

             The Emerging Psychic Challenge   171
             The Interpersonal Challenge   172
             Communication: Its Personal Function   174
             Communication: Its Social Function   175
             Communication: Its Cultural Function   175
             The Comprehensive Investigation of Images
             and Realities   176
             Images and Realities: The Cultural Contexts   179
             Contemporary Social Life: General Symptoms
             of Malaise   184
             Culture-Specific Symptoms of Inadequacy   185
             Two Caveats   188
             The Intercultural Encounter   189
             One Culture or Many?   192
             A Summing Up   193

APPENDIX   **For the Specialist**   197

             References   200

             Index   212

Prologue

As we approach the close of the twentieth century John Donne's prophetic observation—"No man is an island, complete unto himself"—returns to haunt us. It is a pronouncement that gathers force with each passing century, a warning more relevant to our time than to his.

In spite of an expanding population, the increased proximity of people, and multiplication of opportunities for human contact, never has loneliness seemed so widespread or so loudly publicized. Despite all efforts to realize a more humane community by reducing barriers of race and class, wealth and education, such changes have only made us painfully aware of the fragile nature of our ties to other people. Rarely have human relationships seemed so tenuous and transitory as they are portrayed in the closing years of the twentieth century.

Yet personal relations, we are told, are indispensable to health and happiness. Our survival, spiritually and physically, demands that we remain in touch with others. "The most holy bond of society," writes Robert Brain, "is friendship."[1] Along with the families we are thrust into, the most important ties that nurture the individual are the voluntary alliances known as friendships.

Science and philosophy combine to stress the need for human companionship and to expose the sources of this need. We are born into and inhabit a world devoid of meaning, a world that is neutral in all its particulars. As Alfred North Whitehead once noted, "Nature is a dull affair, soundless, scentless, colorless, merely the hurrying of material, endlessly, meaninglessly."[2] Objects and events must be construed in some way in order to act upon them. Meanings arise, in short, from the necessity of acting, but they are situated in the mind of every interpreter, not in the world.

Each of us occupies the center of his or her own experiential world. Each is the creator of that world, its sole inhabitant, and the victim of whatever pleasures or pains it provides. As Gregory Stone and Harvey Faberman emphasize, "the universe presents itself as an occasion for man's creative capacities. *It is there.* It awaits his investiture of identity, meaning, value, sentiments, and rules. It is a convertible commodity—a taken, not a given; a concept, not a dictum."[3] And if all meanings are private and personal, they are also incomplete and unreliable; every interpreter is captive of a particular history and particular motive that shape the meanings events are given.

To recognize the neutrality of the world, and the role each of us plays in attributing meaning *to* events, is to grasp a little appreciated, but essential, truth about communication. It helps to explain the diversity of opinions as each person creates a meaning consistent with their past experience and current motives. But it only accounts for part of the process of communication. To be the authors of our meanings, isolated from every other influence, would condemn us to an autistic existence, not merely islands of meaning in Donne's sense, but islands separated by intervening, unnavigable seas. And such is not the case.

Cultures and Communication

The human community arises from construction of a common reality. Some agency must arise that is capable of transforming private meanings into public meanings so they may become known to others. Culture is the agency and symbols the instrument by which each new generation acquires the capacity to bridge the distance that separates one life from another. Cultures promote the sharing of meanings through creating a broad repertoire of symbolic forms. The most obvious of these is language. Certain combinations of sounds or marks on paper acquire the capacity to *re*-present the thoughts and feelings of their users. The words that make up such languages are relatively few in number and imprecise in meaning; one person can remember only a few thousand words, which must accommodate an infinity of human experiences.

In addition, there are the "languages" of mathematics, music, dance, gardens, sculpture. The multiplicity of such codes in all cultures attests to their unique suitability for giving public form to different types of private thoughts and feelings.

The spoken languages of most cultures are endowed with almost sacred power. Yet people seldom sense the full potential of any language simply by cataloging its words or deciphering its grammar. Meanings are articulated not only by the choice of words but also by their manner of utterance, through changes in stress or inflection, through accompanying gestures, facial expression, or glances. Confusion often results, for example, when foreigners phrase their thoughts correctly but fail to employ the appropriate posture or facial cues. And people often share a meaning without using words at all; an

arched eyebrow, a prolonged stare, and a quiet silence may bind them together.

Far less appreciated and understood are two broader cultural codes that promote commonality of meaning. The first might be called the "interactional grammar" of a culture. It consists of the norms that govern the structure of a conversation: how to initiate conversation, what topics to discuss or avoid, how to shift from one type of message to another, how to terminate a conversation. Human encounters rarely involve a single communicative aim such as complimenting someone or apologizing but proceed through a sequence of exchanges as the aims of the communicants change. The number of such strategies is extensive: It includes how people manage introductions, give compliments, make requests, manage conflicts, offer criticism, make decisions. Each of these strategies has a unique way of opening, a unifying theme and structure, and a conventional way of ending. When people do not agree on these interactional rules, confusion or embarrassment results. While the verbal and nonverbal symbols determine the content of a message, the interactional code determines the sequencing of such messages within extended conversations. Interactional codes are as culture bound as language is, contributing to the sharing of meanings within a culture and to misinterpretation of meanings and motives between cultures.

In addition, there is a "grammar of occasions." Cultures endow certain activities with distinctive meanings, differentiating among parties, funerals, concerts, festivals, and demonstrations. These still broader cultural norms help to define the acts that are appropriate to certain settings and in so doing influence the meanings that evolve in such settings. How people define a social activity—such as shopping, playing, worshipping, fighting—has a profound effect on what people will say and do, and how they will regard and interpret the acts of others. The study of culture in general, and of communication in particular, is concerned with this hierarchy of codes by which people form and share meanings among members of societies.

In short, to make thoughts and feelings intelligible to other people, we must use and respect the same rules for articulating and interpreting meanings. Human societies create a hierarchy of codes for regulating human interaction: Meanings must be cast into words, words arranged into messages, messages positioned in proper sequence, and such sequences situated within appropriate settings. Although such codes require some conformity from their users—whether jazz musicians, ballet dancers, or baseball teams—they greatly expand the collaborative possibilities of human beings. These shared cultural codes give the people of any community a sense of their common identity and a means of relating to one another.

For these reasons we share the view that "culture is communication."[4] In the sounds and syntax of language, the norms of social interaction, and the hierarchy of occasions one confronts a culture in its most tangible form. What the members of a culture share above all else is a way of conducting their affairs, a commitment to similar ways of managing meanings. Mastery of these communicative norms equips each new generation with a way of forming friendships, validating their experience, and contributing to the life of their times. *It is through communication that we acquire a culture; it is in our manner of communicating that we display our cultural uniqueness.*

Yet these linguistic, interactional, and contextual norms are seldom taught formally: They tend to be absorbed unconsciously as the infant matures surrounded by parents, friends, and teachers who model appropriate behavior. Consequently, the members of any society are rarely able to explain the norms governing their conversations with other people; they simply do "what comes naturally" without much awareness of the sources of their behavior. It is for this reason that members of one culture find communicating with members of an alien culture difficult: What one does spontaneously, without thinking, at home, one must be constantly and consciously aware of away from home. Encounters become fraught with hazard when people do not recognize, or cannot employ, the same communicative norms as their associates.

Although intercultural encounters are, basically, interpersonal encounters, there is a difference. When two people of contrasting cultural backgrounds meet they are likely not only to attach different meanings to the same event (because they have acquired unique ways of interpreting the world in their own culture), but also express such meanings in distinctive ways as well (because they obey unique interactional norms). Thus a substantive difference is compounded because they do not share the same rules for addressing such differences. Until they can adapt to differences in their communicative styles there is no way to comprehend or deal with their substantive differences. If two people who speak different languages cannot share meanings, it is equally true that people who observe different interactional rules also are unlikely to share such meanings. What takes place is less a case of *not* understanding (which might not prevent eventual agreement) than of *mis*understanding (which by alienating the two people may exacerbate their differences).

Deciphering Cultural Codes

One of the complications of a shrinking world lies precisely at this point: While we have extensive information about many languages of the world, we are largely ignorant of the interactional norms that might help in communicating across cultural borders. We know almost nothing about how people of various cultures become acquainted. We do not know what behaviors attract or alienate people in forming friendships. Through what stages, in what ways, at what rate do people move from being strangers to being friends? What experiences intensify or terminate such relationships? How, if at all, are people changed by their involvement with one another? These are only a few of the questions to consider regarding personal relationships within cultures.

Even the words used to discuss such matters pose a semantic challange. "Liking" and "disliking," "loving" and "hating," are far from clear. We have only the vaguest notion of what it is to call someone an "acquaintance," "friend," or "intimate." Claims that we "know" what we mean have a hollow ring when we find we cannot specify what we know. And if friendships puzzle the social scientist, they are no less puzzling, and no less significant, for the layperson. It is through our ties with other people that we achieve our humanity and fulfill it; the depth, nature, and quality of our personal relationships are of importance not only to specialists but also to every member of the human race.

Just how might one explore the norms that regulate communication in a given culture? Perhaps the most obvious approach is to let the culture speak for itself. Why not simply ask people to explain their rules of behavior? This is not as easy or as satisfactory as it sounds. Unless people have experienced other cultures they have no basis for comparative judgment. Americans who have never been abroad sometimes describe the United States as a "formal," "cooperative," and "status-conscious" society. After being exposed to other cultures they completely reject the same descriptions. Sometimes one needs to be outside a system to see it clearly.

In addition, natives of a culture are rarely able to account for their own acts. The cultural unconscious—like the personal unconscious—is just that: unconscious. It is enough to know how to act properly within one's own culture; why such acts are necessary or desirable is not at all obvious, perhaps least to the actors themselves.

But the greatest difficulty lies in distinguishing collective myths from collective truths. Popular explanations of Japanese and American behavior are often unreliable: Some are clichés, repeated so often they are finally believed; some constitute the abstract ideals of a given society but are claimed more than they are realized in daily life; still others may offer penetrating glimpses of the cultural ethos. But, in the absence of accurate data, it is difficult to know whether one is dealing with a cultural myth, idealization, or valid insight.

A second way of understanding a culture is through exposure to the comments of sophisticated and careful observers. The cultural profiles of Alexis de Tocqueville (on the United States), Octavio Paz (on Mexico), or Doi Takeo (on Japan) have been immensely provocative. Through specialized training such critics have acquired a unique sensibility to facets of social behavior. Their background equips them with an informed intelligence for interpreting what they observe. But their intuitions, like all intuitions, are born of a singular subjective experience and subject to that limitation. Still, the attention they receive is fully deserved, and their insights offer provocative hypotheses concerning the dynamics of the cultures they have observed.

A third way to approach culture, and the one to be followed here, is to undertake a careful *description* of how people relate to one another in search of the norms that regulate social acts in Japan and the United States. Three features distinguish this approach: It is focused, it is empirical, it is systematic. The aim is to create an agenda for inquiry, design instruments for reporting how people behave with their associates, and identify similarities and differences in behavior in the two cultures.

The pages that follow explore the interpersonal worlds of Japanese and Americans. What is sought, beyond the facts, is the pattern that connects, that links one behavior with another. The approach is unique: It employs neither the psychic focus of the psychologist nor the institutional focus of the sociologist, but looks instead at the social norms that operate when Japanese and Americans communicate with strangers, acquaintances, friends, and intimates.

There is a paucity of just such data. Even in the West, where there is great interest in the factors that govern the choice of friends and spouses, the emphasis has been on experimental manipulation of one or two variables—proximity of residence, physical attractiveness, personal traits, beliefs and values—rather than on describing how companions communicate in real life.

But what behavioral data should be sought? The possibilities are staggering. One might study people at work or play, neighbors or colleagues, in public or private settings, intimate or distant relationships. Some narrowing of the field is essential. Too wide a scope of inquiry sacrifices depth; too narrowing an inquiry may fail to see the pattern that gives meaning to the details. Here we decided to sample Japanese and American behavior across a spectrum of social encounters involving strangers, acquaintances, friends, and intimates. To this end we asked a large number of Japanese and Americans to describe in detail their actual behavior with the people who made up their circle of companions: who they knew, where they met, what activities they shared, what they talked about, what commitments they made, what impact these relationships had upon them.

Before you examine our findings, two caveats are in order. Remember that culture has no objective existence. It is no more than a metaphor, a fiction inferred from consistency in the daily acts of individuals. It is too easy to reify this concept. Cultures are not artifacts but explanatory generalizations based on the way people make their living, compete or collaborate with one another. Consistency in behavior leads to postulating the existence of a culture to account for the similarity in Japanese or French or American behavior.

Similarly, personalities do not have an objective existence. The human personality also is a fiction, an explanatory metaphor inferred from acts over time. What differentiates one person from another—motives, needs, interests—is never directly observable but is derived from consistencies in their actions from one setting to another. Although it is convenient to talk about people as if they *had* a personality or *had* a culture, neither is tangible; they are constructs rather than concretes. Their value lies in the number and importance of the behaviors they explain or predict.

The broad contours of this comparative study are suggested here; the details will unfold in the pages ahead. We look first at the existing images of communication in the twentieth century. Since human relationships do not mature in a vacuum but are shaped powerfully by the environment in which they arise, we next examine the vast changes in the material conditions of life in the twentieth century. Critics maintain that industrialization, urbanization, and bureaucratization have undermined or invalidated traditional forms of companionship, forcing people into dehumanizing ways of relating. Yet these conditions seem to have been assimilated in different ways in Japan and the United States; each culture may throw light on the alternate style of the other. The character of these emerging patterns of human relations is examined through over one million responses to the Barnlund-Campbell Dimensions of Interpersonal Relations inventory in both countries.

These questionnaires, administered to nearly a thousand Japanese and Americans, included eight scales covering a wide span of communicative behavior with the people who make up the circles of acquaintances of these respondents. They reflect on the frequency of social encounters, the content of conversation, the character of physical contact, how space and time are managed, the nature and depth of commitment, ways of accommodating differences, and the impact of involvement on the personalities involved. The relative influence of cultural and sexual identifications is probed. Thus the study attempts both an extensive and intensive look at the communicative styles of members of these two cultures; it affords an opportunity to compare cultural myths and cultural realities in Japan and the United States, and to speculate on their consequences for the individual and society.

Why these two cultures? There are several reasons. Each is a prominent and powerful member of the world community and will continue to be so for decades to come; any improved understanding of their cultural dynamics may provide some glimpse of the future. A more compelling reason is that Japan and the United States each seem to have adapted to the challenges of the modern age in contrasting ways; both have much to offer and much to learn from the other. Further, their cultural distinctiveness is most apparent in their communicative styles. Finally, our respect for both cultures, along with the presence of talented colleagues in both countries, made such a study feasible and appealing.

For anyone contemplating cross-cultural research there should be a flashing light that reads "Dangerous Intersection Ahead!" Cultures are elusive and complex objects of inquiry; they must be handled with care. The manifestations of culture are everywhere, yet this multiplicity of evidence may overwhelm the observer. One must identify certain particulars to study them, yet isolating them may divorce them from the contexts that give them meaning. And even the most prominent features of a society may change as they are being interpreted.

If cultures are awkward phenomena to study, the methodological challenges of cross-cultural study are even more complicated. Which features are to be compared? What may be significant in one country may be trivial in another. There is a major problem in constructing instruments that are sufficiently comprehensive and sufficiently sensitive to cover behavior in both societies. Not only must instruments possess linguistic equivalence—through forward and backward translation—but they must be experientially equivalent as well.

The phrase "forward and backward translation" describes a procedure for making instruments used in two or more cultures linguistically equivalent. After the instrument has been constructed in one language, a copy is given to a bilingual specialist(s) to translate into the second language (forward translation). This second version is then given to another bilingual specialist(s) who independently translates the instrument into the first language (backward translation). The two copies of the instrument are then compared. Where they are an exact copy of each other, it is assumed they are linguistically similar; where they are not, the researchers modify the original instrument until the two versions produce an equivalent test form [often checked by a third bilingual specialist(s)].

While this procedure will assure that the forms used in the two cultures are linguistically alike, there is another form of equivalence that is often more critical. We would refer to this as experiential equivalence. It is not enough that the two forms say the same things or ask equivalent questions with respect to the terms used, but they must be comparable experiences within the two cultures. If people in one culture travel by plane and in the other by train, then finding equivalent terms in both languages is not enough. The experiences referred to in the instrument may have to be adapted to each culture, and that may mean that some items deliberately differ in the two forms used but they do so in the interests of comparability of the life experiences.

Japanese and American Associates

As one might imagine, all of this requires extended sacrifices of time and money. This effort is no exception: It has taken a decade to complete and has involved dozens of colleagues and hundreds of respondents in both countries. Last, there is the necessity of interpreting the results and sharing them with the public. It seems important that behavioral scientists resist the temptation to publish their findings in an esoteric jargon to a minuscule community of specialists; any understanding of what stifles or fosters our humanity rightly belongs to all who might benefit from it. Here we address that wider audience, which requires some adjustment in format and style.[5]

When the subject is human behavior, researcher and reader share a unique relationship. When physicists speak, no ordinary person challenges their conclusions for few know enough to raise objection. This is not the case with social life.[6] As George Homans reminds us, "Nothing is more familiar to men than their ordinary, everyday social behavior; and should a sociologist make any generalization about it, he runs the risk that his readers will find him wrong at the first word and cut him off without a hearing."[7] We are all experts, of sorts, on human relationships: We all have them, have all succeeded in them, have all failed in them.

Yet the socially responsible social scientist would not want it any other way. When the experience of readers confirms or challenges the findings of research, readers ought to talk back. Specialist and nonspecialist alike benefit from such a dialogue: the specialist from sharpening his or her conclusions about human nature, the nonspecialist from the wider perspective that research provides. To obtain a clearer view of our own behavior is the first emancipating step toward choosing rather than blindly following norms that may promote or limit a fuller realization of our humanity.

Difficult and complicated as cross-cultural research may be, the argument for it is compelling. In "Reconstituting the Human Community," the delegates to Colloquium III in Bellagio, Italy, concluded: "There is an urgent need for study and research in the many problems of intercultural relations and the history of culture-contact and culture-change, a field largely neglected by today's social scientists. Here is an area deserving of the highest priority."[8] At present what little cross-cultural research occurs is made possible by the perseverance of a small group of highly dedicated people.

This study, a decade in process, received an initial grant from the Japan Foundation to permit collection of data in Japan. A Faculty Development Grant from San Francisco State University funded the initial phase of computer processing of the findings. The Agency for International Development was instrumental in securing the assistance of specialists abroad.

No prefatory comment can possibly express my indebtedness to Dr. Kay Campbell. Together we spent nearly a year conceptualizing and designing the Barnlund-Campbell Dimensions of Interpersonal Relations inventory, an instrument consisting of eight subscales and over fifteen hundred items. She remained associated with the project throughout the long and tedious process of entering and computer processing the accumulated data. Nomura Naoki and Araki Shoko, although heavily involved in their own graduate research at the time, contributed hundreds of hours to transferring the questionnaire data into suitable form for computer analysis. It is fitting that this collaboration itself reflects the qualities of affection and commitment that the study sought to explore.

In Japan, as well, close colleagues provided continuous encouragement and endless assistance. Without their help so large an undertaking would certainly have failed. Sano Masako and David Reid carried out the forward and backward translation of the research instruments, often making perceptive suggestions for its improvement. Huge Burelson, Chief, Policy and Research Division, USIS, gave the questionnaire its final critical reading in both languages and arranged for its printing and distribution.

In cross-cultural research not only must culturally appropriate instruments be constructed but also equivalent samples must be obtained and the instruments must be consistently administered by speakers of both languages.

In this case over a dozen professionals in Japan and the United States helped. To all the scholars listed below, a note of special gratitude for their critical support of this undertaking.

In Japan

Ayabe Tsuneo, Kyushu University
Erich Berendt, Chiba University
Hashimoto Kayoko, Keio University
Minami Fujio, Tokyo University of Foreign Studies
Mizutani Kengo, Kansai Cultural Education Association of Television and Radio
Murakami Ryuta, Seinan Gakuin University
Naruke Nobuo, Nihon University
Nojiri Yoriko, Sophia University
Okabe Roichi, Nanzan University
Sano Masako, International Christian University
Tsunematsu Masao, Shimane University
Ueda Yoriko, Heian Jogakuin Junior College

In the United States

Milton Bennett, Portland State University
Robert Cathcart, New York University
Alvin Goldberg, University of Denver
James Riggs, San Francisco State University
Lawrence Rosenfield, Hunter College
David Seibert, University of Nevada

Finally, a special note of thanks to the hundreds of participants at a dozen universities in Japan and the United States who completed a long and complicated inventory of their personal relationships. Without their cooperation no investigation would have been possible. We agreed to protect their anonymity, so we can only acknowledge their contribution in a general way.

Cross-cultural research may serve as a model of international cooperation because it involves diverse talents, collaborative effort, empathic communication, and sustained effort. And it creates strong bonds of allegiance distinguished by mutual respect and deep affection.

Communicative Styles
of Japanese and Americans

CHAPTER 1

Images of the Twentieth Century

Modern man is sick in his very soul, and this sickness springs, in its turn, from the sickness in his relations to others. [1]
MAURICE FRIEDMAN

An age, it is said, proclaims and displays its character in every utterance. If true, it is surprising to find that human communication figures so prominently among the preoccupations of our time. Concern for the deteriorating character of human relations seems to lack any factual basis: Radical changes in transportation have obliterated the geographical barriers of seas and mountains that once isolated one community from another; political revolutions have crumbled class and caste barriers; radio, television, and computers have brought us more channels of communication than any other generation has known; illiteracy, the greatest crippler of all, seems conquerable in our time. It appears that human beings have never lived in so promising a time for close and satisfying relations with one another.

Yet the dominant image of our age seems curiously at odds with the realities of life in the twentieth century. Despair, rather than celebration, is the mood of our time. It is the low state of human communication, not its richness or vitality, that is constantly and stridently announced by the leading voices of our age. Pessimism over human relationships seems an

1

obsession of our novelists, playwrights, philosophers, and even our behavioral scientists. These critics provide a point of departure for examining the realities of personal relations as we approach the end of the twentieth century.

TWENTIETH-CENTURY IMAGES: LITERATURE

One place to search for clues to the character of any age is in its literature. The thematic preoccupations of poetry and prose, even though fictional, reflect the subjective experience of their authors. In such recreations of private experience, they cannot help but project the texture and temper of their times. If so, one is struck by the consistency with which estrangement resonates throughout the literature of our day.

Poets

Among our poets, this is an "age of anxiety," the prevailing social order a "wasteland." We, its inhabitants, exist as outsiders and aliens, hiding behind masks of our own invention, nourishing each other with little more than vacuous and banal remarks. Early in the century some lines by T. S. Eliot struck so responsive a chord that for many they characterize life in the twentieth century:

We are the hollow men
We are the stuffed men
Leaning together[2]

If, as Eliot once suggested, "every poem is an epitaph," the gravestones of our age make depressing reading, proclaiming it to be a time when people were never so close physically and never so distant spiritually, separated by anxious silences and sterile phrases. In one of the most incisive and quoted commentaries on modern dialogue, he wrote:

No . . . it isn't that I *want* to be alone,
But that everyone's alone—or so it seems to me.
They make noises, and think they are talking to each other;
They make faces, and think they understand each other.
And I'm sure that they don't.[3]

This mood of pessimism is scarcely confined to poets of Western cultures. Loss of a capacity to communicate in a world of expanding opportunity to do so appears no less vividly in the images of a Japanese poet, Kaneko Mitsuharu.* In "Song of Loneliness" he portrays the Japanese as

---

* Throughout the text, Japanese names are given in Japanese order, that is, family name first and given name second.

"born to loneliness," searching for others "to fill the void of lives not our own."

> Not that I have found loneliness only in Japan's ancient heritage
> I see it just the same in men wearing business suits, smoking
>   cigarettes, mouthing Western ideas.
> At gatherings, in coffee shops, talking to friends, dancing
>   with bobbed-haired girls,
> I see loneliness ooze damply from people's bodies, trail after them,
> Trickling, widening, running deep, flowing on and on forever.[4]

Novelists

Twentieth-century novelists appear equally obsessed with the theme of estrangement. The idea of alienation was anticipated in Dostoyevski's *Notes from Underground* and Marx's "The Alienation of Labor," but rapidly came to dominate much of twentieth-century fiction. It appears and reappears in the works of Franz Kafka, Aldous Huxley, D. H. Lawrence, Herman Hesse, Jean-Paul Sartre, Günter Grass, Albert Camus, and William Golding.

Spiritual crises are the traditional concern of serious writers, but preoccupation with the relations between people seems a unique feature of our times. The central figures of our novels are portrayed as trapped in dehumanizing circumstances, hiding from one another, maintaining a facade of friendship, preserving a fragile peace. The title of Camus's great novel, *The Stranger*, compresses into a single phrase what appears to be the prevailing view of today's citizen, cut off from meaningful relations with nature, with work, with people, with himself, a stranger in a world of strangers.

In these novels human encounters reduce to empty routines that start nowhere and end nowhere, marking the passage of time without satisfying or deeply involving the communicants. Virginia Woolf was among the most incisive in linking loneliness with the character of social conversation, seeing conversation as little more than a chain of clichés with no more significance than the contents of a wastebasket. In *The Moon and Sixpence*, Somerset Maugham posits a world in which people are unable to know or be known, existing "side by side but not together." Among the youth, particularly of the United States, few books have enjoyed the popularity or esteem of J. D. Salinger's *Catcher in the Rye*, a novel tracing Holden Caulfield's fruitless search for a "nice conversation," a true conversation with anyone about anything.

Estrangement might appear, at first glance, to be an affliction endemic to Western societies, an inevitable consequence of commitment to rugged individualism as a primary social value. But contemporary Western novels enjoy wide popularity in Japan and are avidly read and discussed, suggesting that alienation is not confined to a single cultural milieu. Japanese novels, reflecting dislocations caused by abrupt transition from a traditional to an industrial society, seem equally concerned with problems of identity and intimacy. As Arthur Kimball notes, writers from Natsume Soseki at the turn of the century to Abe Kobo today portray the individual struggling to define a "role of himself, his relations to others, and his obligation to society."[5] The same litany of symptoms appears: the monotony of life, the triviality of work, the incapacity to achieve intimacy.

Yamanouchi, commenting on the novels of Soseki, notes his constant reiteration of the difficulties of communication and the need for love combined with an inability to secure it.[6] In the novels of Mishima Yukio alienation is dissected again and again. Sartre's famous line in *No Exit*, "Hell is . . . other people," is echoed in Mishima's remark that "Real danger is nothing more than just living."[7] The central figure of Oe's *A Personal Matter*, the diminutive Bird, is as much an alien in his place and time as any outsider found in Western contemporary writing. Indeed the protagonists of Soseki, Mishima, Tanizaki, Abe, and Oe display a remarkable affinity with those of Kafka, Camus, Grass, and Salinger.

Perhaps no twentieth-century Japanese writer has probed the state of estrangement with as much power and imagination as Abe Kobo. His work, from *The Woman in the Dunes* through *Face of Another* to *The Box Man* dissects the complexities of alienation. If the myth of Sisyphus, in which life is seen as a pointless effort to move a boulder to the top of a hill from which it repeatedly rolls back, reflects a Western view of life, the myth of the dunes, in which an entymologist is trapped in a shifting sand dune, condemned to a barren environment, and forced to relate to a stranger of accident, is a surprisingly compatible Eastern metaphor. In Aldous Huxley's *Chrome Yellow*, the hero dreams of a world when "beautiful machines will take over and nobody will bother us at all," while the protagonist of Osaragi Jiro's *The Homecoming* is willing to settle for an acacia tree as the "perfect friend." The images diverge, reflecting the distinctive artistic heritages of West and East, but the state of mind that is imaged is strikingly familiar. There is a remarkable convergence on the alienating character of modern life, the tenuousness of personal ties, and the inability to share experiences with others through conversation.

Playwrights

Perhaps no form of art mirrors its time with the immediacy and directness of theater. No translation is needed to interpret life on the stage. The moral crises of a period are addressed directly through the words and acts of people as they struggle to survive. The actors and their words must touch the experience of the audience in a recognizable way.

This is an age of great theater and one, therefore, that should expose much about us. No list of the outstanding Western playwrights of this century could safely omit T. S. Eliot, George Bernard Shaw, Samuel Beckett, Eugène Ionesco, Jean Genet, Eugene O'Neill, Arthur Miller, Edward Albee, or Harold Pinter. And yet each of these dramatists, in some or all of their works, directs attention to the superficiality of personal ties, the futility of conversation, the poverty of language.

On the stage, society is shown as an urban wilderness, populated by strangers, out of touch with themselves and each other. People search for an intimacy they cannot find, cannot create, cannot sustain. Jerry, the leading figure of *Zoo Story*, is so desperate to reach someone that he begs, shouts, insults, and finally provokes a stranger into violence in order to elicit some concern. Pleading for connection, Jerry says, "We regard each other with a mixture of sadness and suspicion, and then we feign indifference. We walk past each other safely; we have an understanding."[8] Family life is portrayed by Albee as *A Delicate Balance*, one so fragile it can be destroyed by a single authentic feeling; in Ionesco's *The Bald Soprano*, the Martins gradually discover that since they live at the same address and have the same daughter, they must be married to one another.

It is not merely that we are thrust by birth into a world of strangers, as indeed we are, but that our communicative inadequacy condemns us to remain so. Genuine conversation is subverted by the facades we present, the platitudes we exchange. To many modern playwrights, conversations consist of little more than an exchange of formalities and clichés, the tiresome and empty phrases found in children's grammar books. Yet words are uttered with a gravity and passion that belies their meagre content:

MR. SMITH: One can always be in two places at once.
MR. MARTIN: The floor is below us and the ceiling is above us.
MRS. SMITH: When I say Yes, it's only a manner of speaking.
MRS. MARTIN: We all have our cross to bear.[9]

Conversations seem to start anywhere and end nowhere; words dissolve into gibberish, the sounds of speech but without any substance. Yet the actors go on; they talk and talk and talk. There is, under it all, the hope that someone will finally say something that redeems the effort. That faith, as demonstrated in *Waiting for Godot*, often falters:

VLADIMIR: Say something!
ESTRAGON: I'm trying.
VLADIMIR: Say anything at all![10]

Perhaps the ultimate, terminal conversational cul-de-sac appears in Beckett's *Krapp's Last Tape*, in which a solitary actor is reduced to a dialogue with his own recorded remarks of thirty years earlier. Instead of serving as an agency for overcoming isolation, human speech is seen instead as the means by which we accomplish our estrangement from one another.

Beyond a general concern with the communicative inadequacies of modern human beings lies a questioning of language itself. Every person, in one sense, speaks a foreign language; hence, every voice is the voice of a stranger. While members of a community share a common vocabulary, it is an imperfect instrument for voicing an infinity of meanings. Not only silence divides us but even the most innocent and authentic words may mislead. Eliot, writing early in the century, voiced his cynicism about human speech in this way:

> Words strain,
> Crack and sometimes break, under the burden,
> Under the tension, slip, slide, perish,
> Decay with imprecision, will not stay in place,
> Will not stay still.[11]

When feelings are masked, information manipulated, deceits practiced daily and by everyone, words lose their power to nourish those who use them; they become instruments of alienation rather than of solidarity, disappointing those who place too great a trust in them.

One does not find a parallel concern with the inadequacies of human communication among Japanese playwrights. But neither is the theme overlooked. Perhaps the most noted and most successful of contemporary Japanese plays is *Friends* by Abe Kobo. In it a single man, living alone, is invaded by a family of complete strangers on the pretext of saving him from the unbearable fate of loneliness. Repeated efforts to extricate himself from their oppressive goodwill fail, leaving suicide his only escape. Early in the play, in lines reminiscent of Albee, one of the invading visitors remarks:

> There are millions, even tens of millions of people in this city. And all of them are total strangers. . . . Everywhere you look you see nothing but strangers. . . . Don't you think that's frightening?[12]

The theme of this modern morality play, its dialogue, and its final resolution are so similar to those found in Western drama as to suggest they reflect the same societal malaise.

A final verdict on these playwrights is still out—not with regard to their power to move us, but with regard to the accuracy with which they have reflected modern life. It is also unclear whether these plays expose disorders endemic to our age or are created to incite us to forge new identities, new ways of relating, new respect for the immensity of the communicative act. As with our poets and novelists, our playwrights share certain premonitions about the depersonalizing effects of modern life, but they do more: They situate the threat to our humanity in the character of our personal relationships and, even more precisely, in our inability to communicate authentically and compassionately with our closest companions.

TWENTIETH-CENTURY IMAGES: THE FINE ARTS

The visual arts confirm a melancholy view of our times. Paul Tillich, in *New Images of Man*, notes the concern of modern artists with the "dehumanizing structure of totalitarian systems" in one part of the world and the "dehumanizing consequences of technical mass civilization" in the other.[13] Where painters once portrayed people at home in their environment, secure in their faith, in harmony with their contemporaries, the art of our century shows them alone, tortured with doubt, lacking meaningful connection with one another. The paintings of Mary Cassatt, Pierre-Auguste Renoir, Edouard Manet, and Henri Matisse give way to those of Francis Bacon, Arshile Gorky, Pablo Picasso, Edward Hopper, and Willem de Kooning. When an attempt is made at all to represent human beings, as in the paintings of Hopper or the sculptures of George Segal, they are seen as lonely individuals, condemned to silence and solitude, trapped in oppressive urban settings. Jacques Dupin might have been describing much of twentieth-century figurative art in his description of the paintings of Joan Miró: "His figures are unaware of one another, multiply without seeing one another; their lines do not touch, and their proximity creates no relation between them. They are utterly alone, strangers to one another."[14]

Western sculptors supply a similar view. In the works of Germaine Richier, Marino Marini, Rico LeBrun, Jean Dubuffet, and Eduardo Paolozzi, the individual appears tortured, disconnected, and frightened. But no single sculptor has formed so frightening an image of the twentieth century as Alberto Giacometti. His slender figures, emaciated and fragile, stand alone or stride past one another, unseeing and uncaring, bent on solitary missions. Once characterized by Katherine Kuh as the "apotheosis of isolation," they seem to many to serve as witness to our time. If the artistic intuition is to be taken seriously, ours is an age in which people pass without seeing, listen without hearing, touch without feeling.

To demonstrate the same concern among Japanese artists is more difficult. Traditionally the arts of Japan have focused on nature as their primary subject matter; Japanese art rarely serves as a vehicle for political commentary or social criticism. In the West, all modes of expression tend to serve political or rhetorical ends; in the East, the arts more often serve private or contemplative ones.

Japanese artists, however, have shifted course on many occasions, importing foreign styles and later assimilating them to uniquely Japanese modes of expression. In the past hundred years Japanese artists have confronted and absorbed Western impressionism, cubism, surrealism, dadaism, expressionism, and nonobjective art. Of these, abstract art seems to have been most widely and fully assimilated, perhaps because it is so compatible with features of traditional design in Japan.

Among such painters as Kawara On, Kudo Tetsumi, and Okamoto Shinjiro, who still pursue figurative art, the human being is depicted, as in the West, as tragic, dismembered, and alienated. But abstract paintings are not incapable of articulating the spiritual state of modern man; in this respect the canvases of Yoshihara Hideo, Wakabayashi Tsutomu, Saito Yoshishige, and Nakanishi Natsuyuki seem as filled with a sense of tragic isolation as those of Clyfford Still, Robert Motherwell, Antoni Tapies, or Willem de Kooning. Perhaps few, even in the West, have found a more perfect form to express a crippled capacity for communication than the amputated, gargantuan ears that obsess Miki Tomio.

TWENTIETH-CENTURY IMAGES: THE POPULAR ARTS

A diminished capacity for personal relationships finds expression in the popular arts as well, such as film and song. Film, as Robert Kolker notes in *A Cinema of Loneliness*, is a "carefully crafted lie," a deliberate fiction.[15] But as a fiction, it is never an innocent one, even when its intent is to entertain, for inevitably it mirrors the way we see ourselves and our condition. Such notable film directors as Charlie Chaplin, Jean Renoir, Luis Buñuel, Federico Fellini, Alain Resnais, Michelangelo Antonioni, and Ingmar Bergman consistently expose the triviality of modern life, its dehumanizing quality, its manipulative character. In *Modern Times, Rules of the Game, The Discreet Charm of the Bourgeoisie, La Dolce Vita, La Notte, Blow-up, The Silence,* or *Scenes from a Marriage,* people are shown as lacking significant values, devoid of feeling, incapable of commitment, lacking the will or talent to confirm one another. The search for companionship, and repeated failure in achieving it, is a major theme of the first century of film art; even in Woody Allen's "comedies" the central characters seem incapable of realizing themselves or nurturing one another.

A surprisingly parallel view appears in the great films of Japan as well. Resignation in the face of the conditions of modern life (the spirit of *mono no aware*) often blunts such commentary, turning it toward inner acceptance rather than outward action, but the view is no less bitter in its implications. Not until the unexpected acclaim awarded *Rashomon* did the world recognize the power of Japanese directors such as Kinugasa Teinosuke, Gosho Heinosuke, Mizoguchi Kenji, Naruse Mikio, Imai Tadashi, Ozu Yasujiro, Ichikawa Kon, Kurosawa Akira, and Teshigahara Hiroshi. Films such as *Crossroads, And Yet We Live, Boy, A Man Vanishes, Tokyo Story, Ikiru, The Ruined Map, Kaseki, The Face of Another,* explore the anonymity of city life, disintegration of the family, indifference to suffering, and inability to communicate. The films of this century, perhaps its most pervasive and original art form, present a chilling picture of contemporary life.

Anyone seeking the pulse of a period in history might listen, as well, to its popular ballads. Those who attend to our poets of the street must be struck by similar themes of estrangement found there. Simon and Garfunkel, echoing Eliot on more than one occasion, protest our becoming "strangers out of rhythm, couplets out of rhyme." That this condition might be remedied through conversation is seen as doubtful:

And we sit and drink our coffee
Couched in our indifference
Like shells upon the shore
You can hear the ocean roar
In the dangling conversation
And the superficial sighs
The borders of our lives.[16]

Through employing the common vernacular, folk music remains a powerful and popular medium for voicing anxieties that have no other outlet. The songs suggest not only that "the times, they are a-changin'" but also chorus a wide dissatisfaction with shallow and transitory personal relationships.

TWENTIETH-CENTURY IMAGES: PHILOSOPHY

The widespread dis-ease noted by our writers and artists has not escaped the attention of modern philosophers. According to the dominant philosophical perspective, existentialism, we stand at a critical threshold in our evolution. Dissatisfied with the faiths of our fathers, disappointed with totalitarian promises, disillusioned with technology, skeptical of science, and unfulfilled by material possessions, we seek a new conception of our place in the world. Strangers adrift in a revolutionary age, we seek, in Maurice Friedman's phrase, "a new image of man," a redefinition of what it is to be fully human. The existentialist view encompasses a variety of philosophers and philosophies sharing a number of premises: that the world is neutral, devoid of inherent or fixed meaning; to survive, humans must act, but to act requires the individual to endow events with a particular meaning; the necessity of communicating arises out of the uniqueness of our meanings and the relativity of our values; our humanity is realized not at the level of the abstract, but at the level of the concrete; existence precedes essence.

The existential attack on the institutions and conventions of twentieth-century civilization was a broad and devastating one. First, the decline of traditional institutions and undermining of religious absolutes exposed the meaninglessness of existence. As people become trapped in huge and unresponsive organizations, they surrender whatever influence they might exert for material rewards; they become slaves to routines and roles, and these, in turn, alienate people from each other. An aggravated egoism, born of industrialization, combined with a manipulative view of others, has crippled the capacity to act spontaneously and authentically. "We do not have friends," argues Abraham Kaplan, "We have contacts, connections, clients, customers or constituents."[17]

This emphasis on concrete existence and relationships with others focused further attention on the communicative act. When such encounters were scrutinized they were often seen as perversions of communication, corrupting its potential for securing empathy and intimacy. One such perversion reduced communication to little but an exchange of formalities—preserving the facade of dialogue without its substance. Or conversation was seen as no more than a staged play in which participants adopted roles and recited the lines scripted for their parts. There was only an interaction of performances, not of persons; "seeming" rather than "being" undermined any possibility that conversations might vitally affect the communicants. A more characteristic abuse of communication was its conversion into a means of manipulating others. Behind a display of geniality and apparent sincerity, people masked their motives, fabricating arguments and calculating remarks to secure some material or social advantage. Yet existentialists recognized that there was a kind of "genuine dialogue" whose aim was the sharing of experience, the pursuit of insight, the affirming of a relationship. But such occasions, they argued, were rare in contemporary life because of our social institutions or an inner inadequacy.

Perhaps the most trenchant critic of modern communication was Martin Buber. This is an age, he wrote, in which "we associate, but we do not meet." Our relationships are primarily "I-it" rather than "I-thou" relations. We associate as strangers or as functionaries, but rarely as persons; we use each other as long as it serves our private need and discard each other with the same nonchalance with which we discard paper cups or worn-out clothing. Our encounters are not unfriendly, but impersonal. The sickness of our time, Buber noted, is not in the existence of I-it relations—they are unavoidable given the character of modern life—but the extent to which they dominate our life and are the only form of attachment we know. "Our task," wrote Buber, "is to get in touch," to find ways of creating more open, more enriching, more confirming forms of intimacy.[18]

To some people, existentialism constitutes a depressing, even degrading, view of life. It represents an ontological cul-de-sac from which there is no escape and few options beyond mere survival or suicide. To others it is a liberating perspective that acknowledges the neutrality of nature and thereby invites people to take responsibility for their destiny, to seek more authentic ways of relating, and to create institutions and social norms that promote truly humane ends.

Although the abstract nature of philosophy has held little fascination for the more concretely focused Japanese, existentialism has had its impact in the East as well. And if there are fewer philosophical tracts providing visions of the spiritual state of the Japanese, there is wide recognition that a crisis exists. Japan, according to Michael McIntyre, has been described as "a spiritual abyss," a nation "squirming with cultural indigestion," its people "uncertain of their moorings."[19]

TWENTIETH-CENTURY IMAGES: BEHAVIORAL SCIENCES

Finally, what picture of ourselves do we gain from the disciplines that study people, the behavioral sciences. These disciplines—psychology, anthropology, communicology, sociology, psychiatry—are creations of the twentieth-century, creations that also reflect a concern with the human condition. Unlike their counterparts in the arts, behavioral scientists seek to confront and describe objectively the nature of people and their relationships. Precise description and verifiable explanation are their business.

Surprisingly, the portrait of ourselves that prevails in the behavioral sciences is little more positive or ennobling. People are seen as victims of an inner determinism, every act dictated by some biological drive or combination of drives, or as victims of an outer determinism in which every act reflects the external circumstances of their lives. A third view describes people as self-regulating mechanisms, complicated machines that are programmed at birth and through acculturation maintain their balance by adapting their inner programs (norms and values) to outer contingencies (social pressures). A final perspective, a clinical one, regards people primarily as patients, constantly at risk, defensively oriented to protect themselves against illness and disintegration. Healthy people—a target of amazingly little research or writing by behavioral scientists—make up a residual category, defined mainly by the absence of pathological symptoms.

Traditional models of communication also reflect a view of people as victims or victimizers. From the earliest observations of Aristotle's *Rhetoric* to the contemporary writings of Claude Shannon and Warren Weaver, communication is seen as something one person does to another: A sender produces messages that, when effectively manipulated, produce an intended effect within a receiver. It is an image that reduces human encounters to confrontation between a manipulator and victim.

Although the behavioral sciences occupy a larger place in Western cultures than in the East, their perspectives and methods have spread. Even in Japan, where the group is stressed over the individual, where harmony and commitment might minimize alienation, this theme still appears. Mita Munesuke, for example, finds alienation a universal problem affecting all modern societies. The problem is compounded in Japan by a lower level of conscious awareness of the condition.[20]

Although behavioral scientists, by and large, confine their inquiry to the present, William Schutz has undertaken to place historical periods on an analytic couch. His theory of interpersonal needs posits that three primary drives govern interpersonal relations: the need for inclusion, for control, and for affection. In reviewing Medieval, Renaissance, and Modern periods he concluded that control was the dominant theme of the Middle Ages, affection of the Renaissance, and inclusion of the Modern era. Schutz finds our times preoccupied with "narcissistic self-absorption," "disappointment with fleeting and superficial relationships," "feelings of rejection and being alone," and "deep concern with loneliness."[21]

The consistency among these conceptions of human nature and of human relations leads one to suspect they were born of the same intellectual ancestry that has nurtured the novels, plays, films and songs of our age. No one has yet undertaken to assess the self-fulfilling role of such images in aggravating feelings of alienation or even of creating them. Or, if accurate dissections of life in the twentieth-century, the part these images may play in forcing us to confront realities.

IMAGES OR REALITIES?

One cannot fail to be impressed with the number and eloquence of critics of our age. It is hard to believe they all could be out of touch with our time. There are so many and they speak so persuasively that it is hard to resist the images they offer: disintegration of the human community, exploitation of people, the perversion of friendship, the superficiality of conversation. We have become, in the words of Helen Lynd, "strangers in a world where we thought we were at home."[22]

Estrangement is by no means the only chord struck in twentieth-century art and science; issues of life and death, of success and failure, occupy intellectuals of our day as they have other ages. What is so striking is that at no other period in history has interest in human relations reached such heights, or discouragement with them reached such depths, as at the present moment. While this fact should give us pause, it should also arouse curiosity about the basis of such cynicism. Efforts to diagnose anything as complex as a period in history should be viewed with suspicion until clearly confirmed by data on the actual quality of life. Are these portrayals accurate, an ideological fad, a private confession of their authors, a contemporary myth, or the result of applying obsolete criteria? There are arguments for each of these assessments.

Creative works, arising from the passions of a single author, may readily project onto the body politic what are, in fact, the personal deficiencies of their authors. The artist's crime, as Socrates remarked long ago, is that of misrepresenting reality, thereby misleading people about the conditions of their lives. This confusing of private and public inadequacy forces society to shoulder blame for what may only be the limitations of a solitary person. Artists' works may contain valid insights, but may also give a specious validity to what is only a private vision.

Another possibility is that we have become seduced by the eloquence of such critics, convinced that what is so movingly expressed must be true. Fact is often impotent in the face of a powerful fiction. The rules that govern the writing of a song, play, or film often require some sacrifice of accuracy in the pursuit of beauty and power. Symbols may be manipulated for their artistic effect rather than for their objective validity. Still it is hard to dismiss these critics because their intuitions have sprung spontaneously and widely from the best minds of our time.

The anthropologist Franz Boas warns of another danger. The authors of the greatest literature, art, and philosophy are an intellectual elite, a breed apart from the mainstream of life. Thus they may reflect only the life of a minority, but may mislead readers into believing their works are symptomatic of the majority. Ethnology, as Boas emphasizes, "does not deal with the exceptional man; it deals with the masses, and with the characteristics of their thoughts."[23] This view clearly invites and even insists upon wider testing of such intuitions by more verifiable means. This is a task to which we shall turn shortly.

Perhaps a cynical view of personal relationships is only an ideological fad, a plaything of intellectuals. Each time estrangement is articulated it generates fresh excitement and new converts who see ways of elaborating it further. And such repetition soon elevates it to the level of an unassailable truth. Yet fads, even intellectual fads, tend to pass quickly, and this so-called fad has had a long life.

A more substantial argument might be that every society shares and participates in a collective myth of one sort or another, a myth that helps to frame and explain daily experience. These myths, from animism to the divine right of kings, have comforted those who shared them, but are often seen as misleading or unfounded by succeeding generations. Any theme, repeated often enough, may take on the character of myth. Are we, indeed, only performers, relating superficially? Are our ties precarious, shallow, exploitative? Perhaps. Perhaps not. It is impossible to say without first investigating whether alienation is a myth or reality. Before concluding it is the former, we should seek to know the latter.

Nostalgia is another cause for assuming a censorious view of the present. As with the history of a people, an individual's memory endows the past with such positive feelings that it warps a view of the present. The past, with its simpler life, moral absolutes, lifelong attachments, and predictable future, is sorely missed during an age of transition. The loss of the past provokes angry attack on the present. A romantic view of what *was* makes denunciation of what *is* nearly inevitable. Critics of our day may be prisoners of their own sentimentality, importing criteria from a revered past that are inappropriate or irrelevant for appraising the present.

Still, the past may also remind us of inherent needs that, if disregarded, may cripple our capacity to preserve a sense of community. While a naive person may appear comical and harmless, a naive society, out of touch with reality, is blind to the dangers it faces and helpless, therefore, to overcome them. Whether we are dealing with images or realities cannot be resolved until we secure more objective reports of how people actually form and conduct their relationships with one another today.

ARE HUMAN RELATIONS
AT A POINT OF CRISIS?

If every age characterizes itself by the questions it asks and the way it addresses them, the future will very likely describe this as an age of communication. The artifacts of this century—its poems, plays, films, novels—reflect disappointment with existing institutions, personal attachments, and the quality of human dialogue, all set against a longing for closer, more enriching, and firmer ties with companions. It is possible that our works of art, of philosophy, of social science represent nothing more than an ideological fad, confessions of private inadequacy, nostalgia for a lost past, or the application of dated standards to the quality of life today. It is also possible that these seemingly cynical portrayals reflect a rising sense of isolation and impotence.

Dissecting any age or any culture is a delicate undertaking, susceptible to simplification and distortion by any and all observers. In an effort to strike a balance between image and reality, between fiction and fact, we need first to look at the actual conditions of life in the twentieth century in Japan and the United States because these conditions set the limits and frame the experience of members of these cultures. Personal relationships and communicative acts always reflect the context in which they are set. And a revolutionary age sets new challenges that test the empathic flexibility of its inhabitants.

CHAPTER 2

The Changing Context
of Communication

*Technological change, mobility and the
individualistic ethos combine to rupture the
bonds that tie each individual to a family, a
community, a kinship network, a
geographical location—bonds that give him
a comfortable sense of himself.*[1]
PHILIP SLATER

There are fads in words as there are fads in clothing or humor; these changes in vocabulary reflect no more than an appetite for finding new words for expressing old ideas. Yet this is not always the case. Some new words reflect a rising consciousness, a radical shift in the way people think about themselves and their relation to the universe.

Consider the word *ecology*. It has suddenly become a cult word, familiar around the world, and capable of inciting passions for or against a variety of policies. Yet it signifies a new way of thinking about the relation of living things to their surrounding environment.

Until the closing years of the past century, the prevailing view of the world was of a collection of things: rocks, plants, animals, people. To better understand such objects they were removed from the contaminating influence of their environment and studied in the laboratory. Data began to accumulate, however, that led to suspicion that the world was less a

15

collection of things than a hierarchy of processes, each linked to the other, their destinies inextricably bound together. Change in any part of the system reverberated throughout it, affecting all other parts. The sharp borders that seemed to separate things—that suggested they had independent fates determined solely by their atomic or genetic structures—began to dissolve.

Physical scientists were the first to make this transition, noting that the environment of an atomic particle was as critical as the particle itself in shaping its movement. Biologists, too, gradually recognized that plant and animal were better revealed in their natural habitat than when isolated from it. Students of human behavior now struggle with a similar shift in perspective, away from studying people apart from their environment to studying them within settings and cultures.[2]

There is growing appreciation that the physical environment, configuration of cities, structure of economic institutions, character of families, and patterns of socializing profoundly affect the sorts of people we become. And the resulting personalities, in turn, have a reciprocal effect upon the culture. Organism and environment cannot be divorced without losing something essential; they form a single unitary whole.

Although the full implications of an ecological view need not concern us, that viewpoint is implicated in the comparative study of personal relations in Japan and the United States. No communicative act—be it silence or suicide—is independent of its milieu: Time, place, and culture shape every moment and every human encounter. A vast continent and crowded island constitute unique geographies. This is the twentieth, not the first or tenth, century; communication must be viewed through the lens of the present not the cloudy lens of another time. And the Japanese and American cultures have each evolved unique communicative styles for coping with life in the twentieth century. Social behavior is best seen through an ecological frame, as a response to the possibilities and limitations of a particular context. This context deserves attention.

THE SILENT REVOLUTION

After 15 million years of living as an animal among animals, the first human beings appeared some 250,000 years ago. "It was a revolution without revolutionaries, the most effective kind," as John Pfeiffer put it.[3] From that distant point until a mere six thousand years ago our predecessors were "nomadic, small-group, wide-open-spaces creatures," surviving by hunting and gathering what they needed. If it was a short and rough life in some respects, it was also a life of relative leisure.

The small size of these migrating bands of families had its social consequences: People enjoyed equal status; only the most rudimentary organization of society was required; there were few restrictions on what one might do; communication took place between people who knew and were known to each other; rarely did one encounter a stranger. The population of the world may have numbered no more than the population of New York City or Tokyo today. All the world was frontier and, as nearly as archaeologists can reconstruct it, conflict was avoided by simply subdividing the group and moving to new territories.

THE FIRST CITIES

Then, rather abruptly and for reasons that are unclear, sometime around 3000 B.C. to A.D. 1000 the first ecological revolution occurred. The change, caused by an expanding population and shift from foraging to farming, brought the first towns into existence. This decisive step, from which there has been no retreat, seems to have occurred almost simultaneously in nearly every settled part of the world: Jericho and Uruk in the Middle East; Harappa and Mohenjo-Daro in India; Sian and Chang-chou in China; Monte Alban and Tikal in Mesoamerica; Cahokia in North America. After a millenia people faced the necessity of creating a new social order for which no precedent existed.

A settled life is more risky than a mobile one. There must be food, every day, for everyone, regardless of the harvest. More densely populated centers require manipulation of the environment, new organization of time and space, permanent buildings, management of transport, and maintenance of communication over distance. City life not only changed the landscape but forced a revolution in human relationships: A religious and political hierarchy arose to enforce discipline; enduring institutions were required; political and religious creeds offset a loss of solidarity based on personal contact; specialized duties created inequality in status and power; there was increased communication with others who, if not total strangers, were addressed in terms of their positions rather than their personalities.

Quantity is inseparable from quality; an arithmetic increase in the number of people in any sovereign unit multiplies the problems of coordination geometrically. Each person who joins an existing group complicates the lives of all the others. The birth of cities constituted the first assault on human exclusiveness, on the perimeter of empathy that had earlier regulated the life of the community.

The first efforts at creating viable city life were, in the long view of history, less than successful. These virgin cities, even at their height, rarely exceeded twenty-five thousand permanent residents, and often contained fewer than ten thousand. The vast majority of people continued to live, as in the past, in nomadic groups of foragers or in small villages. All the early cities perished almost as suddenly as they were born, testimony perhaps to the limits of human flexibility in adapting to a fixed territory, specialized roles, unequal status, external discipline, and transient contact with unfamiliar people. Still, the species persevered. Cities continued to be tried with varying degrees of success. After several thousand years of experimentation the transition to larger, permanent cities succeeded although the majority of people continued to live outside them.

THE NEW SUPERCITIES: PRODUCT OF THE POPULATION EXPLOSION

In the past century a third threshold has been crossed: the creation of supercities, urban concentrations that number not in the thousands, or tens of thousands, but in the millions and tens of millions. "In all evolution," Pfeiffer emphasizes, "there is no transformation or 'quantum leap' to compare with this one. Never before has the lifestyle of a species, its way of adapting, changed so utterly and so swiftly."[4] The "rapid urbanization of untold millions" and their need for new forms of affiliation has, according to Eric Hoffer, "shaped the temper of our time."[5]

The population of the earth was an estimated 4 million by 10,000 B.C. When hunters and gatherers became farmers and villagers, Europe grew from 20 to 100 million, Asia increased from 80 to 375 million, Africa expanded from 8 to 55 million, and the Americas, starting from a smaller base, grew to 12 million.

The first stage of urbanization accelerated growth in population: Between 1600 and 1900 nearly every continent experienced a doubling or tripling of its people. But in the past century, along with the birth of supercities, the population rose precipitously: Asia from 970 to 2300 million and the Americas from 145 to 545 million, for example. The population of the earth, estimated at 2.5 billion in 1950, reached 4.3 billion by 1975 and is expected to reach 7 billion by the year 2000. One fourth of all the people who have ever lived are alive today.[6] The population of the planet will increase more in the next 20 years than in the past 200,000 years. (See Figure 2.1.)

Intensifying the effects of this exponential growth in the sheer number of people is their increased polarization in urban areas. Today twenty of our supercities have more than five million; ten have more than ten million inhabitants. Casablanca illustrates how the forces of increase and concentration converge: In 1900 only 600 lived there, 600,000 in 1960, 1 million in 1980; 12 million are expected to live there in the year 2000. To go from farmhouse to skyscraper, from footpath to freeway in a single lifetime tests the limits of human adaptability.

A more revealing figure, however, is that of density, the relation between the number of people and the available land. Even here "theoretical density" is less critical than "nutritional density." The contrast is apparent in comparing Japan's "theoretical density" of 655 people per square mile with its "nutritional density" of 4680 per square mile.[8] In Japan, where only one or two people once occupied every ten square kilometers of habitable land, today roughly five thousand people occupy that same space.

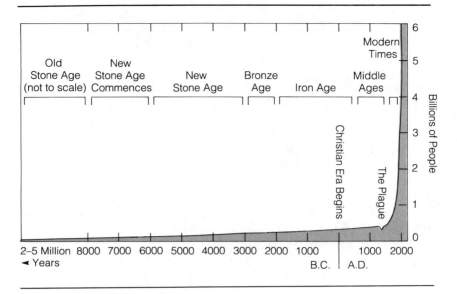

FIGURE 2.1   World Population Growth Through History[7]

The United States and Japan have both experienced the population explosion and urban implosion. Because of its vast land mass the United States falls near the low end of the population density scale among industrialized nations. During the colonial period there was less than a square mile for every settler; today about fifty people occupy that same space. Most Americans experience a far greater density: 65 percent currently live in cities of over a million people, and 80 percent will live in such impacted areas by the year 2000.

To the surprise of many foreigners Japan, too, is a nation of cities. With half the population of the United States, and a land mass smaller than the state of California, the density of Japan exceeds 865 people per square kilometer. Besides Tokyo, candidate for the world's largest concentration of people, Japan has ten other cities of over a million inhabitants. Indeed Japan has a greater number of cities of over a million than the United States has. Increasing numbers of people brought into closer and closer proximity is a worldwide phenomenon, from Mexico City to Calcutta. The "New York–New Jersey agglomeration" with an estimated 1970 population of 16.3 million is exceeded by the "Tokyo–Yokohama agglomeration" of 19.7 million.[9] There is literally "No Place to Hide."

Each of these settings—nature, village, and metropolis—frames life in distinctive ways, altering the forms of society, the human relations that are possible and the traits of personality to be prized or punished. If the context of life and of communication has been so radically transformed, as the facts indicate, what sort of world is taking form before our eyes? How has it affected the way we meet and talk with strangers, acquaintances, friends, and intimates? And how have the cultures of Japan and the United States responded to these challenges?

THE SOCIAL CONSEQUENCES OF URBANIZATION

People face their most painful adjustments during periods of abrupt acceleration or deceleration. A new social order must evolve and new institutions take shape; old values are replaced and social norms are challenged. As Jonas and Jonathan Salk note, an "expansionist epoch," typical of the older world, based on unlimited territory and resources, encourages unbridled independence, a competitive temper, material gains, short-term perspectives, and pragmatic tests of accomplishment. A "contractionist epoch," such as we now face, tends to reverse this orientation, promoting conservation, personal growth, interdependence, consensus and collaboration, and long-term holistic perspectives. [10]

Only a small coterie of specialists, the demographers who study population statistics, seems aware of the devastating potential of this quiet revolution. And even they attend more to its physical consequences—the collision between an expanding population and shrinking resources—than to its social consequences. While we have begun to think about the balance of nature, we have rarely thought about the balance of human relations, about how to address the personal consequences of urbanization. Our humanity, not merely our physical survival, may be at stake. A radical change in population can be expected to revolutionize the way people become acquainted, share experience, accommodate differences, and achieve intimacy. Meeting strangers was once a rare and feared possibility; today it is the most common of everyday experiences. Where communication with familiar people can respond to their unique personal qualities, communication with unfamiliar others tends to be regulated by class, race, sex, culture, or by their status as a clerk, nurse, waiter, or taxi driver.

There is surely some limit to the number of people one can notice and remember, that one can know or become attached to. The main way in which modern urbanites have found to adapt to this condition is through what Desmond Morris calls "anti-contact" strategies. One must learn how to initiate, but also how to block, conversation; not only how to touch but also how to avoid touching. Such distancing tactics seem necessary for limiting potential companions to a manageable number.

Once people were born into an existing fabric of relations simply by the occasion of their birth. And from birth to death they remained a part of that same social fabric, locked into permanent ties with kith and kin. Today personal relationships are more a matter of chance and choice. Everyone is free—or forced—to create his or her own social circle. Almost hourly one must decide to invite or discourage relationships, to contribute to them or dissolve them.

Although the number of possible companions now affords a far wider choice of associates and broader range of social activities, this also demands a greater communicative flexibility of everyone. Conversing with well-known companions requires far less empathic talent than with a constantly changing set of diverse partners. Yet while a traditional social order provided everyone with a permanent cast of companions, it also sometimes strangled or smothered people in an inescapable web of obligation. Modern society may provide people with wider social opportunity and less confining bonds, but may also leave the individual more exposed and vulnerable. In any case a new social context is likely to affect the number, range, intensity, and permanence of human ties.

A Concrete Wilderness
Although the population explosion may be the primary force triggering a new social order, the concentration of masses of people in crowded cities has complicated communication further. "We did not evolve," writes Desmond Morris, "to live in huge conglomerations of thousands of individuals. Our behavior is designed to operate in small tribal groups numbering well under a hundred individuals."[11]

The sheer size of cities, the hundreds of square miles they cover, discourages lasting relationships. Preservation of a sense of community is linked to the limits of our legs: It is difficult for people to share experiences that might bind them together when they cannot reach one another on foot. As Toynbee remarks: "A city that outdistances man's walking powers is a trap for man. It threatens to become a prison from which he cannot escape unless he has mechanical means of transport, the thoroughfare for carrying these, and the purchasing power for commanding the use of artificial means of communication."[12] If one is forced to take a bus, wait for a subway train, then hire a taxi to reach an acquaintance, the relationship may not survive. Inaccessibility has probably destroyed more friendships than lack of communicative skill.

As cities sprawl across thousands of square miles they scatter people related by birth and choice over greater and greater distances. Systems of transportation, constructed to connect parts of a city, are often so confusing, time consuming, and costly to use they are used only for necessary trips. "Dropping-in," which Christopher Alexander argues is essential in preserving friendships in preindustrial society, has all but disappeared, the effort to maintain a friendship often greater than the satisfactions it provides.[13] Distance does not make the heart grow fonder; all the evidence on friendship and marriage suggests it is a major factor in their deterioration and demise. "Distant friends," writes Robert Brain, "are hardly better than no friends at all, since these relationships need contact and constant renewal."[14]

The scale of our cities, sterile steel and glass towers intersected by high-speed freeways, leaves little space for casual conversations. Traffic and crowds fill urban streets and sidewalks outside huge buildings with imposing but distancing facades. One of the first things to disappear in large cities are places for people to gather, to converse, to pass the time of day: Our cities are nearly devoid of public life.

The design of buildings has often added to feelings of alienation. To be cost effective, they grow larger and taller, their forbidding exteriors discouraging anyone from entering except "on business." Inside there is the same isolation of people and activities—cubicle on top of cubicle, cubicle beside cubicle, all designed for machinelike efficiency. Urbanites, as van der Hag has written, "are born in hospitals, fed in cafeterias, married in hotels. After terminal care, they die in hospitals, are shelved temporarily in funeral homes, and are finally incarcerated. On each of these occasions—and how many others?—efficiency and economy are obtained and individuality and continuity stripped off."[15] Our cities increasingly seem designed to promote the "lonely crowd" of which David Riesman once wrote.

"People come to cities," observes Christopher Alexander, "for contact. That's what cities are for: Meeting places."[16] And, since the only true test of a city's viability is its capacity to attract and hold people, our cities continue to flourish. Cities appear to have compensating advantages in offering greater occupational opportunities and an immense variety of companions and activities. Perhaps there is no alternative but to adapt since, as Toynbee sees it, cities "may be man's permanent destiny."

THE SOCIAL ORDERING OF URBAN LIFE

The institutions and forms of communication that serve a band of hunters or villagers are scarcely adequate to manage personal relations in cities of millions. Anonymity was unknown before modern cities; we now live as strangers in the midst of strangers. As Lofland suggests, this new anonymity "has a potential for unpredictability that no one would find tolerable."[17] In many cities talking with strangers is awkward at best and dangerous at worst. According to Milgram, office workers in cities like New York or Tokyo can meet as many as 200,000 unfamiliar people within ten minutes of their office.[18]

One feature that makes cities orderly and decipherable is their physical layout: There are districts for factories, retail shops, cultural activities, financial institutions, and entertainment. The resident soon learns to "read" the city as our predecessors "read" the forest. Appearance was once sufficient to identify and gauge the trustworthiness of strangers because clothing, hairstyle, and jewelry announced their marital status, wealth, social position, and culture. In less industrialized countries, dress may still indicate social rank, but in modern cities, where different clothing styles are widely available and cavalierly adopted, appearance has lost its reliability as a clue to identity. Today, argues Lofland, locale better reflects the probable behavior of others: Certain behaviors belong to certain areas of a city and this affects our openness to, or avoidance of, the people we meet. If anyone doubts the power of locale Lofland suggests, "Ask people who they are afraid of in the city: it depends on where they happen to be. Not who they are with."[19] To be at home in a city is to know how to distinguish one district from another and thus to know how to communicate with its inhabitants.

Another way to reduce stressful encounters is to treat people on the basis of their nationality, religion, race, sexual orientation, profession, or wealth. Communicative encounters are channeled to increase the likelihood of talking with someone who is similar rather than different. Urban ghettos tend to be of two types: Some arise spontaneously out of a common cultural heritage; others arise out of the hostility of the dominant culture toward people who are different and hence difficult or undesirable to know. The effect of segregation has been to foster one-dimensional enclaves within a city so that citizens are insulated against diversity. Urban barriers to communication lie not only in the architecture of our cities but also in the architecture of our minds: in the categories that govern where we live, attend school, seek employment. Whether this selective screening of companions is necessary to protect a fragile social order or is an evolutionary stage toward a pluralistic rapport within the human community is not yet clear.

Urban Institutions: Impersonal Bureaucracies

Complex cities require complex institutions. Villagers are directly acquainted with the problems they face, know the skills of their neighbors, and are familiar with the consequences of failure to act in the interest of all. No such provincial arrangement could produce the mass housing, complex systems of transport, multiplicity of goods, or sophisticated medical care available in supercities. The consequence has been a gradual bureaucratization of urban life. Corps of specialists monitor emerging problems and relay their diagnoses to policymakers, who transmit programs to heads of agencies; these, in turn, draft the rules for executing policies; finally, these rules are administered by cadres of clerks, who apply them to the cases that arise.

The aim of bureaucracy is efficiency through consistency, speed, and coordination. But this efficiency is often purchased at the cost of impaired communication and human alienation. The features that contribute to efficiency—standardized procedures, emphasis on rules, routinization of tasks, circumscribed authority—often make it unresponsive to those who seek assistance. One student, commenting on the depersonalizing quality of university life, wrote: "One finds that the telephone, official transcripts, registration cards and other artifacts command far more respect and immediate response than do human beings. The tyranny of clocks, schedules, forms, IBM procedures, registration cards and calendars has become so pervasive and powerful as to no longer be within reproach."[20] Citizens feel trapped in an incomprehensible machinery that treats them with impersonality, applies rules without qualification, and is impervious to any persuasion.

If the humanity of those who seek assistance is at risk, it is no less true of those who occupy the bureaucracy: Residents of cities include bureaucrats as well as clients and customers. As knowledge of the world expands, each knows more and more about less and less. Specialists tend to develop a narrow view of things, distinctive values, and a jargon all their own, further complicating communication with anyone outside their specialty. Thus an increasing proportion of human contact takes place between people unequal in knowledge and power. And neither Japan nor the United States has been able to avoid bureaucratization not only of government but of education, industry, and social services.

The Restless Urbanite

The smaller population of the past stayed put. Vance Packard once described his parents as living their entire lives within a thirty-mile radius of their home and knowing every person in their county. Today, he writes, they wouldn't recognize half the people within five hundred yards of their home.[21] In earlier generations people often lived and died within the same building. Such a limited physical environment ensured the permanence and intensity of their bonds; long friendships were perhaps due less to an unusual talent for communicating than to confinement to the same place.

Urbanites of today can scarcely confront a more contrasting physical environment. The average American moves roughly fourteen times between birth and death, spending fewer than five years in any single place of residence. Even in Japan, where mobility is less pronounced, the average person will move five times in a lifetime. For many, home ownership has been replaced by leasing a condominium or renting an apartment on a year-to-year basis. The social consequences of this sort of rootlessness are nearly impossible to gauge.

As the accelerating pace of invention condemns technologies and technicians to earlier and earlier obsolescence, companies form and disband overnight, forcing employees to leave jobs in shrinking industries and relocate in expanding ones. Many corporate and public organizations, in addition, pursue policies of "forced mobility," insisting that employees transfer every two or three years to broaden their experience. Often they involve moving across the country or across the world. And to the ranks of the periodically uprooted must be added the permanently rootless: migratory workers, military personnel, airline employees, construction crews, and a multitude of others.

These conditions, suggest Bennis and Slater, contribute to the emergence of a "temporary society," one in which people are constantly on the move and on the make.[22] People will be peremptorily assigned to task forces of strangers to solve specific problems; upon completing a task the group will be dissolved and reassembled into teams of new strangers to accomplish the next task. Such a society would not only foster but require temporary relationships, temporary housing, temporary friendships, and temporary marriages. Although a temporary society does not yet exist, the forces that nurture it are already present in urban society today, according to Bennis and Slater.

Complicating personal relationships still further is increased social mobility. Accidents of birth or of inheritance no longer dictate the status of people. In Japan and the United States opportunities for education, combined with a freer choice of occupation, have given people greater control over their destiny. Yet the fluidity of the social structure intensifies competition for status and encourages a manipulative attitude toward associates. This condition, in both the United States and Japan, would seem to lessen the openness, spontaneity, and trust on which rapport and loyalty rest. An enforced mobility, physical and social, forces people to form their own circle of companions again and again to avoid finding themselves "surrounded by friends one day, and deserted the next," as Brain notes.

The Harried Urbanite

There is a time dimension, as well, to the new reality. "Our problem," reports Delos Three, "is really tempo, not density."[23] The pace of modern life has introduced complications in personal relationships. One is in the lack of historical continuity that characterized earlier times. The French writer Charles Peguy has noted that "the world has changed less since the time of Jesus Christ than it has in the last thirty years."[24] For centuries each generation has inherited the institutions, technologies, and customs of their predecessors. The past was familiar, the future no less so.

Today, life-styles differ between one decade and another. This lack of continuity can make strangers out of people in their own age. "The continually changing scenery of contemporary society," writes Kenneth Keniston, "is one of the deepest strains in our lives."[25] The most obvious social consequence is the widening gap between generations. There have always been complications in communication between people in their seventies and in their twenties. But such complications surface now between people in their forties and twenties; before long it may make foreigners out of people separated by only a decade. The recent battle cry of those in their twenties was "trust no one over thirty"; just a decade was enough to invalidate the experience of anyone ten years older. Margaret Mead, in *Culture and*

Commitment, announced we had reached a temporal watershed dividing cultures of the past in which the young must learn from the old from cultures where the old must learn from the young. At such a time, she wrote, "We are inevitably lonely as we face one another knowing that they will never experience what we have experienced, and that we can never experience what they have experienced."[26] Edwin Reischauer contends that the generation gap is even more serious in Japan, but is obscured by the avoidance of confrontation and the maintenance of outward cordiality there.[27]

Accompanying the dizzying pace of change is a far wider involvement with the world. The crises of life were once local and manageable within the community. Today the neighborhood extends to the perimeter of the planet. A border clash, an oil embargo, a crop failure, an epidemic may be more devastating in its impact than what happens next door or across town. But the media that disseminate information—radio and newspaper, television and film, satellites and computers—often overwhelm us with capsule accounts, superficial explanations, and partisan judgments. It is not surprising that modern citizens are bewildered in obtaining guidance from an output of over a hundred thousand books annually in both Japan and the United States, especially when combined with publication of over 30,000 periodicals and the airing of half a million radio and television broadcasts yearly. If, as Toynbee suggests, the prime requisite of a satisfying life "is the ability to resist distraction," the technology of communication seems to confound the very process it is designed to promote.

To relieve urban congestion the Japanese and Americans have spread out across the land in search of affordable housing. This has forced the construction of ever more extensive freeway, rail, subway, and bus systems. Yet each extension sentences people to spending an increasing proportion of their waking hours to an endless to-and-fro. Commuting is a distancing experience in more than one way: Millions commute by private automobile, cut off from all who pass or are passed; those who rely on public transportation cultivate strategies to counteract the enforced physical intimacy of crowded subways and buses. On the sidewalk, the urban pedestrians rely on still other avoidance tactics: walking fast, averting eyes, hiding behind newspapers, feigning distraction, even talking to themselves. Modern urban life spent more or less constantly on the move—a life of arrivals and departures—may not be conducive to deep or fulfilling attachments.

A complex urban life would scarcely be tolerable unless millions of people standardized and coordinated their activities. A natural rhythm of life, one dictated by inner need, gives way to a life tuned to external controls. Activities are segregated in time as well as in space: There is a time to wake, eat, commute, work, sleep, even a time to arrive at the tennis court, cinema, and concert hall. Rarely have people been so subject to the dictation of clocks, calendars, schedules, and appointment books. In both Japan and the United States a premium is also placed on speed: Any act that can be performed faster is rewarded, adding more impetus to the rush, rush, rush called the "rat race." Time becomes a commodity: It is "spent," it is "saved." Yet few, if any, human encounters appear to benefit from being speeded up, from making conversation to making love. The urgency that pervades urban life means that conversations may be forced rather than spontaneous, more informative than insightful, more incomplete than fulfilling. They take place on the run to somewhere, or someone, else; they often begin abruptly and end prematurely.

THE NEW SOCIAL REALITY

When society consisted of small enclaves where people knew one another for a lifetime, social life may have been boring, the choice of companions limited, invasions of privacy commonplace, pressures to conform confining, people often being trapped in relationships that were tiresome or trying. Social conventions may have been sterile or even stifling.

The supercities of today, with their monumental scale, mounting congestion, massive institutions, and accelerated pace, have challenged the norms that for centuries have regulated human affairs. What sort of social life is evolving in this new context? Does it serve the needs of urban residents?

Although there may be much to decry about life in large cities, the ultimate test of their vitality lies in their capacity to survive. Do our cities work? The answer clearly is yes. Periodically we ask if Tokyo or New York is governable or habitable, but most large cities not only survive, they grow in number and size. If they are not always attractive, or pleasant to work in, they are stimulating and invigorating places to be; there is an energy and excitement about them that draws people to them even while loudly protesting their inconvenience.

Cities offer a variety of jobs, recreation, housing, schools, and cultural activities unmatchable in smaller communities. There is a far wider choice of compatible companions. The city dweller is free to expand or contract his or her circle of friends at any time. Increased mobility, while it strains existing bonds, releases people periodically from soured relationships and permits them to form new circles of companions. Interdependence is not less critical today but arises more often from a choice of responsibilities than from enforced obligation.

Still no one would argue that adaptation to this new age has been an unalloyed success: Adaptation is rarely accomplished without some pain. Learning to live in villages under a stable social order took thousands of years. Many of these experiments failed and we have only a few artifacts to testify to their existence. To live in the midst of millions of strangers during an era of radical change is another matter.

Urban Isolation and Loneliness

One of the alleged costs of urban life has been an increase in the extent and depth of loneliness bred among city dwellers. Many like the privacy the city provides; being alone is less a problem than is the lack of deep involvement with one or two close companions. We have a powerful need for another person to talk to and listen to, to nurture and be nurtured by, to provide connection with the larger community. "People are more frightened of being lonely," says Frieda Fromm-Reichman, "than of being hungry, or being deprived of sleep, or having their sexual needs fulfilled."[28]

Evidence of isolation is not hard to find: Sociologists, from the classic Middletown studies of the 1920s to the past decade, report one fourth or more of the population with "no intimate friends" or "no friends at all." The expanding services legislated by government, from suicide clinics and drug rehabilitation programs to family counseling, are aimed, at least in part, at providing the nurturance that previously came from families and friends. Where public efforts stop, private enterprise encourages companionship through singles bars, computer dating, encounter groups, retirement associations, travel tours, classes, and study groups. All, to some degree, attempt to redress the communicative failure of neighborhood, home, school, and office. Even the current fascination with objects—television sets, records and tapes, sports cars, and home computers—may reflect dissatisfaction with personal relationships; purchased objects are sometimes treated better than acquaintances.

Many explanations are offered for the anomie of city dwellers. Loneliness is not a simple consequence of rootlessness; those who move frequently appear no more lonely than those who do not. Many people have superficial or fleeting involvements with many other people, but no deeply satisfying ones. Vance Packard describes the plight of many urbanites when he writes, "He drifts between communities of amiable strangers. He may be immensely affable . . . but he finds a sense of community only on the occasion of accidents, dog fights, wife beatings, flash floods, fires or earthquakes."[29]

There is a paradoxical quality, as well, to loneliness. In one of the more provocative analyses of modern life, Philip Slater has argued that loneliness is of our own creation, that the cultivation of independence terminates in loneliness as surely as dependence ends in slavery: "We seek a private house, a private means of transportation, a private garden, a private laundry, self-service stores, and do-it-yourself skills of every kind. An enormous technology seems to have set itself the task of making it unnecessary for one human being to ever ask anything of another in the course of going about his daily business. We seek more and more privacy and feel more and more alienated and lonely when we get it."[30] In the modern city there is virtually nothing that a solitary person cannot do or provide for himself or herself except affection and intimacy.

For those who are not lonely, the bond with others is often precarious. Ours is an "Age of Transience" when all ties with places, objects, and companions may be temporary. Our mobility encourages the making of "contacts," but these contacts may be shallow and opportunistic.

A high rate of divorce characterizes most industrial nations but is at its highest in the United States and has doubled in the past decade in Japan. But because divorce is the only form of detachment that is ritualized and recorded, it may greatly underestimate the frailty of personal affiliation. If a rate of disengagement could be calculated for broken friendships as well as marriages, the rate might be even more astonishing. Mobility and the fast pace of life may promote "Kleenex friendships," "one-night stands," and "serial monogamy." It would not be surprising if urban life cultivated a reluctance to invest in relationships that have little chance of enduring. But whether this is true or not awaits the collection of data.

Contact with Strangers

Part of the problem is traceable to increased contact with strangers. The urban resident meets hundreds of unknown people every day and must acquire ways of dealing with them. The twentieth century, writes Ronald Laing, is unparalleled in the cultivation of "tactics of nonmeeting."[31] City life seems to require a mastery of the communicative arts of noninvolvement such as the defensive stance, impatient gait, or glazed expression of the pedestrian. Once home, the unlisted phone and locked door with spy hole protect the privacy of the resident. For the strangers one must meet on a functional basis—cashiers, bus drivers, salesclerks, waiters—a cautious amiability allows tasks to be completed pleasantly but also sets clear limits on involvement. A growing guardedness seems to characterize daily life in a large city.

Dehumanizing Relationships

A complex technology also replaces many encounters with people with encounters with machines: automatic tellers, recorded messages, programmed elevators, factory robots, ticket machines, televised lectures, food dispensers. Computers now cash our checks, or lose them, analyze our blood pressure, test for pregnancy, reply to inquiries and answer complaints, verify or invalidate signatures. At the supermarket or self-service gas station we are encouraged, however, to "Smile! You are on camera!" A classic student film, *Have I Told You Lately That I Love You?* records a day in the life of an urban family who, surrounded by radio alarm, thermostat, automatic coffee maker, ticker tape, food freezer, microwave oven, television set, and electric blanket, find it unnecessary to talk to each other at all.

Mechanization, of course, contributes in another way to the objectification of humans; the more society relies on machines, the more such machines require machinelike behavior from their users. Machines, employing the crudest of languages and possessing minimal flexibility, cannot deal with unique or capricious operators; users must conform to the primitive vocabularies and narrow options of the machine. The advantages these devices offer—precision, consistency, speed—are precisely those that make for a dull and predictable person. What is required for healthy personal relations—spontaneity and individuality—are the very qualities that technology cannot tolerate. Yet an increasing part of daily life is spent with switches, knobs, and keyboards, none of which cultivates the empathic depth that makes one an interesting companion.

The scope of contemporary organization appears also to diminish occasions for truly personal encounters: Massive bureaucracies are not, in the way they function, very different from machines. They favor the category over the individual, rulebook over reality, fact over feeling, routine over novelty. Those who inhabit such organizations—and most of us do—as well as those who approach them, rarely meet as persons but only according to the script and role demanded by the offices we serve.

As a consequence, there is growing dependence on contracts and courts for regulating the conduct even of people who know each other well. Mutual obligations in the classroom, office, and even the home are put into writing and subject to court action if violated by either party. Contracts replace the commitments that tempered relationships in earlier times. The United States has roughly twice as many lawyers as physicians. Where Americans are defended from each other by one lawyer for every seven hundred people, the Japanese get along with one for every ten thousand citizens. But the number grows in both countries.

Urban Pathologies
Is there any evidence that growing congestion, rootlessness, or mechanization has increased the incidence of physical and mental disorders? Some indexes of pathology—rates of violence, psychiatric disorder, and drug addiction—suggest this is the case. Studies show that single, divorced, and widowed people, those without permanent attachments, are more prone to illness, premature death, cancer, and heart disease. James Lynch, writing in *The Broken Heart: The Medical Consequences of Loneliness*, claims loneliness kills.

There is accumulating evidence that to be without frequent communication with close friends contributes to emotional disturbances. In an early study by Herman Lantz, one thousand men referred to a mental clinic were classed according to the severity of their illness and number of friends they had when they were between four and ten years of age. Of those classed as "normal" or "mild neurosis," 61.5 percent had five or more friends, but of those diagnosed as "severe neurosis" or "psychosis" 85 percent reported having no friends during that period of their lives.[32] In one sense insanity is the ultimate form of loneliness. The growing number of the homeless, the unemployed and unemployable, and those addicted to self-destructive drugs may also comment on the extent of malaise.

No evidence of social failure is as dramatic as the rising incidence of physical aggression against other people, against public property through vandalism, or against the self in the form of suicide. Americans own an estimated 90 million guns, about one for every two adults, and kill around ten thousand people a year with them. More and more residents are afraid to enter certain areas of their own cities, refuse to go out at night, or remain barricaded behind locked doors. Even in Japan, where crime is at its lowest among industrialized nations, the number of offenses steadily increases and is at its highest level in postwar years.

Although the United States has the highest, and Japan the lowest, rate of homicide, the pattern reverses itself somewhat with respect to suicide. If aggressive acts arise from the frustration of human needs, as they are thought to do, the supercities of today appear to contribute to these high levels of intrapersonal and interpersonal violence.

CULTURES: THE MEDIATING FACTOR

How have the United States and Japan responded to the unprecedented challenges of life in the twentieth century? Although the United States is a huge land of immense resources and Japan a country of limited habitable land and resources, the two countries resemble each other in many ways. Both possess large populations, although the American population is more heterogeneous and Japan more homogeneous. Both are highly industrialized and employ the latest and most sophisticated technology. Both are highly urbanized with a comparable number of supercities. Large and complex bureaucracies in both countries administer the policies of government, industry, and education; tens of thousands are employed in these massive institutions. A highly educated population, with specialized skills, has developed equally in both societies. Both share a practical pragmatic approach to problems.

In both countries the standards of living are extremely high, although economic differences are more marked in the United States. Mobility is greater in the United States, but the requirements of modern industry are fast making greater mobility a feature of Japanese life as well. The mass media provide the bulk of information and entertainment in both countries, although control of them is far more centralized in Japan. Personal achievement is prized in both societies, and material success is the major form of recognition.

Yet the two countries have allegedly created distinctive social systems, contrasting patterns of personal relationships, and somewhat different styles of communication. Japan, particularly since Nakane Chie's classic work, has been seen as a vertical society, one in which relations between people are highly sensitive to distinctions based on status. The United States, from de Tocqueville's early assessment to the present, has been regarded as a horizontal society in which social advantage based on age, sex, or affiliation is actively resisted.

For us, a more significant difference lies in the importance attached to the group and to the individual: In Japan the impulses and needs of the individual tend to be subordinated to the good of the group; in the United States any intrusion by the group on the rights of the individual is regarded as unwarranted. (If one is the land of the big WE, the other is the land of the big I.)

Compatible with these orientations is a concern in Japan for minimizing differences, preserving harmony, and reinforcing group loyalty; in the United States for maximizing differences, confrontation, and compromise. The aim of decision making in one is to avoid discord in pursuit of consensus, while in the other it is to promote competition in ideas in pursuit of objective truth. Despite equally pragmatic goals, decisions in Japan according to Nishiyama tend to be based on "mood" but in the United States on "arguments."[33]

PERSONAL RELATIONS: JAPAN AND THE UNITED STATES

In personal encounters many observers claim there are striking differences in the styles of the two cultures. Writers on Japan stress the strong ties to pivotal groups such as the family, school class, work group, and corporation. Americans, in contrast, are seen as maintaining looser and more provisional ties to others. The bonds that matter most in Japan are said to be less a matter of choice than of birth, school, or employment; a large proportion of marriages continue to be arranged by others. Personal relations in the United States are largely matters of choice, and they shift with the changing interests of the partners. Among the Japanese friendships are reportedly more comprehensive and more durable; with Americans they are held to be less comprehensive and less permanent, temporary alliances of tennis players, work colleagues, and photography enthusiasts who do not expect to share their lives totally. The Japanese are supposedly indifferent toward people they do not know, while Americans are more open and trusting of strangers.

Observers of both cultures claim the manner of conversation also differs. If Americans are often described as assertive, the Japanese are described as conciliatory; if Americans favor a rhetoric of exclusion, emphasizing differences, the Japanese favor a rhetoric of inclusion, emphasizing similarities of viewpoint. Where Americans indulge in overstatement and self-congratulatory remarks, the Japanese are said to be inclined toward understatement and self-depreciation.

Even with respect to verbal and nonverbal communication there appears to be some contrast in cultural styles: Among Americans there is great respect for the power of words, for eloquence of expression; among the Japanese there is a corresponding skepticism concerning the authority of words, with noble phrases seen as oversimplifying events. If clarity is the path to truth in one culture, ambiguity is more highly cultivated in the other. Where Americans emphasize the verbal code, what is said, the Japanese place their trust in the nonverbal code, what is left unsaid. If intellect is an instrument of understanding for Americans, it is intuition that is valued among the Japanese.[34]

FROM CONJECTURE TO FACT

Roland Penrose once noted that "the ruthless changes that happen in the external world usually have their counterpart within us."[35] That we confront a new reality in the twentieth century seems undeniable, one marked by congestion, urbanization, industrialization, and bureaucratization. That it will have repercussions on the relations between people seems equally probable. A new level of social organization is likely to breed new forms of social behavior.

Here our concern is with the patterns of human relations in two cultures that confront the challenges of this new reality: Japan and the United States. How do people in each country form ties with one another? What kind of people make up the social circles of Japanese and Americans? What activities do companions share? How intimate are their involvements? How are differences addressed and decisions made? How deep and lasting are their commitments? How, if at all, are people changed by their involvement with one another?

We seek to explore these questions in the following chapters, not at the level of speculation and imagery, but at the level of fact and experience. Critics of every persuasion have offered endless speculations on the character of social life in these two countries. The bulk of the commentary has been negative, focusing on the loneliness, manipulation, and exploitation alleged to result from the quantum leap from village to metropolis. An occasional voice has found compensating benefits in a more stimulating environment, greater diversity of companions, wider range of activities, and expanding latitude of personal freedom. But these conjectures, persuasive and provocative as they are, fail to provide a factual base for evaluating personal relationships today in either country. No one has yet asked Japanese and Americans to describe in detail their actual conduct with strangers, acquaintances, friends, and intimates. It is this challenge, in all its complexity, that this initial exploration seeks to address.

CHAPTER 3

Exploring Social Space:
Japan and the
United States

Although love has been an almost exclusive
preoccupation of literature and legend,
objective reports on human love are
conspicuously scarce. [1]
HARRY F. HARLOW

Cultural patterns appropriate to nomadic life evolved over thousands of years; centuries were required to perfect the institutions and practices appropriate to life in small villages. The pace of change—of challenge to human flexibility—has continually accelerated; no longer evolutionary, providing sufficient time to create new social norms, it must now be described as revolutionary, suddenly confronting people with unforeseeable challenges to traditional ways of conducting human affairs. Today in our supercities we only vaguely sense the consequences of these changes as we rush to avoid becoming victims of our inventions.

SIMILAR FEATURES
OF TWO SOCIETIES

Two modern societies that epitomize this revolution, the United States and Japan, are instructive case studies: Both have been in the vanguard in

35

forming this new reality. They share a remarkable number of features. There are few physical differences visible upon arrival in Tokyo or New York: There are the same skyscrapers, same office buildings, even the same films playing in downtown theaters. Thousands jam the streets, crowding onto buses and subway cars, clustering in bars and coffee shops, wearing similar clothing, and hurrying to similar deadlines.

This similarity is not a result of Westernization of Japan or Easternization of the United States, although there is influence in both directions. It is because modernization has followed a similar course in the two countries: Both are highly industrialized, exploiting every technical innovation to its fullest; both are populous nations with huge urban concentrations of people; in both large-scale institutions—industrial, financial, governmental, academic, medical—dominate the social scene; both cultivate high levels of specialization; both rely on the mass media to supply information and entertainment; both use sophisticated systems of transportation and communication; both have capitalistic economies and democratic political structures; both emphasize productivity and efficiency along with an accelerating pace of life; both experience the increasing social and mental pathologies that accompany life in mass society. Together Japan and the United States are nearly without equals with regard to productivity, accounting for a large proportion of the world's automobiles, computers, aircraft, ships, robots, cameras, and appliances. Although it is easy to become preoccupied with differences, we should not disregard underlying similarities. [2]

There are other respects in which they resemble each other with some qualification. Both enjoy high standards of living; but the somewhat higher per capita income in the United States is offset by the greater contrast between rich and poor; Japan's status as the third most productive nation in the world is offset somewhat by the lower per capita income and more modest material advantages of its citizens. Industrialization, it is said, creates a more egalitarian social order; if so, Japan, with its highly homogeneous population, seems freer of class consciousness (most Japanese see themselves as middle class), while the United States, with its more heterogeneous population, seems more willing to accept and assimilate immigrant populations. Both societies have been described as pragmatic, though in Japan this seems to spring more from a preference for the concrete over the abstract and in the United States from an emphasis on short-term results. In both countries there is considerable social mobility, status being determined more by education and accomplishment than by birth or caste. In the United States there is greater mobility of residence and occupation, while in Japan movement is more limited to changes of status within a framework of lifetime employment with a single organization.

Universal education is a feature of both societies, although literacy is more completely achieved in Japan; in both countries a large number of the young attend universities, although the proportion is markedly higher in the United States. Another sign of a sharp break with the past lies in the emergence of the nuclear family; the United States illustrates its most extreme development, but mounting evidence indicates a parallel change occurring in Japanese families. Since the nuclear family is everywhere stronger in urban than in rural settings, it is not surprising that as people converge upon cities they would share this cultural feature.

That the forces of industrialization and urbanization should have led to similar adaptations in these two countries is not entirely surprising. But it is only part of the picture. As William Caudill observed: "As countries develop a modern social structure in line with the requirements of increasing industrialization and technological advancement, then they do thereby become more alike; but at the same time this does not mean that the traditional culture is lost. Rather, it persists in many important ways that deeply influence a person's way of thinking, his emotional response, and his behavior."[3] Material similarities in the two societies have left sufficient latitude for considerable cultural divergence. Each, as we shall see, has made unique adaptations to the twentieth-century and these may prove instructive in displaying alternative ways of accommodating the drastic changes in the material conditions of life.

CULTURAL PROFILE: THE UNITED STATES

Profiles of cultures are always open to challenge—there are always exceptions—but some appreciation of the general social milieu is essential in understanding the behavior of any people. With regard to the United States one is struck by the diversity of its population, a mosaic of races, religions, nationalities, and languages. It is—if it is not a contradiction in terms—a nation of aliens, settled by waves of immigrants who are still coming in record-breaking numbers to its shores. Yet the Judeo-Christian religious tradition unifies major segments of that population and provides the underlying premises that shape its institutions, laws, and social structure. Out of this ideological heritage comes a deep respect for the individual, one so profound as to resist all limitations on personal freedom. As Emerson wrote in a line that is dear to most Americans, "Whoso would be a man must be a nonconformist."[4] An independent, self-realizing person, faithful to his or her own inner truth, is the ideal. Implicit in this focus on an independent human being is insistence upon equality of treatment without which the fullest personal growth is impossible.

Commitment to individualism and equality is buttressed by a high regard for the values of competition—between persons, between groups, between institutions. (Even the balancing of political power among executive, legislative, and judicial branches of government reflects this.) A rugged individualism, combined with belief in the value of competition, inevitably produces strains and conflicts. To prevent the destructive consequences of unbridled competition, and to keep the contest fair, laws, contracts, or elaborate agreements specify the "rights" and "obligations" of competing or cooperating parties. Justice is considered best served through frank and direct confrontation between opposing parties and opinions. Arguments are offered and rebuttals are heard, leading to some form of compromise that reflects the merits of the case and the power of the contending parties.

Truth, it is believed, is most likely to emerge from a competition of ideas: It should rest on the quality of the evidence marshaled, the logical adequacy of the arguments, and the persuasive appeal of each case. The ability of every person to act as his or her own advocate, to articulate personal opinions trenchantly and persuasively, is cultivated throughout the educational process. The constant encouragement to express one's self, to be heard and felt, understandably promotes a certain assertiveness and propensity for overstatement. Rarely does one gain a position of power without a gift for articulating ideas clearly and eloquently. Underlying all of these cultural features is a deep commitment to the desirability of change, an almost missionary zeal for reforming society, reforming one's companions, and even for reforming one's self. If this accounts for some of the faddish enthusiasms of Americans, it also accounts for their ceaseless pursuit of social reform.

CULTURAL PROFILE: JAPAN

While participating just as fully in the revolutionary changes of the twentieth century, Japan has addressed them from a perspective that contrasts sharply with that of the United States. Here a highly homogeneous population, resistant to invasion and immigration for thousands of years, has cultivated a society that, with only slight variation, shares the same values, norms, language, and aesthetics. There is a strong sense of national identification, and a somewhat greater ease of communication may result from this shared tradition. Its cultural premises have been shaped not by a single religious faith, but by three: Confucianism, Shintoism, Buddhism. Yet all have a form and a content that are uniquely Japanese, and they converge more than they diverge. Out of Confucianism has come what Nakane Chie has called a "vertical society," a hierarchical ordering of society based on status differences with regard to age, tenure, sex, and ability.[5] Out of the Shintoist tradition has arisen an empathy with nature and a search for harmony. Out of the Buddhist tradition has come a sense of humility and of fatalism and a preference for the simple and concrete over the abstract and theoretical.

At the core of the culture is the group rather than the individual. The family not only dominates; it is the prototypic model for society. All large organizations from the school to the corporation, even to the state itself, are modeled upon it. Independent behavior is seen as a threat to the solidarity and performance of the group. While competition is no less a feature of Japan than of the United States, it is a competition between groups rather than individuals, and rewards accrue to the group rather than to a single member. Since group affiliations tend to be permanent, loyalty to the group and conformity to its norms are essential for success.

Conflict is far less common in Japanese society for a number of reasons. First, the emphasis on the group instead of the individual reduces interpersonal friction. Second, an elaborate set of standards emphasize "obligations" over "rights," what one owes to others rather than deserves for oneself. Third, the value attached to harmony cultivates skill in the use of ambiguity, circumlocution, euphemism, and silence in blunting incipient disputes. The ability to assimilate differences, to engineer consensus, is valued above a talent for argument. During the process of acculturation, schools emphasize the cultivation of intuition and respect and the avoidance of words or acts that might antagonize others.

It is as if one society, promoting the expression of differences, must train its citizens to develop compensating strategies for resolving them while the other cultivates strategies for assimilating differences before, or without, their having to be articulated. Truth is seen as more attainable from combining individual viewpoints than from compromising them. In personal relations there is a reluctance to evaluate or change others, especially through confronting them directly.

INTERPERSONAL PROFILES: JAPAN AND THE UNITED STATES

In view of the striking similarities in the material aspects of life in Japan and the United States and the striking differences in their cultural heritages, what might one expect with regard to communicative styles? Who do Japanese and Americans know or not know? How do they meet? How do casual and close relationships differ? How are companions treated? How do friendships evolve over time? How do acquaintances spend time together? What do they do or talk about? What obligations do they assume and what consequences do such attachments have for both parties?

Relations with Strangers

Some speculations about personal relationships can be projected from existing commentaries on Japan and the United States or are implicit in the deeper motives that drive these two social systems. With regard to meeting strangers, for example, one might expect a striking contrast: Americans, it is said, are open to a wider range of possible partners, interacting more easily with strangers on the basis of their attractiveness; the Japanese, because of the importance attached to group affiliations and the obligations associated with them, may be more restrained or even indifferent toward strangers. As one Japanese student put it, "When Americans need a friend they simply go out and meet someone. In contrast, we Japanese are reluctant to *do* anything actively to find a friend."[6] Thus accidental contacts may figure more prominently in the choice of companions in the United States, while in Japan the choice may be more restricted and based on age, class in school, and, later, company affiliation. Such speculations, however, provoke inquiry into the actual behavior that Japanese and Americans display toward strangers.

The Choice of Companions

A hierarchical society is as deeply rooted in Japan as is the egalitarian view held in the United States. As a result, says Reischauer, "it is as natural for a Japanese to shape his interpersonal relations in accordance with the various levels of hierarchy as for an American to attempt to equalize his interpersonal relations despite differences in age and status."[7]

For the Japanese, suggests Nakane, there are three distinct worlds of others: the first, those in one's primary group, one's closest friends and family with whom one has the most informal and intimate ties; a second world includes associates with similar backgrounds and interests where somewhat greater formality prevails; a third category is the functional contacts one has with people whose services are needed, where excessive politeness is appropriate. Those in the last category, including strangers, are not seen as different so much as they are seen as "outsiders," often regarded as "nonpersons."[8]

The criteria by which people select companions also appear to differ. Nakane points out that "attribute" (qualitative features that distinguish one person from another such as "sincere" or "capable") and "frame" (rank or role within a reference group such as vice president or personnel manager) influence the choice of companions in all societies.[9] But in Japan the frame tends to take precedence over the attribute. The habit of exchanging identity cards (*meishi*) during introductions illustrates the extent to which this mediates social interaction: The Japanese, she notes, cannot talk to each other until their status is clarified. Such matters as appearance and similarity of personality might, therefore, have less relevance in the choice of associates. In the United States evidence suggests greater importance is attached to attributes rather than to frame—to individual attractiveness, similarity of attitudes, compatibility of life-styles rather than status. Preliminary visual appraisal may supply enough information about such attributes to prompt an American to talk to or avoid a stranger. In the most intimate of bonds, that of marriage, the cultural contrast is still more striking: In Japan a large proportion of marriages are arranged by third parties, family members, relatives, or employers and are arrived at through collaboration; in the United States the choice of spouse is a spontaneous decision and the exclusive business of the couple who will marry.

In the American view, friendships develop over time. Strangers become acquaintances, acquaintances become friends, and friends become intimates. As people expand the activities they share, self-disclosure is supposed to promote closer relationships. Spontaneity and informality are

cultivated as signs of growing attachment. Talking about the relationship is thought to encourage deeper involvement. In contrast the Japanese may prefer relationships that remain at the same level throughout their duration. Constancy rather than change, with all the risks it involves, may be preferred. Greater formality and respect for social conventions, rather than impulsive and unpredictable acts, may promote this ideal.

Independence and Dependence

Few differences in the cultural ethos may have as profound social consequences as American emphasis on independence and Japanese emphasis on dependence. When Urie Bronfenbrenner visited the People's Republic of China, he was told that the guiding principle was "to serve the people." When asked for the guiding principle of American society, he answered, "to do your own thing."[10] This reluctance to subordinate personal to social needs is captured in an oft-repeated "prayer":

> I'll do my thing
> and you do yours
> If two people find each other—
> it's wonderful—
> If not, it can't be helped.[11]

Friendships are highly valued, but not if they cramp one's personal freedom. Yet this attitude is balanced by a respect for the integrity of others.

Central to understanding Japanese relationships, suggests Doi Takeo, is the principle of *amae*, the effort to establish a protective relationship with others; it is a preference for mutual dependence over mutual independence.[12] To the Japanese ear, says Robert Ozaki, the idea of an independent person "connotes an attitude of defiance, a lack of concern for others." Such Japanese words as *on* (obligation), *giri* (indebtedness), *ninjo* (humanity), *kao* (face), *sekenin* (responsibility), and *gimu* (duty) all emphasize dependence on others and the importance of adapting one's actions to the needs and moods of others.[13] To a Japanese, American preoccupation with the self appears to diminish concern for others; to an American, Japanese sensitivity to others may seem oppressive and crippling. Indeed Ozaki himself questions whether the close-knit bonds of dependency that worked so well in small stable societies can survive in the more complex and mobile societies of today. A nation modeled on the household may be endangered by modernization.

Compromise and Consensus

Another wide cultural difference appears in attitudes toward personal disclosure and the approach to differences. A Japanese student in the United States observed that "the topics talked about are quite different for Americans and Japanese. There is greater frankness between Americans and less inhibition about sharing negative kinds of information."[14] Harmony is valued, but not at the price of disguising or concealing inner convictions. A

EXPLORING SOCIAL SPACE: JAPAN AND THE UNITED STATES   41

tradition of freedom of expression and faith in a dialectical approach to truth, make conflict an often unavoidable feature of friendships. As I noted in an earlier study:

> Interaction among Americans provides an opportunity for the expression of personal meanings, hence becomes an arena for confrontation. Ideas are its subject matter. Argument is its means. Valid conclusions are its aim. The maintenance of rapport is less important than stimulating a variety of points of view.[15]

"Telling it like it is," even if that sometimes complicates relationships, is often valued.

With respect to his own culture, the Japanese student quoted earlier remarked, "With Japanese I talk about less personal and less serious topics when we meet." This tendency toward limited disclosure, combined with a desire to avoid or absorb differences, promotes the harmony so valued in the Japanese culture. "To avoid friction," Kurt Singer noted, "seems more important than to eradicate evil."[16] Japanese conversation appears to possess unique characteristics:

> For the Japanese, conversation is a way of creating and reinforcing the emotional ties that bind people together. Interpersonal attitudes are its content. Intuition is its mode. Social harmony is its aim. Differences of opinion, and particularly arguments, since they disrupt the atmosphere and divide the group, arouse apprehension.[17]

The course of conversation in the two countries appears to follow a different rationale: In the United States communicants listen for what is invalid and unacceptable about a remark; in Japan they listen for what is acceptable and agreeable about it. Both seem to serve their users well, although they provoke different levels of animosity and different truths.

Even the tools of communication—words and gestures—seem differently viewed by the two cultures. In the United States language is respected as a way of clarifying positions, of comparing and contrasting views, and a way, ultimately, of testing the relative merits of divergent opinions. Words are the primary tool of discourse. In Japan words are somewhat distrusted and seen as less reliable guides to a complex and elusive reality; words are *a*, but not *the*, means of communication. The nonverbal channels, though less precise, seem better suited to the expression of feelings, and feelings may be more significant than facts. "One crucial thing about learning to be Japanese," writes Harumi Befu, "is to know what people mean without (their) saying it."[18] Where one society seeks clarity, the other is more comfortable with ambiguity; where one attaches importance to what was said, the other is more tuned to what was implied. Each style appears consistent with their distinctive views of communication, one seeing it as an instrument of analysis, the other as a means of promoting harmony.

Transient and Permanent Ties

A cultural difference appears to affect the permanence of personal bonds as well. As Jack Seward notes, "While most Westerners believe that the more friends we have, the better off we are, the Japanese tend to shy away from additional acquaintances, feeling that each is more a burden than a pleasure or source of gain."[19] Hesitancy about forming new relationships, as Seward suggests, may be linked to the heavier obligations Japanese assume for their companions. When asked to describe how friendships might end, one Japanese was astonished at the question: "The ending of a relationship . . . it is a strange thing even to think about." It is claimed that Japanese friendships involve a lifelong responsibility for others. Among Americans such ties are claimed to be more tentative and temporary. The greater geographic and occupational mobility of Americans may make permanent ties less feasible, or it may reflect a feeling that changes in one's self and others make permanent commitments problematical.

Interpersonal crises, too, carry different implications in the two cultures. Friendships in the United States are assumed to involve conflict. A certain amount of tension and disagreement is viewed with both resignation and excitement: resignation because it is an unavoidable consequence of two people sharing their lives and excitement because it offers a chance to learn more about themselves and each other. To Japanese eyes one of the most shocking features of American social life is the way friendships survive frequent and even violent confrontations. The Japanese view of conflict is dramatically at odds with this. As Robert Ozaki emphasizes: "One wrong phrase may sever the human connection. One inappropriate gesture may turn out to be a fatal mistake, the beginning of the end of a warm friendship. In Japan, no one can afford to take a chance. A Japanese is compelled to be polite and reserved."[20] While Western observers are prone to write this off as evidence of Japanese insincerity, it is better explained by a desire to avoid hurting others unnecessarily and because their identity rests in such affiliations rather than an isolated self.

Of course friendships do end in both cultures—and for a variety of reasons. Unless a friendship involves very close companions, Americans tend to view it less as a tragedy than an inevitable phenomenon. Some end because of external circumstances, others because the connection no longer seems promising. Once ended, new friends are sought. Separations also occur in Japan, but they appear to be more strongly resisted and are rarely seen as truly terminated. Even when distance makes contact difficult, friendships remain on "hold," ready to be renewed should circumstances change.

A still sharper contrast appears in the process of reconciliation. The rugged individualism and assertiveness of Americans produces not only opposing opinions but clashes of will as well. Although these conflicts more often strain than rupture friendships, breakups do occur. Once broken, however, they may be rather easily restored. A greater fear of such rifts makes

Japanese relationships less subject to breakdown. But when breaks occur the friendship is less likely to be restored. A recent effort to study reconciliation aborted after extensive interviews failed to reveal a single case of a broken Japanese friendship being reestablished.

That Americans choose companions from a wider range of people, select on the basis of impulse, confront differences frankly, see friendship as a source of personal growth, and prefer more informal and disclosing encounters *may* be true. That Japanese acquire friends more through accidents of schooling and employment than by choice, more sharply differentiate between strangers and acquaintances, avoid unpredictable encounters, find dependency satisfying, and prefer harmony to periodic crises and conflicts *may* also be true.

But we do not know. Reasonable as these observations seem, they lack objective confirmation. And such profiles may exaggerate or minimize—may even overlook—features of social life in these two countries. We need broader and more reliable data on the actual interpersonal behavior of Japanese and Americans.

THE PARAMETERS OF INQUIRY

Many accounts of the two societies contrast them in global terms as vertical and horizontal cultures, shame and guilt cultures, or exterior and interior cultures. But such generalizations reveal little of the conduct of daily life, of how ordinary people meet, spend their lives together, and, in the process, enrich or impoverish one another.

Culture is, above all, a way of living. Only through examining the ordinary and the mundane can we confront culture at its most elemental level. Two people in creating a relationship are a microcosm of the larger society—reflecting it and creating it—in the way they communicate with one another. If friendships become more formal or manipulative, the society becomes more formal and manipulative; if they become more informal and harmonious, the culture becomes more informal and harmonious.

In venturing into this unfamiliar territory there are few tools to assist us. All suffer from one or more limitations. Emory Bogardus, one of the first to explore social life, used a Social Distance Scale to measure the psychic distance people wanted to keep between themselves and people of other nationalities and life-styles. People were simply asked if they wanted certain people—agnostics, communists, Bulgarians, and so on—in their country, city, neighborhood, and homes. It measured the intensity of prejudice against various "outsiders."[21] Later Paul Wright developed an Acquaintance Description Form, which elicited the broad characteristics of friends but revealed little of their activities together.[22] Clifford Swenson's Love Scale contained a hundred questions about the attitudes and activities of specific intimates. But it focused only on certain types of companions, sampled only a few kinds of behavior, and has not been validated for cross-cultural comparison. [23]

Arguing that the process of forming attachments is an orderly one in which two people gradually expose more facets of their lives and at deeper levels, Irwin Altman and Dalmas Taylor have developed an Intimacy Scale for measuring closeness. It, too, is limited by its emphasis on attitudes rather than actions and by its lack of cross-cultural sensitivity. [24] Still the idea that intimacy deepens gradually over time is an important assumption to test. Taking almost the opposite view, N. A. Polansky and associates hypothesize that relationships progress through a series of stages or steps, periods of uncertainty and instability followed by periods of integration and stability. [25] Friendships, thus, might remain for long periods, even permanently, at a stage that was comfortable for both people. Confirmation of both hypotheses awaits an instrument capable of testing the relative merits of these two explanations.

Perhaps the most extensive probing of friendships was reported recently by Mary Parlee. [26] Questionnaires mailed to forty thousand subscribers to *Psychology Today* were asked a battery of questions about traits of their friends, attitudes toward friendship, and "liked" and "disliked" behaviors. Overall these studies demonstrate the feasibility of exploring personal relations, but have also exposed a number of difficulties in doing so.

The first limitation results from focusing too often upon friendship as an idea, rather than as a concrete experience. Statements such as "Describe what friendship means to you" may provoke discussion but reveals little of what happens in real life. More pointed inquiries such as "What do you seek in a friend?" elicit only ambiguous traits and presume that choices are conscious and deliberate. Attraction to others is often a mystery, as we are often a mystery to ourselves. Often people confess, "I haven't the faintest idea why I like her, but I do" or "I know he is irritating sometimes but that won't stop us from being friends." Focused questions such as "What are your friends like?" tend to elicit a list of static qualities that do little to reflect the ebb and flow of thoughts and feelings in real encounters. Friendships are with particular people, not with types, and consist of an exchange of actions that promote or discourage attachment.

Even when behavior is the focus (as it rarely has been), there is a chance of semantic slippage. People tend to be asked about particular categories of partners—acquaintances, dates, parents, friends—but it is doubtful that these terms carry precisely the same meaning or identify people of similar status for each respondent. Every person within such categories may arouse quite different feelings. The difficulty cannot be overcome by using hypothetical situations or partners because they often provoke idealized or socially appropriate answers rather than describing how people act in relation with their actual friends and associates.

A final difficulty is the lack of suitable instruments for studying communicative behavior across cultures. Existing instruments are not only unsuitable, they also lack cross-cultural validation and translation. None have been used outside the cultures that created them. Yet cross-cultural comparisons of bonding behavior might reveal what is universal and what is culturally unique about personal relationships.

If one wants to find out about people, one of the best ways to do so is to ask them. But what is asked, and how it is asked, affects the quality of the answers. Our aim was to create an instrument that might be used to explore social behavior in Japan and the United States, but to do so in a way that would minimize the sources of error just noted. Consequently, we observed the following criteria in constructing the Barnlund–Campbell Dimensions of Interpersonal Relations instrument. First, respondents rather than investigators, should name the people who made up their circle of companions. Categories such as "relatives," "friends," and "work associates" force people to employ categories that may be differently interpreted or irrelevant in their choice of partners. Second, it should be a multidimensional instrument to capture the variety of ways people initiate and conduct their social lives. As in a "multiphasic physical examination," which tests the sight, hearing, heart, and lungs of a patient, the assessment of social life should include the diverse ways people affiliate. Our third requirement was that the instrument focus on acts, on what people have said or have done rather than on their conceptions of intimacy, ideal relationships, or the traits of desirable companions. To reduce errors of recall the questions should only refer to the recent past in asking what people have said or done, how often, and with what partners.

Finally, completing the Dimensions of Interpersonal Relations questionnaire should not only yield a rich body of cultural data but also benefit those who complete it. It is paradoxical that people who regularly submit to physical checkups rarely subject their social lives to scrutiny, reviewing who their associates are, how often these people are seen, how time is spent with them, and how they enrich or diminish their lives. The questionnaire, thus, should put people in closer touch with themselves and the realities of their social lives. This appears to have been the case for many who completed the Dimensions of Interpersonal Relations questionnaire.

THE INSTRUMENT: DIMENSIONS OF INTERPERSONAL RELATIONS

One way to explore cultures is to examine them at a macroscopic level, seeking to identify the broadest norms that regulate social life: Ruth Benedict's *Patterns of Culture*, Margaret Mead's *Social Organization of the Manu'a*, and Gerardo Reichel-Dolmatoff's *The Amazonian Cosmos* illustrate this comprehensive approach. Another is to select a simple critical event and subject this fragment of social life to microscopic analysis. "How to Enter a Hakan House" by Charles Frake and "Pattern of Criticism in Japan and United

States" by Nomura and Barnlund illustrate this narrow approach.[27] We chose a middle level of analysis, one that was neither macroscopic nor microscopic in perspective.

Even with the level of inquiry specified, there are still many strategies for obtaining information on the conduct of personal relationships. They range from unstructured interviews to the design of laboratory experiments. To conduct hundreds of interviews in Japan and the United States was impractical not only because of the costs involved but also because of the difficulties in generalizing from the different ways people might describe their behavior. And the experimental mode, while the most rigorous in testing hypotheses, is less suited to generating hypotheses and seems better suited to the final stages of scientific inquiry. For these reasons a comprehensive questionnaire was desired, suitable for use with large samples of Japanese and Americans, that would explore behavior in social encounters with a variety of companions. The aim was to gain a clearer view of the social norms operating in these two countries but one based on how Japanese and Americans actually behaved with their close associates.

Central to this inquiry were two questions: (1) Who are the people who make up the social worlds of Japanese and Americans? (2) How do Japanese and Americans communicate with companions at various degrees of intimacy? The Dimensions of Interpersonal Relations questionnaire explores these issues through a series of eight subscales that probe different facets of social behavior.

Although we are born into some relationships—with parents, siblings, and other relatives—for the most part we are born into a world of strangers. Some will become members of our circle of friends, most will not. A Stranger Scale examines Japanese and American attitudes toward strangers, the bases of selection or rejection, and the frequency with which these result in closer ties.

Next an Acquaintance Inventory identifies the attributes of the people chosen to play a significant role in the life of the respondent. What specific persons are found at the periphery and at the center of the social circles of Japanese and Americans? What are the demographic characteristics of these companions? Where did they first meet, and where do they spend time together? How long has the relationship lasted? How much time is spent with each partner?

An almost totally neglected feature of social life is how we spend time with friends. What sorts of activities are representative of various degrees of closeness? People who like one another usually arrange to pursue certain interests together. An Interact Scale was created to examine the types of activities and the nature of involvement in them. How often do people participate in physical, cultural, spiritual, and sensual activities with their companions? Do these experiences promote independence, competition, or collaboration? Are there similarities or differences in the activities, or in the form of relationships, favored by Japanese and Americans?

Although people who feel some affection for each other do many things together, closer companions are distinguished by their capacity to talk to each other, to understand and respond empathically to what each says. Our Verbal Communication Scale explores the variety of topics discussed and the depth of disclosure with the closest and more distant partners.

For other ways of sharing experience a Physical Communication Scale assesses the way time, space, touching, gift giving, and silence were employed as alternative channels of communication.

Friendship carries certain responsibilities with it. The closer the bond, the stronger the commitment to promoting the welfare of the other person. Hence an Accommodation Scale evaluates how Japanese and Americans take responsibility for their friends. The questions examine the extent to which material possessions are shared and the extent to which respondents sacrificed time and effort to help their partners.

Since conflict is nearly inevitable in any relationship, people must find some way of accommodating it or risk terminating the bond. A Difference Scale surveys the dominant ways of managing conflicts over leisure time, personal habits, financial matters, and everyday tasks of Japanese and Americans.

Any significant attachment to another person is also likely to change the people involved. The closer the bond, the more deeply are unique ways of thinking and acting likely to become incorporated into the personalities of close companions. Although it is one of the most elusive of all consequences of intimacy, an Affiliation Scale explores the extent to which the ego boundaries of respondents have remained unchanged or have expanded to assimilate traits of their partners.

Two other features of the Dimensions of Interpersonal Relations questionnaire deserve comment. One is an item that asks respondents if they would prefer to have more or fewer friends and acquaintances. The second item appears at the end of the questionnaire. All participants were asked to indicate if their answers gave an "accurate" or "inaccurate" picture of their behavior. If the latter was the case they were asked to indicate what had been overlooked, minimized, or maximized. Too rarely are participants in scientific studies asked to offer their own insight into the procedures followed; in this case their assistance was encouraged and provided another measure of the quality of the data.

THE SAMPLE: JAPANESE AND AMERICANS

Many features of the scientific enterprise have their parallel in everyday life; like scientists, laypeople must identify problems, collect relevant information, and interpret what they have found. One of the critical steps in all inquiry—whether it is testing the bath water, reckoning the moisture content of grain, or predicting the outcome of the next election—is to secure a representative sample that will give a reliable estimate of the large population of which it is a part.

The testing of millions of Japanese and Americans would be prohibitively expensive and time consuming. And the processing of the quantity of data obtained might be less accurate than more careful testing of a smaller but representative sample. Is it possible to secure such a sample? Perhaps not if one insists on including every segment of the population, but it is feasible to study a limited yet significant part of the whole in considerable depth.

Our focus was on college students in the social sciences and humanities in Japan and the United States. While they are not representative of their cultures as a whole, they constitute a large and important part of it. More significantly, any findings are likely to underestimate rather then overestimate cultural differences in the population as a whole. Acculturation has already taken place in large part, but it is still not complete. And, since we seek the shape of the future rather than of the past, their patterns of communicating with one another may suggest its direction.

The size of a sample is always controversial to some degree. No one has yet specified the perfect sample size; it depends on what is being studied. From a theoretical standpoint, the larger the sample, the better; from a practical standpoint, the smaller the better. It should be large enough so that extreme cases—individuals who are overly sociable or overly withdrawn—do not unduly bias the results. The size of samples employed here, 423 Japanese and 444 Americans, seems more than adequate.

The samples were also as similar as possible with respect to all but their cultural backgrounds. One requirement was that they be drawn from different geographical areas and cities of different sizes. Japanese participants were enrolled in public and private universities in Fukuoka, Kyoto, Matsue, Tokyo, and Chiba City. The American sample included students enrolled in public and private universities in New York, Minneapolis, Denver, Reno, and San Francisco.

Preliminary testing for comparability of the two samples showed no significant differences in the age range (eighteen to twenty-four), or in their mean ages (Japanese = 19.99 years; American = 20.44 years). Nor was there any significant difference in the proportion of males and females (Japanese males = 207, American males = 204; Japanese females = 216; American females = 237). They were alike also with regard to their years of education (Japanese = 14.02 years; Americans = 14.62 years). And they were raised in families of remarkably comparable size (Japanese family size = 5.3; American family size = 5.4).

As one might expect, there were some differences. The first concerned "place of residence." Although both samples included about the same number who lived in houses, apartments, and dormitories, more Japanese lived at home with their parents while a greater proportion of Americans lived in apartments with peers. Another difference appeared with respect to birth order: The Japanese sample included more first-born and only children while the American sample was almost equally divided between first-born and only children and later borns. Yet there was no difference in the proportion of eldest children in the two samples.

There is good reason to conclude that these samples are sufficiently alike with regard to age, sex, home environment, education, and family size to attribute any differences in their communicative styles mainly to the influence of culture.

THE QUALITATIVE-QUANTITATIVE DILEMMA: A FINAL NOTE

It is understandable if people feel some misgivings about the capacity of quantified data to capture the elusive qualities of human acts. Yet numbers are often a more, rather than less, sensitive tool for describing human experience than are words. To characterize a friendship as "close" or a companion as "a lot like me" may sound precise until one probes the meaning of "close" and "a lot like me." How close? And in what ways? If a friend is "a lot like me" we need to know "in what respects" and "to what degree." If, instead, we can specify that someone is closer than five other acquaintances but not as close as two other acquaintances, then we have gained, not lost, precision. If "a lot like me" means two people are similar in five of seven respects but differ in two, we have, again, increased the quality of our knowledge.

Whether or not the Dimensions of Interpersonal Relations instrument provides an accurate picture of the subtle and complex ways people relate was raised during the pilot states of the investigation. The question deserved a serious answer so a number of questionnaire responses were converted into prose remarks of the kind one person might make in telling someone about a social encounter. When read, these paragraphs seemed remarkably similar to what one might casually and spontaneously say to someone who inquired about an encounter. For example:

> I met a woman, about twenty, before class yesterday. She opened the conversation because she needed some information. We talked for about half an hour. She was not attractive but not unattractive either. She probably had less schooling than I, but the way she was dressed suggested a better income. I would guess we probably have similar social attitudes, political views, and life-styles, but that we belong to different religions and probably have different interests. I wouldn't mind seeing her again.

Participants in the study were also asked into a collaborative relationship with the investigators in completing the questionnaires. First, their participation was invited, never required, and their anonymity protected by immediately substituting identifying numbers to replace their names. Second, they were asked to use this as an occasion for examining their manner of socializing with others for the insight they might gain from it, and a number of them commented on how much they had learned from the experience. Finally, the last page of the questionnaire invited each person to evaluate the extent to which their answers gave an accurate or inaccurate picture of their relationships. If inaccurate they were asked in what respects the questionnaire gave too much or too little importance to various facets of such relationships or had failed to include relevant features of them. The evaluations were very reassuring: A large majority of all respondents indicated that the Dimensions of Interpersonal Relations instrument gave an accurate picture of their interpersonal communicative behavior.

Students of social behavior often face this dilemma of the relative value of qualitative and quantitative information. It is why many investigators favor both modes of inquiry wherever possible. Each has its place, its special form of knowledge, and each suffers from inherent limitations; both deserve to be respected and, at the same time, to be viewed with caution. Here, for various reasons, the approach is more quantitative than qualitative, but the findings address, and hopefully illuminate, issues of deep humanistic concern.

CHAPTER 4

A World
of Strangers

The streets are full of people,
So full of people, they're ready to burst

But everywhere you go
They're nothing but strangers.[1]
ABE KOBO

At one time, almost until the day before yesterday, nearly all the people one might meet in a day, or a lifetime, were familiar. On rare occasions strangers might appear and one had to decide whether to welcome them, worship them, or attack them. But, as Lyn Lofland notes:

> It's one thing to kill such persons when they appear infrequently; it's another when they are constantly about. It's quite possible to provide every stranger one meets with bed and board and good fellowship, but only as long as one doesn't meet too many. It's plausible to believe that the first stranger one sees is a god; it strains one's credibility to think that 100,000 gods have congregated in one place.[2]

On an average day a resident of our large cities is unlikely to talk with or even notice most of the people who share the same sidewalks, offices, stores, or dwellings that he or she does. Truly we inhabit a world of strangers.

As more and more people press into less and less space, they are forced

53

to invent new modes of accommodation: involvement must be limited, spontaneity curtailed, psychic distance created to counteract the effects of physical proximity. Arnold Toynbee, concerned with the psychological challenge of metropolitan environments, observed:

> It is in this environment that civilized man has to live—safe from infections but threatened by degenerative diseases; safe inside his home, but not in the streets, isolated in the crowd, exposed to neuroses and psychoses. How many of these conditions are caused by the fact that our children must be caught by the hand in the streets and taught that they live in hostile surroundings?[3]

What was once communal space has become dangerously uncommunal. No one yet knows the extent to which training children to avoid the overtures of strangers will, in later life, encourage social paranoia toward anyone who is unknown or different. Despite the safety of its streets, Japan has cultivated an attitude of indifference toward strangers; even the United States, once the most open of societies, is forced by rising violence to discourage openness toward strangers. Yet indifference and mistrust are precisely what encourage the image of city life as characterized by isolation and aloneness. "To experience the city," writes Lofland, "is to experience anonymity."[4] The stranger is no longer the exception but the rule.

The character of human relationships, however, is no more than a reflection of the context of village and supercity; each has its attractions and each its drawbacks. If small towns promote familiarity, they also afford a narrower range of companions and subject residents to almost constant scrutiny and control. Deviation from communal norms not only arouses stronger censure, but can be more devastating because all of one's companions are acquainted; disapproval comes from every point in the social matrix. And the stability of village life forces one to put up with the consequences of any indiscretion for as long as one lives in the community.

Large cities offer a far wider choice of companions among a far more diverse set of eligible partners. But this variety requires more communicative flexibility to initiate conversations with a more differentiated and transient population. Acquaintances and friends are people with whom, by definition, we have already experienced modest communicative success, but with strangers we have no way of knowing how efforts to talk with them will turn out. As a result, city friendships are more often based on only one or two shared interests or activities. People are less completely involved with one another, less totally dependent. But that also means they are less subject to censure and control by any single person or group: If existing companions fail to satisfy one's social needs, it is always possible to drop them and search for more compatible associates. At the same time, such temporary friendships appear more fragile and less capable of supplying the deepest confirmation and support.

URBAN INDIFFERENCE

The greater interdependence of village life may encourage greater sensitivity to others while city life may discourage one from becoming one's brother's keeper. In the city, private tragedies may go unnoticed; even those that occur in public are met with indifference. The Genovese case in which dozens of bystanders watched a woman being murdered without so much as informing the police is an extreme instance, but not without precedent in police files. Responsibility for others in times of tragedy—unemployment, catastrophic illness, physical assault, accident and injury, senility—tends to be transferred from kith and kin to the impersonal welfare office, emergency services, the police, and nursing homes.

The indifference of residents of large cities, according to Margaret Wood, "is an impersonal attitude born of necessity for conserving his own energies and for preserving a measure of freedom and of privacy even though living in the midst of crowds."[5] Where small towns may provide a less stimulating environment, large cities overpower their residents with sensory overload. Where small towns are congenial to spontaneous encounters between friends and to conversations that proceed at a slower pace, city life may force people into scheduled, often interrupted, and abruptly concluded brief encounters with even close companions.

Neither village nor metropolis has any monopoly on virtue or vice, but each creates a radically different setting for social life. "The city is," according to Wood, "at once more personal and more impersonal in its relationships than the country, more lenient and more critical in its judgments of others, more tolerant and more intolerant in its attitudes toward outsiders."[6] To exchange a world that was populated more with friends than strangers for one populated more with strangers than friends is to test the adaptability of humans to a new social order.

The city dweller of Osaka or Chicago may daily encounter hundreds, even thousands, of unknown and unpredictable others. Yet the probability is that nearly all of them, with only an occasional exception, will remain strangers. To test this, Elaine and William Walster suggest this simple experiment:

> Tomorrow as you go about your daily activities observe *everyone* you encounter—on the bus, on the street, at work, at school, at the supermarket. Keep a running total of those men and women you would be willing to date. You'll be startled to find out just how incredibly fussy you really are.[7]

Yet at some time, somewhere, somehow, such strangers—at least some of them—must become friends, although the rules that govern this passage may vary from one culture to the next.

ENGAGEMENTS WITH STRANGERS

We are oblivious to most of those who pass us in the street or who live in the same building; they are, for the most part, treated little differently from the furniture we detour around. They are unnoted and unremembered; they have no status whatsoever, not even that of stranger. The mere presence of people occupying the same space is not enough to produce involvement.

There must be some sort of engagement, an awareness of the unique physical identity of the other. This sort of visual identification, of noticing the specific others one meets in an elevator or a hotel lobby, constitutes what Erving Goffman has called "unfocused interaction." Something about the appearance, stance, or movement of the other person makes us aware of their presence. Each perceives the other and becomes aware of being perceived. It is prerequisite to further involvement.

As two people notice each other they may begin to edit their behavior to influence the inferences and judgments made about them. They may change their posture, adjust their clothing, stare at each other. At some point the behavior of each becomes influenced by what the other is doing. "Focused interaction" is the result as two people share a single focus of attention or participate in some shared activity.[8] Thus involvement with strangers begins in the perception of their unique qualities, the deliberate monitoring of one's own behavior, and finally, in coordinated acts in which what each person does is influenced by what the other is doing.

As Goffman suggests, some people such as police officers, priests, and shopkeepers, by virture of their uniform or role, are inevitably exposed to communication from strangers; most people, however, through their posture, gait, or facial expression announce their accessibility or inaccessibility to intrusion. The need to inquire for the time of day or for directions increases the need to initiate contact with strangers, while accidents such as falling or dropping a package invite help from others. A special case occurs with seatmates on planes or trains where one is forced into a physical intimacy that makes nonrecognition of the other difficult, and strangers must soon decide on a mutually acceptable level of involvement with each other.

This heightened self-awareness and social anxiety experienced during exposure to strangers seems to arise from a dilemma: One is attracted to some strangers, but at the same time, wants to avoid some who are attracted to one's self; even with those one would like to meet there is anxiety over being too forward and risking rejection, or of being too reticent and missing an opportunity to know someone who might become a valued friend. Some catalyst—a power failure or a humorous incident is often necessary to induce people to breach the fictional border that insulates them from one another. There is the fear, writes Goffman, "of being thought too forward and pushy, or odd, the fear of forcing a relationship where none is desired—the fear, in the last analysis, of being rather patently rejected and even cut."[9] There is evidence of a "greeting gradient" that requires acquaintances to acknowledge

each other while people who are unacquainted must have some justification for exchanging greetings.

In the absence of such catalysts people move through a city vacantly, intent on their inner thoughts or next destination until such time as they receive an indication that overtures will be favorably received. Thus an aura of uncertainty surrounds encounters with strangers and complicates communication with them. Perhaps this is why people are so reluctant to initiate conversation unless the need is overpowering—we are lost or suddenly ill—or confidence in our social skills is very high. Their unpredictability may also explain why such conversations are so gratifying when they turn out well. To reduce this anxiety people try to acquire as much advance information about strangers as possible to guarantee a successful outcome; without such information talking to strangers may prove too great a gamble.

Strangership: Rites of Passage

What we seek to understand is what the anthropologist calls the "rites of passage"—not the thresholds in life—birth, childhood, adolescence, adulthood, old age—but those rites signaling changes in the status of personal relationships. These are not the stages in a singular life but in our life with others.

Just as nations designate borders and establish credentials for crossing them so, too, do individuals maintain standards, albeit unconscious ones, regarding whom they will admit into their circle of friends. To do so they must learn something about the people they meet. Within a small band of foragers or farmers this knowledge was readily available; there were, at best, only a few hundred people to know and their traits were observable day in and day out. The anonymity of life in huge cities requires new strategies. Yet privacy must be breached if people who are strangers are ever to become acquaintances, friends, or lovers. Often there is no more than a split second in which to decide if someone is to be approached or avoided, to be trusted or feared. As Leonard Doob puts it: "No additional data are going to be available; you just have to force yourself to make a decision, you cannot inquire into his life history, you cannot force him to take a paper-and-pencil test, you cannot ask him whether he has a psychiatrist or priest who knows him well and then, if he says yes, consult that expert."[10]

Usually we make such decisions with little awareness that these global judgments rest on such precarious information. In an unusual experiment American high school students described in detail the attributes of a fictitious person after being told only that his name was "Jim." Added details about him changed their preconceptions somewhat but their judgments, even ten weeks later, showed how profound was the influence of these initial images.[11]

Apparently one leaps from clue to clue: The stranger is a woman, in her thirties, wears no wedding ring, is casually but carefully dressed, wears an exotic necklace, is impulsive, has an expressive face. We observe, interpret, compare, evaluate, and conclude that she is liberal or conservative, outspoken or reticent, interesting or dull. And then we decide if she will be friendly or antagonistic, helpful or not. Every facet of appearance and behavior serves as a point of conjecture about her communicative manner.

There is no more time to collect information or to test the data one has; to initiate a conversation, one must project some image of the other. Such images—often confused with stereotypes—are unavoidable; they are prerequisite to dealing with anyone or anything.[12] One has to form some impression of what the other is like to know how to behave. Should one approach or withdraw? Speak in Greek or Spanish? Greet the person by bowing or shaking hands? Talk about this topic or that? One cannot confidently act without some estimate of the consequences of one's acts. Such images should be tentative so that when they prove wrong, oversimplified, or incomplete (as they almost certainly will), they can be revised as people get to know each other. Some disparity between our image of others and their image of themselves will always exist no matter how long or how well people become acquainted. But the smaller the disparity the more empathically they will communicate.

First Impressions

Strangership in the twentieth century has added a new dimension to human relationships. To cope with hordes of strangers, many city dwellers have opted for selective indifference because it seems impossible to respond to the thousands of passersby and bystanders one sees for a second and may never see again. As Fosco Maraini notes, "It enables a seething mass of humanity to rub shoulder-to-shoulder without creating so much friction that the machinery of city life breaks down altogether."[13] This indifference, he adds, keeps Tokyo—or any modern metropolis—from having a complete nervous breakdown. But this highly selective boundary occasionally admits some strangers and even encourages some border crossings. There are recognized strategies—a smile, appreciative wink, nod of the head—used to approve the credentials of those who might cross from strangership into acquaintanceship.

At one time it was possible to learn a great deal about strangers simply by looking at them. The style of clothing, quality of material, combination of colors, hairstyle, and accessories were enough to announce the village, occupation, age, religion, sex, marital status, rank, and power of the stranger. Most of what we now call "demographic information" was decipherable from appearance alone. It was on public display.

The number and reliability of such clues has steadily declined. In an age of international fashions, cosmetics, costume jewelry, face-lifts, and hair dyes, appearance has become a less reliable guide to forming a correct image of others. It is relatively easy to mask one's status by conforming to current standards of taste, obscuring one's identity behind a standardized uniform. Even such obvious characteristics as age, race, and sex have become less predictable from appearance alone. This has undoubtedly contributed to greater anxiety and confusion in public settings.

Even though apparel has lost some of its potency as a clue to character, appearance has not lost all influence in the selection of companions: Research shows it to play a significant role in first impressions, and these impressions are either remarkably insightful or remarkably persistent over time. A recent study by the Roper organization asked American males and females what they first noticed about strangers. Men were most aware of the figure, face, and dress of females (in that order) while women were most aware of the dress, figure, and face of males (in that order). Both most often noticed the dress, hair, and face of others of their own sex. But the declining reliability of traditional signs of status has, if anything, intensified the search for other clues to the character of strangers one meets.

People also give clues to their identity through their behavior. They may be aware of it, or may not, but they cannot avoid standing or sitting, smiling or frowning, speaking or remaining silent. In their manner of relating to others, people cannot refuse to communicate about themselves. The compatibility of strangers may be gleaned, thus, from their way of behaving with others: Are they talkative or silent, warm or cold, impulsive or poised, formal or informal? "The moment a conversation begins," writes Myron Brenton, "all kinds of signals and cues, verbal and nonverbal, are exchanged that let each of the two parties know something about the other, something of the hidden as well as of the overt person; thus we pick up nuances, we begin to sense whether this is 'our kind' of person or not."[14] People sense a common interest in sports or music, that they may have similar backgrounds or occupations and spend free time in similar ways. Each detail confirms or disconfirms an initial impression gained from observation alone. With surprising speed strangers decide to commit themselves to deeper involvement, to limiting the relationship, or to withdrawing from it.

Locale Versus Appearance

"We can live in a world of strangers," writes Lyn Lofland, "only because we have found a way to eliminate some of its 'strangeness.'"[15] People tolerate the anonymity of city life by giving order to the mass of unavoidable strangers. We do this, she contends, by relying upon location as an indicator of status:

> In the preindustrial city, appearances were critical, but location was not; in the modern city appearances may deceive, as nearly anyone may dress any way, but the locale is often a clue to identity. Thus persons may not know the individual, but know the type of people likely to be encountered in parks, libraries, slums, ghettoes, universities, office buildings, concert halls.[16]

Spatial segregation of markets, factories, nightclubs, schools, and financial centers has dispersed people according to ethnicity, religion, class, and age, thus encouraging place-based identities.

City residents often become upset when the "wrong people" get into the "right places" because they confuse predictions based on locale. No one is prepared to communicate successfully in every urban setting so people avoid places where they are likely to meet incompatible communicative styles. Foreigners who do not know the spatial organization of the inner city sometimes risk their lives by intruding into places normally off limits.

Attitudes Toward Strangers: The United States

When no physical barrier separates one person from another, a very real psychic or social barrier may exist. That such a barrier is real is evident from the different way people treat others within their circle of acquaintances and those outside it. Enemies are rarely approached, and contact is limited to hostile acts. Strangers, too, usually keep their distance from each other, avoiding physical, verbal, and even visual contact as they pass one another. Where the line is drawn that separates strangers from acquaintances (how *many* and what *kinds* of people are excluded) and how permeable or crossable the boundary is (how *often* and how *easily* strangers may become acquaintances) appear to be subject to cultural constraints.

Over 150 years ago Alexis de Tocqueville remarked that in hierarchical societies citizens occupy distinctive ranks—dependent on the patronage of those above them and obligated to those below them. Although such people are more securely woven into the social fabric, they lack the equality essential to friendship. Americans, he noted, have no higher ideal than that of equality, followed by insistence on independence and a distaste for formality. The first tends to reduce social barriers, the second to favor spontaneous relationships, the third to encourage frankness in communicating with others. In America, he wrote, where rank confers no privilege, people are ready to frequent the same places and to exchange opinions freely: "If they [Americans] meet by accident they neither seek nor avoid intercourse; their manner is natural, frank, and open. . . . They converse, they listen to each other, and they are mutually stimulated to all sorts of undertakings."[17] While acknowledging that equality and independence do not attach citizens strongly to one another, he concluded, "it places their habitual intercourse on an easier footing."

One of the first social scientists to take a serious interest in the cultural aspects of social behavior, Kurt Lewin, observed that an American is more willing to be open and to share certain situations with strangers than a German is: "People waiting for a bus may start to discuss the weather, and in the train, conversations between strangers start more easily than in Germany. . . . The American seems more . . . ready to help a stranger. It is more customary in America to invite a visitor, who is not a personal friend, to lunch or to one's home, than in Germany."[18] The average American, he suggests, has less need for privacy in certain areas of his life.

Attitudes Toward Strangers: Japan

To the Japanese the word *tanin*, or *stranger*, carries a "chilling connotation," writes Robert Ozaki, suggesting that someone who lies outside the circle of intimates provokes no feeling whatsoever:

> For a Japanese to be sociable is an ordeal. Confronted with an outsider, he does not know what to say or how to behave. . . . In Japan, members of a group are forced to keep close contact with one another for the sake of group solidarity. To do so is a matter of necessity for a stable, unified group is the source of each member's sense of security. Knowing your colleagues is all that is required. There is no need to be sociable with outsiders.[19]

Other observers of Japan have similarly noted a tendency to avoid strangers, a hesitancy in speaking up in public, and a polite reserve displayed in unfamiliar settings or with unfamiliar people. This image of the Japanese as shy and reserved, reluctant to initiate conversation in ambiguous social settings, Kitano found, was largely an accurate one.

The distinction introduced by Nakane Chie between cultures dominated by the "frame" (Japan) or "attribute" (United States) also suggests that Japanese might treat strangers with greater indifference because they lie outside the frame that is relevant in regulating social acts. Sharp borders, she claims, separate three interpersonal worlds of the Japanese, each with its own distinctive communicative styles: a primary world of people to whom one is bound closely and affectionately and to whom one is obligated; a second world of people with whom one interacts on the basis of roles and functional needs; and a third world of strangers who are virtually ignored and who rarely become intimates. Of the latter Nakane writes, "The consciousness of 'them' and 'us' is strengthened and aggravated to the point that extreme contrasts in human relations can develop in the same society, and anyone outside 'our' people cease to be considered human."[20] Thus discomfort in the presence of strangers may prompt great reticence, rudeness, or excessive politeness. One of Japan's leading psychiatrists, Morita Shoma, one characterized this anxiety as the "*taijin-kyofusho*," or "people-phobia," of the Japanese.[21]

Japanese indifference toward strangers seems as natural and understandable as American openness toward them. Each reflects the cultural premises that govern behavior in the two countries. Japanese neutrality appears to arise from an inability to fit strangers into the category of "friend" or "associate" for which standards of social behavior exist. "A Japanese tends to be insecure," writes Kano Tsutomu, "unless he can clearly define his relationship with others around him."[22] Relations with strangers may also be confounded by language: Japanese is a highly sensitive language for coping with specific people—older brother, younger sister, teacher, section chief, parent, spouse—but is more awkward in addressing statusless strangers. And, adds Ozaki, "There is little training, formal or informal, in how to deal with people who lie outside the perimeter of groups in which everyone has a well-defined status."[23] Nor is such skill needed as long as one remains within the protective embrace of family and work group. Finally, the strong loyalties and heavy obligations that surround attachment may prompt the Japanese to be reluctant to initiate conversations that may impose a burden of lifetime responsibilities as a consequence.

The hostility toward strangers that some observers ascribe to the Japanese seems exaggerated, yet insensitivity to others is often apparent in Japanese behavior in public: Outside the confines of the home and primary group, Japanese often seem unaware of the rights of others, shoving people aside, pushing their way on to buses and subway cars, staring and making audible cutting remarks about strangers.

Yet loneliness, so long considered a feature of urban life in the industrialized West, is by no means unknown in Japan. Indeed it seems as widely experienced and deeply felt there as anywhere in the world; it is a theme of Japanese popular music, poetry, novels and plays. Edward Seidensticker refers to Japan as a "lonely crowded country," noting that the Japanese fear and experience loneliness most intensively when they no longer enjoy the support of an enclosing group, gang, or family.[24]

Clearly the two cultures seem to regard strangers in distinctive ways, one more receptive to contact, the other more reluctant to interact with unknown people. Yet in both cultures, contact with strangers is not only unavoidable but essential for the health of the individual and of society. Out of the pool of strangers one meets, people must continuously create, and recreate, their circle of intimates. Not only the ordinary contingencies of life—marriage, divorce, death—but residential moves, changes of employment, promotions, and transfers that are characteristic of a technological age regularly decimate the ranks of our friends, making it necessary constantly to recruit new companions to take the vacated places. Attitudes toward strangers may facilitate or frustrate this process.

STRANGERSHIP: THE CULTURAL VARIABLE

How have people in Japan and the United States adapted to this world of strangers? At first glance it would seem that in Japan, with its greater homogeneity, its singular language, and conformity to social norms, talking with strangers would be easier and more likely to be rewarding. At the same time the immense importance attached to close and permanent group ties, combined with the difficulties of talking with people of uncertain status (and for whom one might then have to assume some responsibility), would seem to discourage such openness.

In the United States, the heterogeneity of the people, their cultural diversity and ethnic consciousness, and the variety of life-styles would seem to complicate communication with strangers. Yet there are compensating tendencies in Americans' presumption of equality, the high value placed on spontaneity and informality, and a basic openness and trust in even the people one does not know.

Thus a number of questions about relations with strangers seem worth pursuing: How frequently do people in both countries talk with strangers? What motives prompt such conversations? What fears or inhibitions discourage such contacts? What is learned from these conversations? How do such perceptions of others influence the decision to extend or terminate the relationship? How fragile or how substantial is the boundary that divides the world of strangers from the world of acquaintances?

The Stranger Scale:
Attitudes Toward Strangers

Upon opening the Dimensions of Interpersonal Relations booklet, respondents were asked to complete a Stranger Scale. They were instructed as follows:

> When we are exposed to other people—on a street, in a store, at a concert—we are often unaware of them. On other occasions we notice their presence and even individual features—the way they are dressed, their way of talking, what they may be doing. The questions below concern such encounters with strangers during the past month. [25]

Participants were then asked to indicate how often in the presence of strangers they had "*noticed* and thought about their personal characteristics," had "*considered* talking to strangers they had noticed," had "actually *started* conversations with such strangers," and had "*responded* favorably to strangers who started conversations with them." To minimize errors of recall the questions focused on experiences of the past month.

The findings reveal that Americans consistently were "more aware of" and "responsive" to strangers than the Japanese were. This was demonstrated in two ways. First, Americans scored higher in every category; the cultural difference between the two countries is a highly significant one, and the probability of error is less than one in a thousand. Second, because respondents indicated whether they manifest such behavior "never," "seldom," "occasionally," or "very often," one could compare the frequencies in each category. Americans, without exception, scored higher on "frequently" and "very often," while the Japanese scored higher on "never" and "seldom." The results are mixed, as one might expect, with regard to the middle category, "occasionally," with Japanese scoring higher on "noticing" and "responding" and Americans higher on "considering" and "starting conversations" with strangers.

The answers expose a broad difference in attitudes toward strangers, with the Japanese less disposed to notice, consider, initiate conversations, or respond to strangers. While members of both cultures more often noticed and responded to strangers without actually starting conversations, the greater cultural disparity lies in "considering interacting" and "actually interacting" on which Americans consistently scored higher. Although a definite barrier exists to discourage conversations with strangers in both countries, it is clearly a lower and more permeable boundary for Americans.

The Motive to Communicate with Strangers

Why do people start conversations with people they do not know, or why do they avoid such opportunities? Participants in the study ranked twelve reasons that prompted them to talk or not to talk with strangers in the preceding month. The Japanese and Americans agreed on the most important reason for talking with strangers: "to give information or help." For the Japanese the next three most often cited motives were "to get to know others who might share my interests," "to confirm my attitude or opinion about some event," and "to be courteous and sociable"; for Americans it was "to be courteous and sociable," "to get to know others who might share my interests," and "to pass the time more interestingly." The first motive on the list provoked the widest cultural contrast: Americans ranked "to attract someone who appealed to me" fifth while Japanese ranked it eleventh, or nearly last among the reasons for talking with strangers.

With regard to the motives that caused people to *avoid* talking with strangers, a wide contrast was expected but this was not the case. Although a reliable difference appeared, it was not at the highest level of statistical confidence. Three out of four of the reasons for not talking to strangers were the same, although ranked differently in the two countries. The Japanese reported "I could not think of a suitable way to begin the conversation," "It wasn't an appropriate time or place," It wasn't appropriate because of our positions," and "I was uncertain how it might turn out" as their major reasons. These responses suggest sensitivity to the social appropriateness of conversations with strangers. Americans avoided strangers principally because "I was uncertain how it might turn out," "It wasn't an appropriate time or place," "I was afraid of being misunderstood," and "I couldn't think of an appropriate way to begin the conversation." Here there is a suggestion of possible embarrassment as an inhibitor of conversation. The widest contrast was in the higher ranking given by Japanese to "It wasn't appropriate because of our positions" and by the Americans to "I was afraid of being misunderstood."

Overall, the answers reveal contrasting cultural motives prompting an approach to, or avoidance of, strangers, but there are similarities as well. A further analysis, clustering motives that arise from inner need or outer pressure, was made but no further conclusions were warranted from reordering the data.

The Initial Encounter Explored

To look more closely at the content of initial conversations with strangers, Japanese and Americans were asked, on a second scale, to describe three of their last encounters with strangers. They were given the following instructions:

> This section concerns specific people with whom you talked recently that: (1) you did not know and to whom you were not introduced; (2) you did not talk with simply to carry out some task (mailing a package, paying for groceries, ordering a meal).
>
> The conversations with these strangers may have taken place anywhere—at work, while waiting for a bus, between classes, at a concert. You may have started the conversation, or they may have. You may have talked for only a few minutes or for much longer. But these conversations were with people you did not know and were not required to talk to by the circumstances.[26]

Respondents were asked to identify the three strangers with whom they had talked most recently and to specify when these conversations took place. A series of questions followed concerning the stranger's age, sex, dress, education, where the encounter occurred, the motive that prompted it, who started the conversation, how long it lasted, what was learned, the perceived degree of similarity, and the future of the relationship.

Nearly all Japanese and Americans recalled talking with three strangers in the past year, suggesting there is regular recruitment of new acquaintances to one's circle of friends in both countries. People in both cultures talk with strangers, and this occurs more frequently than one might expect from descriptions of Japanese indifference or hostility toward strangers. There is, however, convincing evidence of a dramatic difference in the frequency of encounters with strangers: Over 90 percent of the Americans had met three strangers within the twenty-four hours preceding the testing; this was true of only 50 percent of the Japanese. Clearly Americans approach and talk with strangers more frequently.

A closer look at the time intervals shows that Americans, on the average, had their most recent contact in the preceding five hours, Japanese in the past eleven; the second most recent American conversation occurred within the preceding thirteen hours, for the Japanese it was within the past twenty-four hours. Generally, Japanese took about twice as long to meet three strangers as Americans took. The findings clearly show a difference in communicative accessibility.

The Attractive Stranger

With regard to age the data suggest that the dominant pattern in both countries is to talk with strangers of about the same age, though there is a slight tendency to select strangers who are perceived to be a little older.

Members of both nations also prefer talking to strangers of their own sex. Within Japan the tendency was somewhat stronger for females to prefer females and males to prefer males; in the United States the tendency to approach members of the opposite sex was more pronounced. But neither of these tendencies was strong enough to counteract a general preference for same-sex encounters.

Who initiated the contact? The results are clear on this point and consistent with prevailing images of the two cultures. A highly significant cultural difference appeared with more Americans reporting they initiated the conversations, while more Japanese reported it was initiated by the stranger. This finding could suggest that people recall incidents consistent with their own cultural values, but it seems more likely to reflect a greater reticence among Japanese in confronting strangers.

To identify the motive that caused these encounters, the reasons cited earlier were repeated in two forms, one for when the respondent opened the conversation, the other for when the stranger did, for example: "I needed help or information" or "They needed help or information," and "I wanted to pass the time" or "They wanted to pass the time." This time a much sharper cultural difference was apparent. For the Japanese the two most often cited reasons were "They needed help or information" and "I needed help or information." For Americans "I wanted to get to know them" and "They wanted to get to know me" were the dominant reasons for talking. Apparently, necessity breaks the barrier between strangers among Japanese; among Americans it is simply the desire to make a new acquaintance.

The Pursuit of Similarity

To study the role of similarity, this factor was approached in several ways. The first was to ask whether the strangers had greater, similar, or less schooling, higher, similar, or lower incomes, and dressed more conventionally, similarly, or less conventionally. Here the two cultures were alike in preferring to talk with strangers seen to have similar education, income, and dress. A slight, but not significant, tendency to prefer strangers of a higher, rather than similar, income appeared in the Japanese responses.

A subsequent set of questions returned to the issue of similarity by asking for estimates of similarity in values between themselves and the three strangers with regard to "leisure activities," "political views," "religious views," and "life-styles." The results do not support a simple conclusion: Japanese females perceived similarity more often in political views, religious views, and life-styles but not in leisure activities; Japanese males saw their partners as more similar in religious views and life-styles but different in leisure activities and political views. American males and females again responded more similarly, perceiving the three strangers as resembling them in leisure activities and political views but different in religious views and life-styles. Thus the factor of similarity that emerges so clearly from laboratory studies using artificial encounters or bogus strangers appears to be a more complex phenomenon in real life. People approach strangers who share some values but who also differ, and the two cultures do not agree on which similarities or differences matter.

Where do people meet strangers? Respondents were asked to indicate whether they met at work, in a store, in a restaurant or coffee house, in a recreational setting, in an auditorium or theater, in a public area (such as a street or park), on public transportation, in an institutional setting (such as a library or hospital), in a private residence, or in a government or business office. Although Japanese and Americans met strangers most often at school, Americans next most often met them at work or while shopping, while Japanese did so in public settings or on public transportation. The coffee houses of Japan, which have impressed so many observers as centers for socializing, apparently are used more for gatherings of friends than for meeting strangers. And the work setting, so frequently mentioned by Americans, may be explained by their tendency to hold jobs while attending universities.

The Consequences of Talking to Strangers

It is difficult to measure the success of encounters with strangers without relying on highly subjective evaluations. But a somewhat objective indicator might be the length of the conversation. A very short or very long conversation suggests that it may have been painful or pleasant. Consequently, respondents were asked whether their conversations lasted one to five, six to fifteen, sixteen to thirty minutes, or longer than an hour. In both countries conversations were typically under five minutes in duration. (Fifty percent of the Japanese and 61 percent of the Americans reported the minimal length.) They also decreased proportionately up to one hour. There was a reliable cultural difference, however, in the patterns of talking: Americans had a larger percentage of conversations of both the shortest and longest duration, while Japanese had more conversations lasting between six and thirty minutes. One of the intriguing findings is that although the number of conversations decrease as the interval lengthens, as one might expect, there is a sizeable increase in conversations lasting more than an hour.

Another way of estimating the success of conversations with strangers is to find out what people learned about each other. If they learned a great deal it is reasonable to assume the stranger proved interesting or likeable or why continue talking? If they learned little one suspects the two people were less than compatible or other needs prevailed. Participants were asked, therefore, what they learned about each stranger they met: "I learned their name," "I learned where they live or their phone number," "I learned about their marital status," "I learned about their occupation," "I learned about their activities and interests." Again a reliable cultural difference appeared: The most frequent information acquired by the Japanese (55.9 percent of all cases) concerned the occupation of the stranger; for Americans the most frequently acquired information, again in over half the cases (55.6 percent), was the name of their partner, followed closely by their activities and interests (54 percent). That occupation figured so prominently among the Japanese may affirm the critical importance of status in regulating communicative behavior in a vertical society. In both countries the phone number and address—important facts for further contact—was the least often acquired information (though nearly one third of the Americans obtained this information compared to only one fifth of the Japanese).

The last question on the Stranger Scale was a final effort to assess the success of these meetings with strangers. This was done by asking how respondents felt afterward about future encounters with each of the three strangers: "I hope not to see this person again," "I would not mind seeing this person again," "I hope to see this person again," and "We arranged to meet again." Once more a consistent difference was found in the probability of future encounters: The Japanese scored higher in the first two categories—"I hope not to meet this person again" and "I would not mind meeting this person again"—while the Americans were higher on "I hope to see this person again" and "We arranged to meet again."

All of this suggests that Americans are more likely to convert chance encounters into continuing acquaintanceship and friendship. Although one might expect that the longer someone talked with a stranger the greater the likelihood of meeting again, this was not the case. Qualitative considerations—the style and content of the stranger's remarks—rather than the length of the conversation seem to better predict the future course of such relationships.

JAPANESE AND AMERICAN PROFILES

How does each country cope with an urban environment filled with strangers? On attitudes toward strangers the findings clearly confirm the images of the two cultures: Americans are more aware of strangers, more open to approaching them, more often start conversations, and are more responsive to strangers who approach them; the Japanese are more indifferent toward strangers, are more reluctant to approach them, and respond less favorably to conversations initiated by people they do not know. There is a striking cultural contrast in the frequency with which Japanese and Americans talk with strangers; Americans report almost twice as many encounters or, to put it another way, meet twice as many strangers within the same time frame. The assumption of a psychic or communicative boundary separating acquaintances and strangers appears valid in both countries, but where one culture adapts to the press of strangers by discouraging contact, the other seems to permit or even welcome movement across this boundary.

The motives that prompt people to approach or avoid strangers are both similar and different. The Japanese were more hesitant about approaching strangers because of the inappropriateness of the setting or status relation, while Americans avoided such encounters because they were unsure how they might turn out or feared being misunderstood. When asked about recent encounters with strangers the Japanese felt they occurred because "I needed their help" or "They needed my help." Americans more often engaged in such conversations because "I wanted to get to know them" or "They wanted to get to know me." The former seems to emphasize external factors while the latter appears to reflect inner impulses.

Where one society favors a higher, less permeable border between self and stranger, the other favors a lower, more permeable one. These represent two unique adjustments to the pressures of being surrounded by thousands of unknown and unpredictable people: one protecting against being overwhelmed by interaction with people of uncertain origin, status, and motives and providing greater personal privacy, the other encouraging openness to strangers even though such exchanges might prove superficial or occasionally risky.

Since similarity has figured so often as the principal factor in the forming of human attachments in laboratory studies, Japanese and American participants were asked about the extent to which strangers they met were of the same age, sex, education, dress, and income. Japanese and Americans both preferred talking with strangers of the same level of education and same economic status. Deeper attitudes and values produced more complex findings, both confirming and disconfirming similarity of values as a factor in attraction. But initial contacts with complete strangers are generally of such short duration that they may provide few clues to deeper values.

There was agreement and disagreement also over the settings in which conversations with strangers were likely to occur. While Japanese and Americans both reported such incidents occurring mainly at school (an understandable outcome with student respondents), Americans were also more likely to meet at work or while shopping, and Japanese were more likely to talk to strangers on public transportation or in public settings. Clearly, environmental settings do encourage or discourage conversations with strangers, and the two cultures designate somewhat different sites as appropriate places for such encounters.

Three measures of varying objectivity were used to estimate the relative success of conversations with strangers. The first, the length of the conversation, showed that conversations of less than five minutes were the most common in both countries—a natural outcome considering where such conversations take place, the motives that prompt them, and the unfamiliarity of those involved.

A second measure of satisfaction was inferred from what respondents learned about the strangers they met. Again there was a reliable cultural difference: The most frequent information acquired by Japanese concerned the occupation of the stranger, a relevant fact in a society where status is said to mediate personal relationships; for Americans it was the name and interests of the stranger. The address and phone number, essential to continuing the relationship, was least often learned in both countries, suggesting that most contacts with strangers are transient.

Perhaps most significant was the cultural contrast found with regard to the future of the relationship: Japanese scored notably higher on "I hope not to see this person again" while Americans more often reported "We arranged to see each other again."

Clearly, cultural attitudes toward strangers differ markedly in motives for talking with them, in the frequency of such encounters, and in the future of these relationships. There is some cultural similarity in attraction to strangers of similar appearance and social status, although the evidence with regard to similarity of values is less clear.

STRANGERSHIP: THE FIRST STAGE OF INTIMACY

Whether greater accessibility to strangers is desirable or not, to be encouraged or discouraged, is a question of some importance but one that goes beyond the capacity of data to answer. Perhaps some distance in the congested cities of today is needed to preserve privacy and to reduce stimulus overload or simply required to conserve time and energy for friends with whom there is a deeper and longer commitment. "The human personality," Emil Durkheim reminds us, "is a sacred thing; one dare not violate it nor infringe on its bounds, while at the same time the greatest good is in communion with others."[27] Perhaps a capacity to communicate with strangers when these are met in increasing numbers is a requirement of an age in which the pace and mobility of life demand some facility for "instant friendships." Descriptive data provide some basis for reflection. If they do not make such decisions for us, they help to clarify the communicative challenge we face. And the fact that these two countries follow a somewhat different path in accommodating this new challenge broadens the alternatives to consider.

Yet the need for privacy should not obscure the equally pressing need to overcome the isolation and loneliness of urban life, conditions that grow out of an inability to meet strangers and to transform such encounters into more enriching and lasting bonds. We need to remember that people are drawn to and congregate in large cities not only to enjoy the wider economic opportunities they provide, but for social reasons as well—as Wood reminds us:

The loneliness of city life, which is a frequent theme of literature, is more often the loneliness of the stranger heightened by the contrast of his position with that of the hurrying multitudes about him, all of whom seemingly belong somewhere and to someone while he alone does not. The poignancy of such loneliness is not to be denied; but it seems reasonable that if this were the common lot of those who lived in cities, urban life would not be as attractive as it is actually known to be.[28]

Remember that through fleeting conversations people take their first tentative step toward intimacy, the selection of people who in the future will become their acquaintances, friends, and lovers, who will shape their social life and personal destiny. The persistence of cities, their increasing number and size, suggests that in spite of the social challenge they pose, they remain viable settings in which to live. If in ages past we learned to regard strangers with fear and to treat those who were different with hostility, in this age we may have to learn new lessons—that those who are strangers are potential friends and those who are different may prove to be interesting. It is doubtful that nostalgia for the past is going to return us to village life.

Speculating on the connection between attitudes toward strangers and the quality of cultural life, Abraham Kaplan makes this provocative observation:

> Recently someone proposed what I think is a brilliant numerical measure of the degree of civilization of any society: the number of strangers whom you can trust, or, as I would prefer to say in this context, the number of strangers whom you can talk to, whom you can talk with, whom you can understand and know that they understand you. This, of course, is another way of saying that you enter into community with them.[29]

Since this exploration of strangership opened with some lines of Abe Kobo, it seems fitting to close with another thought of his. In his play *Friends* he reminds us that "if you trace strangers back far enough you'll find they were once brothers."[30]

CHAPTER 5

Profiles
of Intimacy

Some friends arrive all at once, setting off
an interior fanfare of immediate
recognition. Some arrive slowly, by dint of
simple continuity, the accumulation of
shared experience gradually stretching to
new intimacies. Some arrive dramatically,
unexpectedly stepping out from behind a
disguise they had previously elaborated. By
whatever route they come, friends join us
in a kind of conspiracy against the world,
circumscribing with us a private space filled
with mutual concerns. [1]

TONY JONES

If we are to believe our social critics the modern world is
hostile to living things, including human beings. The litany is familiar: A
growing population surrounds us with anonymous others; urbanization forces
contact with more strangers in a week than our predecessors met in a lifetime;
an accelerating technology and burgeoning bureaucracy force us into manipulative and superficial relationships; specialization of roles and segregation of
activities fracture our lives; a surfeit of information provides no sense of
direction or significance; the media sap our capacity for spontaneous and

creative expression; a competitive and acquisitive materialism replaces attachment and commitment to one another.

The net effect, say the critics, gives rise to a sterile environment for people. In 1844 Karl Marx gave early warning of the dehumanizing effect of industrial society by converting people into mere producers and consumers; the religious philosopher Martin Buber saw a growing dominance of "I-it" over "I-thou" relations among people; the poet W. H. Auden wrote of the increasing proportion of human ties that serve to satisfy needs for power or profit. And there seem to be other grounds for such doubts: Families have diminished in size and permanence; ties with kith and kin seem less secure; "contacts" seem to be emphasized over "friends."

How much of this is true? How much of it is fantasy? Except for figures on decreasing family size and increasing divorce rates, little hard evidence supports such grand indictments of our age. Some of these pronouncements may rest on myth. Some draw their appeal from the eloquence of their authors. Some may have a firmer foundation in the details of daily life. But which are true, and which are fiction?

We know astonishingly little about the facts of social life. As Roger Barker once observed, we know a great deal about the elements that make up our physical world: "We read, for example, that potassium ranks seventh in the order of abundance of elements, and constitutes about 2.59 percent of the igneous rocks of the earth's crust" as well as where it may be found. But, he adds, the same is far from true of our knowledge of the social world: "The fact that there is no equivalent information in the literature of scientific psychology about playing, about laughing, about talking, about being valued and devalued, about conflict, about failure confronts the psychologist with a monumental incomplete task."[2]

FORMS OF ATTACHMENT

What we seek, in short, is acquaintance with the contours of social life in Japan and the United States. What can we learn of the circle of companions that Japanese and Americans construct for themselves to satisfy needs for attachment to other people? We have seen something of the way these two societies regard strangers. The overwhelming majority of such strangers will remain unknown due to lack of social opportunity or because such strangers fail to attract strongly enough to overcome the inertia of isolation. Some, however, will be approached. A smaller fraction of these will be engaged in conversation. Following an initial exchange, a few will be admitted to that inner circle that constitute the social world of each person. Who will be selected? Why will they be selected? How close or distant will they become? How will the intimacy of these relationships be secured and reflected in what they say or do together as companions?

Unfortunately, there is danger of running aground before getting started. The moment we try to identify the people who make up our circles of acquaintances, we encounter semantic confusion. We may describe a particular person as a "relative," "friend," "associate," "acquaintance," or simply "someone we know." Although these words fall easily from our lips, people do not use them consistently. As Mary Parlee, author of one of the most extensive studies of American interpersonal relations, warns, "surprising differences in people's conceptions of friendship emerge when people begin to talk about what it means to them."[3] Or we may reach out for labels such as "parent," "employee," "teacher," "neighbor," "daughter," "lover." Some have a shred of objectivity about them: One becomes a husband or wife only through marriage, a son or daughter only through birth, a colleague or associate only through occupation. But do these words reveal or obscure the variety of relationships they identify?

Perhaps the most basic distinction drawn in the scientific literature, and in ordinary conversation as well, is between those to whom one is formally related by blood and those to whom one relates informally through choice. But is this distinction as reliable—or as useful—as it appears? Although children do not choose their parents nor parents their children, how should one regard adopted children? Even husbands and wives are not related in the sense of sharing the same blood. And second or third marriages scarcely meet the criterion of permanence. Do people who are assigned the same office, attend the same school, occupy adjoining apartments really "choose" their associates and friends? How adequate are such labels in accommodating homosexual or heterosexual pairings where no civil or religious ceremony binds two people who live together permanently? Finally, is there any reason why a mother, neighbor, teacher, or colleague cannot serve equally as a friend, acquaintance, or confidant? In any human relationship one may find laughter, tears, argument, confession, embraces; companions may be superficially or deeply committed to one another, may provide various kinds of physical, material, and emotional support for each other. "We are not so very different," writes Myron Brenton, "in the way we behave with family and with friends."[4] The exclusiveness of our labels seems to lack any solid basis in real life.

The social experience of any person is, in short, likely to be diverse and complex. Recognition of this fact should be the starting point for investigating the social worlds of Japanese and Americans. In view of this, we should make explicit the assumptions that have shaped this exploration of social behavior in these two cultures.

First, there appears to be no objective basis by which to classify the people to whom one is attached. Whatever labels are used—relative, friend, acquaintance—mislead as much as they help. The boundaries that separate our companions are vague, tenuous, arbitrary, and of dubious value in exploring personal relationships. The use of such labels, by framing the answers, tells us more about our categories than about the behavior by which people satisfy their needs for companionship. As Graham Allan notes, "The assumption that people labeled in a particular way necessarily have a given type of relationship and provide a specific form of service is too rigid."[5]

Even within a single category, relationships are unique. No acquaintance is a perfect substitute for any other. No two parents are alike, nor any two lovers. Each relationship is born of a particular time and occasion, each traces a trajectory that is unique, and each carves out a special niche in our social life. "Any relationship," writes Erving Goffman, "can be seen as having a natural history: it starts, develops, has turning points, attenuations, and one of a small set of available terminations. Relationships are not born and they do not die; however, like social persons they must have a beginning and must come to an end."[6] Our attachments to people are as varied as people are. With some it is deep, with others superficial; with some it is steady, with others volatile; with some there is constant involvement, with others only periodic encounters are needed to nourish and sustain them.

Finally, what is appropriate in a particular friendship is not dictated by society, or by investigators, but by the people who experience them. What people say and do may be observed, but the meaning of these acts is an internal matter: The parties themselves are the ultimate judge of their significance. What a marriage, friendship, or a parent-child relationship is like is best judged from inside it by the people who live it and derive satisfaction from it.

THE ACQUAINTANCE INVENTORY

To study the character of personal relations, it is essential first to identify the people—the significant others—who figure prominently in the social lives of Japanese and Americans. Only after such identification can specific behaviors within such relations be studied. If we are to avoid the biasing effect of categorizing companions, how might we identify such significant others? The simplest approach might be to have people name those companions whose telephone numbers or addresses they know by heart. That would be objective but hardly exhaustive. Another would be to use proximity of residence as a criterion—precise, but given our urban mobility, questionable. Participants in the study might be asked to identify only those acquaintances whose favorite foods, leisure activities, religious views, or political attitudes they know. But a person may feel close to someone without such knowledge about them. Another, more objective criterion, would be to list only people with whom one has spent fifty or a hundred hours in the past year. But frequency of meeting, or quantity of time shared, may be less important than the quality of such encounters. Circumstances often force people to spend a great deal of time with people they dislike and may make it difficult to be with those they like immensely.

So, to encourage the listing of all significant partners while avoiding the distorting effects of such terms as *relative, friend,* or *acquaintance,* respondents were asked to name and rank order their companions on the basis of a single subjective criterion: *closeness.* They were instructed simply to identify "the fifteen persons you have felt closest to in the last twelve months, placing them in the order of their closeness to you." To provide some guidance on the way this term should be interpreted they were further advised: "These should be the fifteen people you like best, who know and understand you best, with whom you feel most comfortable, and with whom you feel closest."

Lest any participants still might bias their choices toward or away from a particular category of acquaintances, they were given an additional warning:

> The persons you name *may include anyone*—a relative (brother, wife, father, grandmother, daughter), a member of either sex, someone older or younger, a work associate, a neighbor, anyone.
>
> It is not important how often you see or talk with them, but how close you feel to them. Do not identify any relationships you have maintained only through writing letters or telephone calls.[7]

Although a limit of fifteen persons was imposed for practical reasons, this number permitted close comparison of relationships that extended from the center to the periphery of the social worlds of respondents. (An earlier form that asked for a ranking of the twenty closest acquaintances brought complaints of the difficulty of identifying the outermost four or five people.) See Figure 5.1.

PARAMETERS OF PARTNERS

What, precisely, would we like to know about the "fifteen closest companions" of Japanese and Americans? A sizeable literature has accumulated in psychology and sociology describing the process by which people select their friends and marriage partners. The findings have led to a number of tentative conclusions about who people will meet, become attached to, and marry. "Tentative conclusions," of course, is another way of saying incompletely tested hypotheses. What are some of these hypotheses for which we might obtain facts drawn not from the laboratory but from the actual life experiences of Japanese and Americans?

One of the most solidly confirmed features of social life is that people become acquainted on the basis of physical proximity. People who live close to one another are likely to get to know each other, the probability of meeting enhanced by their proximity. To test the role that distance played in these friendships we asked Japanese and American participants to indicate the distance between their own residence and that of each of the fifteen

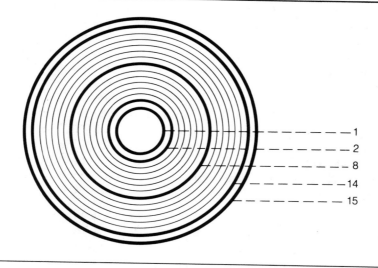

FIGURE 5.1 Circle of Acquaintances*

people in their circle of associates. Further evidence on the role of proximity was sought by asking where the people met originally and the settings in which they meet most often.

An opinion shared by many laypeople and a conclusion drawn by many behavioral scientists is that people are attracted to those of the same age, nationality, and sex. The role of demographic similarity can be estimated easily from the Acquaintance Inventory by calculating the proportion of the listed companions who are of the same age, nationality, or sex.

One of the simplest and seemingly relevant distinctions is between kith and kin. It is usually assumed that relations with parents, brothers, and sisters, even distant relatives, differ inherently from relations with other people. The former are inherited rather than chosen, and the role they play in infancy and childhood is thought to endow them with a special emotional significance. Commitments to relatives are unique and permanent. The Acquaintance Inventory permitted exploration of this issue as well. After identifying their fifteen closest companions, respondents identified those who were relatives and those who were not so their respective roles in the social life of Japanese and Americans could be examined: Which relatives are

* Although all fifteen relationships are explored in the Acquaintance Inventory, relations with the two closest acquaintances (#1, #2), an intermediate acquaintance (#8) and with two more distant acquaintances (#14, #15) are examined in depth in the remaining six subscales of the Dimensions of Interpersonal Relations questionnaire.

included? Do they rank as closer or more distant companions? How does behavior differ with them, if at all, from behavior with peers?

The Acquaintance Inventory explored other features of personal relationships. One of these concerned the role of sex in personal relationships. Do males and females differ in their choices of companions? Do males or females prefer relationships with the same or opposite sex? In what respects do the two sexes act alike or differently in encounters with close or distant acquaintances?

Time is one of the more intriguing features of personal relationships. One facet of this factor concerns the relative importance of quantity and quality of communication. One might assume that people would interact more frequently with people they are closest to and less frequently with more distant acquaintances. On the other hand, some have argued that the quality of interaction, not its frequency, creates intimacy. Since respondents were asked to indicate the number of hours they spent with each of their fifteen closest companions during the preceding month and year, it should be possible to estimate the relative importance of quantity and quality in personal relationships in the two cultures.

Do friendships progress slowly toward intimacy or do they abruptly shift from one level of intensity to another? That is, does strangership evolve into intimacy *gradually* as two people come to a deeper understanding of themselves, appreciation of each other, and awareness of the importance of their relationship, or do they rather quickly ascertain the appropriate level and move *suddenly* from one plateau to another? Are there "thresholds of intimacy" that hold relationships at a particular level of intimacy unless some crisis provokes an abrupt advance or retreat to other levels? Does intimacy grow by degrees or steps? There is support for each speculation: Sharing experiences over a long period of time does seem to solidify and deepen our ties with others, but there are also occasions when people seem, from a single encounter, to move closer or farther apart with astonishing suddenness. Although the Acquaintance Inventory does not address this issue directly, the answers to "years known" and "time spent together" provide some clues to the relative claims of these contradictory hypotheses.

CHOOSING COMPANIONS: SEVEN KEY CHARACTERISTICS

As Pascal once wrote, "To be born is for the individual the prime contingency, since it means to be born of this time, in this place, of these parents and this country—all of these brutally given facts on which his life has to seek to found itself."[8] Though born of a particular age, place, and culture, we are far from prisoners of these particularities. Such contingencies, without doubt, limit who we will become and the scope of people from whom we will construct our circle of intimates. The persons we elect to be our companions will constitute only an infinitesimal fraction of the possible people we might know. Who we choose to meet, talk with, spend our lives with is still largely a matter of choice. "You meet people by chance," notes Graham Allan, "but you do not form a friendship by chance."[9] To establish a close bond with another person involves a personal decision, indeed a whole series of mutual decisions regarding its potential value.

The Acquaintance Inventory in which Japanese and American respondents identified their fifteen closest companions explored a number of factors that might account for the choices made. As one might expect, the companions ran the gamut of possibilities. Among them are grandmothers, tennis partners, neighbors, classmates, children, car poolers, fellow employees, teachers, club members, priests. Despite this diversity some consistency in these choices is evident.

Age

With respect to the age of their companions, Japanese and American respondents show no overall cultural difference in their choices. In both countries there was a distinct tendency to interact with a somewhat older circle of acquaintances: While the participants averaged twenty years of age, the age of Japanese partners averaged 26.5 and of Americans 25. When the findings were divided into smaller units of plus or minus five years, fifteen years, or forty years, some cultural differences do appear: The Japanese have a greater proportion of companions between fifteen and twenty-five years older, while Americans have a greater proportion of companions who were more than forty years older. The greater affinity of Japanese for similar age partners and of Americans for older partners does not fit existing images of the two cultures in which the closer family ties of the Japanese should increase age discrepancies with their acquaintances and the looser family commitments of Americans should decrease them. While there is a tendency toward homogeneity of age among close companions in both cultures, there is also a far greater heterogeneity than the similarity hypothesis proposes. In neither culture did age appear to dictate whether another person will be known or not, will become an intimate or not.

Nationality

Much is written these days about the profound impact that international travel will have upon the visitor and the visited. As millions travel abroad or take up residence in a foreign country, the proportion of people who will include someone of another nationality among their circle of friends should change radically. But the profiles of acquaintances provide little encouragement for this conclusion. Japanese and Americans did not differ significantly in the number of their foreign companions: 98 percent or more of the people identified in both countries were of the same nationality as the respondent; the likelihood of having a foreign friend was roughly one in fifty. Although this may represent a slightly greater degree of heterogeneity than one might have found a century ago, it hardly confirms that greater mobility has had a profound impact on human relationships. The results here strongly confirm the tendency of people to prefer one's own kind as close companions and to do so equally in both cultures.

Sex

The influence of sex on the choice of companions is neither as clear nor as consistently confirmed as in earlier studies. Again the issue is one of homogeneity or heterogeneity: Do we prefer people as acquaintances who are of the same or opposite sex? Or, more correctly, in what proportion do people choose associates who are male or female?

The data indicate there is no difference in the pattern of choices with regard to the sex of companions in Japan or the United States. Further, males and females are chosen in almost exactly the same proportions in both samples; roughly 50 percent of the named companions are female and 50 percent male. This conclusion held true of the Japanese with regard to all fifteen companions; Americans tended to prefer a slightly greater number of females in the six closest relationships. Thus there is evidence of great cultural similarity combined with almost equal choice of male and female associates.

Propinquity

People must be physically accessible if they are to become acquainted, so it is not surprising that propinquity has been so consistently confirmed as a cause of friendship. While its influence upon encounters with strangers and casual acquaintances is well documented, its role in longer and more significant relationships—where personal factors such as talent, temperament, attitudes, and values may be more critical—has not been as thoroughly tested. (The strong correlation found between proximity of residence and choice of marriage partners is an exception.)

The role of physical accessibility was explored in three ways. After listing their fifteen closest companions, Japanese and Americans were asked to indicate the distance separating their own residence from that of their close acquaintances. The results provide partial but far from overwhelming support for proximity in the forming of friendships: Roughly 24 percent of Japanese and Americans lived in the same building or within walking distance (0 to 150 meters) of their closest companions; the largest proportion, however, 48 percent, lived at a sufficient distance to require local transportation (1.5 kilometers to 50 kilometers); an additional 19 percent lived far enough apart to require long-distance transportation (51 to 500 kilometers), and a final 9 percent lived in another province, state, or country (500 to 15,000 kilometers).

Proximity plays *a* role but far from *the* critical role in determining which residents of a large city will become companions. Perhaps modern transportation has indeed reduced the powerful effect that residence once played in determining the choice of companions: Three quarters of the identified partners had to overcome substantial distances to share activities or experiences with a friend.

Other data were used to explore further the effect of environmental constraints on close relationships. We found out where the two people first met and where they interacted most frequently. Although both Japanese and Americans identified home and school as the principal settings in which they socialized, nearly twice as many Japanese met their companions at school rather than at home; Americans met their companions more often at home, with school and home ranking more equally. Among Japanese the coffee shop ranked third in importance as a setting for meeting acquaintances while for Americans the workplace ranked third (possibly reflecting the larger number of American students who work while attending a university).

The same pattern holds for current communication with close companions: School and home constitute the most common meeting place, with coffee shops ranking third for the Japanese and the workplace third for Americans. After initial encounters both Japanese and Americans report that the home dominates as a setting for spending time with friends; 40 percent of Japanese and 64 percent of American contact takes place there. Although the place of residence may influence initial exposure, it appears to play a diminishing role in longer and deeper relationships. School, home, coffee house and workplace clearly promote social interaction, but the two cultures have different profiles of preferences for them as communicative settings.

Durability of Relationships

In view of the perception of Japan as a country that cultivates close and permanent ties with a limited circle of acquaintances, and of America as a country of wide but transient interpersonal ties, the data regarding the permanence of relationships in the two cultures is striking: There was no significant difference between the two cultures with respect to the length of interpersonal relationships. This cultural similarity in the durability of ties with others held true across the entire scale: There was no cultural difference in the length of affiliation with the closest companions (persons ranked one and two), moderately close companions (the person ranked eighth), or those at the outer perimeter (the people ranked fourteenth and fifteenth).

This holds true as well when comparing Japanese and American relationships lasting one to five years, six to ten years, and eleven to fifteen years. Clearly, personal relationships last no longer in Japan or are any more transient in the United States. Whether this would hold true for other age groups, particularly for older persons, cannot be projected beyond this college-age sample, but it raises some doubts about existing stereotypes. Despite the mobility of people, or perhaps because of it, friendships appear to be more resilient than expected. And it bears out the findings of the *Psychology Today* study, which found that "close friendships can transcend geographic distance and persist over time with impressive robustness."[10]

Frequency of Interaction

The Acquaintance Inventory incorporated two further measures of the role of time. While experts disagree about the nature of friendship, there is universal agreement that it requires contact between the two people. All other features of friendship depend on the two people having opportunities to communicate with one another face to face; the greater the frequency and length of such encounters, the deeper the involvement in them. How often do people who are close companions get together weekly, monthly, yearly? How much time do close relationships normally require?

Japanese and American respondents estimated the time they spent with each of their fifteen closest companions during the preceding month and year. A highly significant difference separated the two cultures: Americans spent a consistently greater amount of time with their companions in the preceding month than the Japanese did; this was particulary true for the closest partner, but held also for the partner occupying the middle position and for the partner at the outer edge of the circle of associates. Over the longer period of a year, however, the cultural contrast diminishes considerably. Americans still spent slightly more time with their closest partner, but the Japanese spent slightly more time with their second closest. Over the longer time interval the cultural contrast tended to disappear.

Apparently the supposedly dehumanizing pace of modern life does not prevent people from having close contact with valued partners. Within the preceding month Japanese and Americans spent about an average of one hundred and fifty hours with their closest companions, roughly thirty hours a month with more distant ones; in the preceding year members of both cultures arranged to spend well over a thousand hours with their two closest acquaintances and about three hundred with the least close members of their social circles.

Both countries show evidence that intimate relationships are highly valued and maintained for equally long periods of time; there is frequent and lengthy involvement in shared activities. If over the short term Americans appear to be more active socially, over the longer term this cultural difference disappears.

Kith and Kin

The transition from extended families to nuclear families combined with the high divorce rate in the United States and rising divorce rate in Japan are often cited as showing the diminishing role of inherited relationships. "As families decline in size and importance," writes Jane Howard, "peers become more important."[11] How many of the close companions of Japanese and Americans are relatives, and how many are not? Which relatives appear most frequently, and at what level of intimacy, within the circles of acquaintances?

After naming their fifteen closest companions, Japanese and American respondents were asked to identify those who were related to them and those who were not. In the former case they were then asked to specify the precise nature of the kinship tie.

Again, despite existing images of the Japanese as much more closely linked to their families and Americans as having more tenuous ties to their families, Americans consistently named a larger proportion of relatives among their closest companions (27 percent related; 73 percent unrelated) while the Japanese named a smaller proportion (22 percent related; 78 percent unrelated) among their intimates. It appears again that some of our cultural images rest on a fragile basis of often repeated but rarely tested projections.

By extending the analysis to the particular relatives who are named among the closest companions, we learn something further about the place of relatives in the lives of Japanese and Americans. The relatives named most frequently by Americans are those who compose the nuclear family (mother, sister, father, brother) while the Japanese name a greater number who make up the extended family (particularly aunts, uncles, cousins). The cultures did not differ with respect to grandparents or relatives acquired through the marriage of brothers or sisters (in-laws). The data clearly contain some surprises for those who have long accepted descriptions of Japan as a country with close family ties and of America as a country in which family ties are strained or distant.

More importantly, the findings challenge the distinction so often drawn between kith and kin. The data suggest that being a relative neither *guarantees* nor *excludes* one from closeness. If choosing to spend time with another person, disclosing yourself to him, sharing activities with him, and assuming responsibility for him cultivates a strong bond with another person, there is no inherent reason why this cannot involve parent or peer.

You may be born without choice, may share a residence without choice, but parents or siblings become close only through choice; rapport cannot be imposed, it must be earned. Status is an external description of a relationship, intimacy an internal description of its meaning. It is not uncommon in either Japan or the United States to hear a parent or other relative described as "my best friend," and the data here confirm that possibility. Japanese and Americans commonly include among their closest companions members of their immediate or extended families. Relatives are distributed across the entire range of intimacy, sometimes accorded the closest position, other times a more distant one; occasionally respondents failed to place any relative among those admitted to their circle of intimates.

HIGHLIGHTS OF THE FINDINGS

What can we learn from this assessment of the social circles of Japanese and Americans? Perhaps, first, that there is little evidence here of the loneliness and alienation thought to be so characteristic of modern life. None of the respondents apparently had any difficulty in identifying fifteen people with whom they enjoyed varying degrees of intimacy. The fact that a few participants had some difficulty in the ranking, but not the naming, of the fourteenth and fifteenth acquaintance only suggests that the Acquaintance Inventory was approaching the perimeter of the inner circle of intimates. Fewer than 1 percent reported difficulty in ranking any but the most distant companions, which suggests that people can and do see their relationships in terms of closeness rather than the category into which their companions happen to fall. People who were relatives and nonrelatives, older and younger, same sex and opposite sex, who lived nearby and who did not composed the social worlds of these Japanese and Americans.

Evidence here supports the notion that similarity is a factor in forming friendships, but it also raises some questions as to whether similarity is not currently overstated as a factor in attraction. The two cultures were alike in the average age of the listed companions (about five years older on the whole). But there was also considerable divergence in the ages of the people identified: They included infants and friends eighty years old. Similarity of nationality was found consistently in both samples, although if ethnicity, race, and sexual orientation had been included the results might show greater contrast. In spite of an occasional person whose companions were all of the same or opposite sex, the prevailing tendency was to choose male and female companions about equally. Geographical proximity, which may affect initial more than long-term contacts, was partly confirmed and partly disconfirmed; one fourth of the listed partners lived within walking distance. But a substantial number lived a country or a continent away. Home and school, as one might expect, were the most important places for meeting people (and for continuing relationships), but in reverse order of importance in Japan and the United States.

The two cultures resemble each other with regard to the durability of personal relationships; in both countries the length of such ties is much longer than might be predicted, and holds true for all partners and all time periods. Members of both cultures communicate with their closest companions regularly; the somewhat greater investment of time by Americans over the short term disappears when the two cultures are compared over the long run.

Japanese and Americans are surprisingly alike with respect to the number of relatives listed among their closest companions; Americans cite a somewhat larger number of relatives than the Japanese and there is some difference in the particular relatives named most often. The importance of the household, so long assumed to be a unique feature of Japanese society, was not confirmed; family members appear to play no more, and perhaps a less, important place in Japan than in the United States. Members of the family are not consistently ranked among the closest or least close partners; they appear across the entire range of companions. It was relatively rare for neither parent to appear in the list of fifteen partners, and often (especially among Americans) both parents were named among the closest companions. Fathers were named slightly less often than mothers among close companions, especially by the Japanese, but not significantly so. Whether the family is declining in importance and peer relationships growing in importance cannot be answered; there are no figures from the past to compare with the present findings.

Some evidence here supports two other speculations about modern social life. Data from the Acquaintance Inventory indicate that a number of respondents named among their closest companions people they had met less than a year before and in some cases a month before, suggesting that personal relationships today often evolve over a very short time. Commenting on the alleged superficiality of transient relationships, Joel Block warns against any flippant equating of the two:

> Those of us raised on the notion that friendship is for the long haul believe that stable and enduring relationships are the only ones in which we can have commitment. Short-term and temporary relationships are considered necessarily superficial. Long-term relationships do offer a kind of anchoring and an opportunity for development that is unique, but the assumption that temporary relationships *must* be devoid of commitment needs to be reconsidered. [12]

There is indirect evidence, as well, to support the idea of "suspended relationships," friendships being placed on "hold" during periods of reduced opportunity to be together but reactivated later with no substantial loss of rapport.

THE INTERACT SCALE

It is unfortunate that the only words we have to describe our relations with others, such as *friend* and *companion,* have no parallel verb form like *friending* or *companioning* because to become a friend or companion is an active process rather than a static category.

Knowing something of the age, nationality, sex, and status of others may help us form an impression of them; such features help us estimate the likelihood that others may share our values and interests and therefore might be worth knowing. Thus demographic features, no matter how unreliable, often provide the only basis for initial attraction.

Extended relationships, however, depend on actually spending time together in satisfying ways. To become a friend requires some face-to-face involvement. The social exchange theory of George Homans argues that activity, interaction and affection are interdependent: Each breeds the other. The more people like one another, the more they try to spend time together; the more activities they share, the more they become involved emotionally.[13] The extensive survey reported in *Psychology Today* revealed that 78 percent of their forty thousand respondents felt that "sharing leisure and cultural interests" was critical in creating close friendships.[14] The Acquaintance Inventory also confirmed the importance of shared activities in the development of intimacy: Japanese and Americans spent over a hundred hours a month and over a thousand hours a year with their closest companions. The average number of hours spent with friends correlated so highly with their rank on closeness that the rank of a particular companion could be accurately estimated from knowing the amount of time spent with that person compared to the others listed.

However, the amount of contact does not by itself reveal much about the actual form and content of their involvement. We need to look beyond the frequency and duration of contact and into the specific activities that are shared to obtain some idea of the nature of their attachment. People not only select their companions but they also construct the social life they will share with them. Every activity shared by two people is a way of defining the self, defining one's partner, and defining the sort of relationship that is to be. Surprisingly little effort has gone into studying the importance of common interests in the forming of friendships. An exception is found in a study by Carol Werner and Pat Parmalee. They found preference for similar social activities a better predictor of friendship choices than that two people have similar attitudes or beliefs.[15] Do two friends spend their time attending concerts, building a cottage, studying together, playing with children? How diverse or similar are these shared activities? Do they facilitate intimacy or discourage it? What relational orientation do they require?

It would be hard to overestimate the bearing such shared social activities have upon the health of any individual. For example, Derek Phillips, in studying the relation between the social life of an individual and his or her level of happiness, found that the higher the level of involvement in social activities with acquaintances, the higher the level of satisfaction with one's life.[16] Whether social activities cause higher morale or high morale prompts wider participation in social life is unclear, but the fact that both rise and fall together underscores the importance not only of who we know but also of how we relate to them.

Shared Activities

When cartographers set out to map a plot of land they must first agree upon a set of indexes—length, width, height—to use in measuring the terrain. Students of human behavior must also postulate the range of social activities they will explore and the criteria to be used in measuring them. To do this one must develop a catalog of basic types of social activity: What are the things companions can, and do, do together? The list should be extended enough to include representative forms of social activities but short enough to make measurement feasible.

Accordingly, our Interact Scale included the following set of social activities: "routines" (shopping, cleaning, cooking), "primary" (working together at school or office), "leisure" (playing games, watching television, listening to records), "physical" (flower arranging, playing an instrument), "personal" (sharing doubts, hopes, fears), "inspirational" (meditating, worshipping, contemplating nature), "sensual" (embracing, massaging, making love).

First, we focused on what kinds of activities played the largest part in the lives of people who know each other well. How frequently are such activities pursued? In some relationships most of the time may be spent working together; in others the two people spend their time pursuing common leisure interests; in still others people may seek sensual satisfactions. Does the social life of Japanese and Americans differ with respect to the character of activities that are shared and their perceived importance in fulfilling needs for companionship?

Interpersonal Relations

Another, heretofore unexamined, feature of social life deserves attention. It has to do with the manner in which an activity is pursued. What sort of relationship between two companions is created in pursuing a particular interest? Most social activities permit a wide variation in the way two people engage in them; some do not. But each type of relationship promotes a different sort of rapport, and each reveals more or less about the people who are involved. There are five basic relational orientations that companions can create in pursuing any common interest.

Two people may come together at the same time and place but act *independently* of one another. Friends often arrange to be together, but the time is spent in each "doing their own thing," pursuing his or her own interests more or less unaware of what the other is doing. They may read, work, meditate, write, or sketch, but each is preoccupied with his or her own thoughts and feelings. They do not share a focus of attention or even interact. The behavior of each is not a response to what the other is saying or doing. Though physically close, they are subjectively apart. Yet there is a difference between doing things alone and acting independently in the presence of another person. The presence of another person, even if only subliminally noted, is part of the context that frames the experience and, for that reason, may influence one's mood or motivation. When two people share a physical presence but pursue activities that are independent of one another there is opportunity for individual insight and satisfaction but little likelihood of insight into one's companion.

There are occasions, however, when the relation of the two people constitutes a case of *co-presence*. Two acquaintances decide to attend a concert, see a film, listen to a lecture together. Here there is a common focus of attention to which both are simultaneously exposed. Each person, by noting the reactions of the other, is likely to learn a little more about their companion—his or her sense of humor, likes or dislikes, objectivity or emotionality—and so gain insight into and appreciation of the personality of the other. Similar responses such as laughing or crying at the same moments cast at least an oblique light on their compatibility; widely differing reactions may distance the two parties or endanger the relationship.

A *competitive* relationship constitutes a third form of involvement. Most games and sports and many leisure and cultural activities—even arguments—pit one person against another. Here, too, there is a single focus of attention. There is interaction. And both people are reciprocally involved, each determining and dependent on what the other says or does. Emotional involvement is often high. All these features of a competitive relationship mean that the temperament of companions is likely to be sharply exposed. One cannot compete effectively without gaining insight into the motives and attitudes of an opponent. Although the aim of such insight is to gain advantage over each other, competitors often acquire acute insight into the other person and learn something about the meaning of their relationship.

A fourth relational orientation is a *hierarchical* one, in which one of the two companions assumes a greater role in guiding, directing, supervising, or evaluating the acts of the other. Hierarchy usually reflects an inequality of power between the two parties—as with parents and children, supervisors and employees, sellers and buyers—but it need not. Many of the ordinary activities people engage in, such as performing a play or preparing a meal, are ones in which one person assumes greater responsibility because of his or her greater knowledge, experience, skill, or motivation. A hierarchical relationship may not only reflect unequal status but also may be preferred as a way of creating unequal status. Nevertheless, out of hierarchical relations may come insight into both persons and the nature of their relationship. Hierarchical relations are by no means entirely devoid of respect or rapport.

A *collaborative* relation may be the most revealing and hence enriching of all. Two people share a common goal and seek to achieve it through combining their insights and integrating their talents. They share a common focus. There is reciprocal influence and equality of opportunity to participate in the final outcome. The greater the challenge and more intense the involvement, the wider the exposure to one's partner's limitations and potential. The most serious forms of collaboration—creating a work of art, seeking a scientific breakthrough, managing a personal crisis—may be among the more painful social experiences, but are likely also to be the most

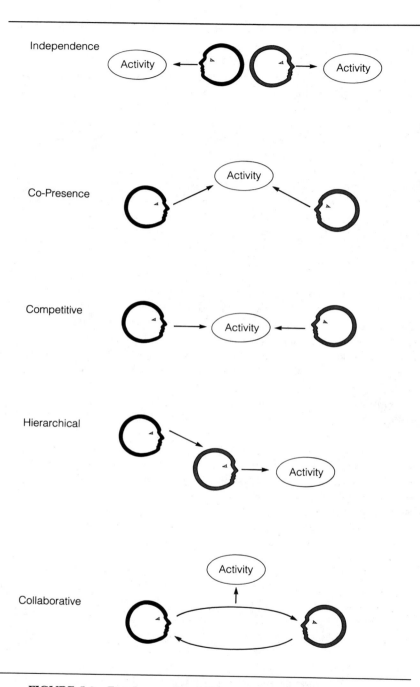

FIGURE 5.2   Five Interpersonal Orientations

enriching experiences that can be shared with another human being. (Figure 5.2 represents these interpersonal orientations.)

The Critical Companions

The Interact Scale was designed to assay a variety of social activities and to identify the dominant social orientations of Japanese and Americans. Throughout the remainder of the study five companions were scrutinized in particular in the Dimensions of Interpersonal Relations questionnaire: the two people identified as the closest companions (number one and two of the target persons listed), the person occupying the middle of the scale of intimacy (number eight), and the two people named at the outer edge of the circle of companions (number fourteen and fifteen). Refer again to Figure 5.1. These five seemed to constitute a reasonable sample of the circle of acquaintances, permitting an intensive and comparative analysis of communicative behavior with associates of different levels of intimacy. This strategy also brought the testing of a large sample within feasible bounds. These five "target persons" permitted the testing of a number of speculations about the character of human relationships in the two countries. Do relationships mature slowly or abruptly? How do relationships with the most and least intimate companions differ? How do close and distant relationships of Japanese and Americans compare?

The following list illustrates the format of the Interact Scale.[17] The five selected partners were identified across the top of the scale, the forms of activity made up the major divisions, and a series of five questions explored the relational orientations that occurred most frequently during the past year. The questions were ordered so there is increasing intimacy examined with each subsequent question.

	Target Persons				
Physical Activities	1	2	8	14	15
1. We have participated independently in sports					
2. We have attended sporting events together					
3. We have competed with each other in sports					
4. We have participated in sports activities one of us led					
5. We have participated in sports as members of the same team					

Thus the frequency of any activity should decrease as one moves from close to distant relationships reflecting less extensive social involvement and should decrease as one moves from less to more intimate involvement reflecting more intensive involvement. And this is, with occasional exceptions, what the responses of Japanese and Americans indicated.

With regard to each partner, participants recorded the frequency with which each activity occurred during the preceding twelve months: 0 = This has *not* occurred in the past year; 1 = This has *rarely* occurred in the past year (one to five times); 2 = This has *occasionally* occurred in the past year (six to fifteen times); 3 = This has *frequently* occurred in the past year (sixteen to thirty times); 4 = This has *very often* occurred in the past year (over thirty times). The recall interval was limited to the past twelve months to counteract distortions of memory, and frequencies were used to avoid discrepancies in the interpretations of "rarely," "occasionally," "frequently," and "very often."

ENCOUNTERS WITH CLOSE COMPANIONS: THREE PROFILES

A highly significant cultural contrast appeared with regard to the ways in which Japanese and Americans spend time with their closest companions. The two cultures appear to favor different norms with regard to the social activities they share with friends, the forms of relationship preferred, and their frequency of contact. But which of these—activity, relation, or frequency—is the principal source of the difference?

Profile of Activities

For activities pursued with close companions Japanese respondents ranked them in the following order of importance: personal, leisure, routine, primary, physical, sensual, cultural, and inspirational. Most of the socializing with close friends involved sharing personal experiences, leisure interests, and routine tasks or was associated with work. Americans ranked these social encounters in almost the same order of importance, reversing only the order of leisure and personal activities. The same three were also ranked as least popular although they followed a slightly different order, with inspirational, sensual, and cultural occupying the lowest ranks. There are only minor discrepancies in the priorities of Japanese and Americans with respect to how they spend their time with acquaintances.

Profile of Interpersonal Orientations

There is even greater agreement between the two cultures on the types of relationships favored with close associates. The Japanese prefer the following: independent behavior in the same setting; co-presence, as in observing a performance together; collaborative situations in which both parties cooperate; hierachical relations of unequal status and responsibility; last, competitive relations.

Americans agree with respect to the three most preferred interpersonal orientations—independence, co-presence, collaboration—but they reversed the order of the last two; hierarchical relations ranked last among Americans while competitive relations ranked last among Japanese. In spite of the last exception, which fits the contemporary images of the two societies, there is surprising agreement on how members of both cultures prefer to relate and the activities they pursue with their closest companions.

That these orientations rank overall as they do is not surprising. We may spend most of our lives in less intimate encounters simply because more intimate involvement carries greater risk. Further, to pursue one's own interests, or simply to observe events with friends, is far less demanding of communicative skill than to collaborate. Since the deeper the involvement with others the greater the exposure of the self, less intimate activities may provide a margin of protection against premature termination of friendships that might be promising in the longer run.

Profile of Intensity

The pattern of involvement with the five target persons is similar in both countries: The most intensive activity occurs, as one might expect, with the two closest companions, then drops off precipitously with people at the midpoint or outer perimeter of the social circle. There is evidence of a very sharp "threshold of intimacy" that differentiates activities shared with the two closest companions and those of lower rank. This sharply dropping curve of involvement will appear again and again with respect to other dimensions of human relationships in the two countries.

It is when we examine the amount of social activity that a cultural contrast, and a substantial one, appears. The Japanese "less than rarely" (one to five times a year) participate in such activities with their acquaintances; the rate of such activity for Americans is 50 percent higher. And this difference overall holds for all partners from the closest to the most distant, although the cultural contrast diminishes as intimacy decreases.

The same pattern holds with regard to preferred ways of relating to partners: While both cultures prefer independent and collaborative encounters with friends, the frequency is significantly higher with Americans. Thus we can conclude that although Japanese and Americans favor engaging in similar sorts of social activities with their friends, and prefer similar ways of relating to them, they differ significantly in the extent to which they participate in such activities.

PERMUTATIONS

Japanese and American profiles of socializing seem to offer something for everyone: The data confirm some hypotheses and raise doubts about others. Members of the two cultures share remarkably similar ways of spending time with their companions; there is great similarity in the relative popularity of socializing through leisure, personal, work, and routine activities. One might have expected somewhat greater interest in physical activities among young adults and a greater interest in cultural activities in a college population. The low status of inspirational activities may confirm the diminishing importance of religion in this generation. That sensual activities do not figure prominently in the social life of Japanese and Americans may be because they tend to be focused on only the closest companions rather than diffused across the entire field of acquaintances.

A British sociologist, Graham Allan, recently published results of interviews with middle-class and working-class adults in Selden Hay. He found a striking difference in the character of affiliation in the two classes: Working-class people tended not to identify their closest companions as "friends," but as "mates"; middle-class people tended to do the opposite. In pursuit of this distinction, Allan found that in the working class relationships were "context specific," a consequence of occupying the same setting (workplace, church, local pub). In the middle class, relationships were "person specific." Although originating in a specific setting they were quickly elaborated so that people chose to meet in a variety of settings. In context-specific relationships the choice of a setting rather than the choice of a partner brought people together; in person-specific relationships the choice of a person prompted the selection or creation of social activities to share with him or her.[18] Whether this observation will hold for other cultures is not yet known, but the distinction is a provocative one. In the present study the relationships described clearly qualify as person-specific relationships; Japanese and American respondents shared a variety of settings and variety of activities with their closest companions.

There is, as well, surprising consistency in the type of relations favored by Japanese and Americans in their social activities. In both countries independent, co-present, and collaborative relationships were preferred. Americans, however, are more active socially with each of the partners across the scale of intimacy.

The apparent conflict between the "incline" hypothesis and "step" hypothesis was noted earlier. The former argues that there is a gradual, incremental increase in intimacy over time; the latter argues that personal relations shift more abruptly from one plateau of intimacy to another triggered by external circumstances or internal changes in the people. The data so far seem to favor the step hypothesis: Social activity with the two closest companions is distinguishably different, followed by a sharp drop in involvement with the middle companion, and another drop with respect to the two partners at the outer limit of the social circle. A sloping line of gradually increasing intimacy does not seem to best represent the course of friendship; it is more accurately represented by a broken or interrupted line that jumps from one plateau of intimacy to another. If social involvement with all fifteen companions were included, this line might smooth to some extent, but it would still have to indicate thresholds of change in evolving relationships. Additional data on this issue will come from examining other facets of communication with differently distanced partners.

One of the interesting consequences—and beneficial effects—of completing so exhaustive a description of communication with close companions is that it enables people to reflect on the scope and quality of their social lives—often for the first time. Participants often volunteered comments that reflected insights they obtained from completing the Dimensions of Interpersonal Relations instrument. One respondent, for example, found she had never realized the extent to which her relations with nearly all her companions were competitive. Others remarked on how narrow or how broad was their acquaintanceship with people around them. Some were surprised to find that the people they knew were closer or more distant than they previously assumed they were. As Myron Brenton observed, "When we talk about our friends—more to the point, when we think carefully about them and about our relationships with them—a little magic occurs. We are forced to think more carefully about ourselves. We learn something new about ourselves."[19]

In neither the Acquaintance Inventory nor the Interact Scale results was there more than isolated evidence of the alienation, anomie, and estrangement so often claimed to characterize life in the twentieth century. It appears, as Saul Bellow noted in *The Adventures of Augie March*, that everyone "sees to it his fate is shared."

CHAPTER 6

Intimacy:
Its Verbal Dimension

Whether clear or garbled, tumultuous or silent, deliberate or fatally inadvertent, communication is the ground of meeting and the foundation of community. It is, in short, the essential human connection.[1]

ASHLEY MONTAGU and FLOYD MATSON

Every person is born of a particular time and place and circumstance and each is forced to come to terms with his or her experience of the world. Condemned by our biology and our separate nervous systems to a solitary spot from which to view events, we stretch out to others seeking to confirm our identity and validate our beliefs, reaching for the support and encouragement of others in the destinies we pursue.

To overcome our inescapable isolation, and to make our experience comprehensible to others, humans are endowed with a unique capacity: the capacity not merely to signal one another—to cry, growl, or shout—but to *re*-present experience symbolically so it may become known to others. Symbols are simply a way of giving outward form to inner meaning and, in turn, of giving meaning to the behavior of others. These symbols, these fragile and arbitrary sounds, scratches, and gestures, make it possible, vicariously, for one person to enter and glimpse the subjective world of another—and, on some occasions, to participate in the richness and subtlety of another's view of events.

97

Language is the primary mediating agent that makes it possible for one person to experience the private world of another; words transform what is private into something public. In so doing they vastly expand the scope of human collaboration, making it possible for each person to plug into and use the experience of every other. But no tool is without its limitations, and this has led to a proliferation of symbolic codes. Over time the species has learned that some meanings cannot be written or spoken but are better danced, blown through a horn, painted on a canvas, put into an equation, or realized through a caress. We speak not in a single tongue but in a variety of tongues, each capable of helping us to articulate our own thoughts and feelings and to participate in the thoughts and feelings of others.

One of if not *the* primary function of culture is to create and preserve such communicative codes because they alone make possible a universe of discourse within any community. Those who observe these conventions of meaning agree to transform similar inner states into similar symbolic acts and in the presence of such acts agree to construe their meanings in similar ways. On some occasions an exchange of symbols produces an exquisite resonance of meaning. More often we fail in some degree. There is always some slippage when subtle and complex experiences are forced to fit the limited vocabulary and grammatical constraints of such codes. As Eduard Lindeman and T. V. Smith once remarked, "No two hearts ever beat as one, no two minds ever share a single thought. Sharing points to unanimity is a lovely limit, but a limit never reached."[2] Imperfect as our symbols are, they remain the best and only bridge linking the private world of one human being with that of another.

As two people become known to each other, come to appreciate what they share in common, and learn to accommodate what they do not, there is increasing closeness and confidence in the relationship. Yet this growing intimacy is a product of the simple things that people say or do in each other's presence. If we are to learn something about how relationships mature, or how distant and close relationships differ, we need to look at how people actually communicate: What do people who have a close relationship talk about, and how does such talk differ between close and distant companions? Are there differences in the conversations of Japanese and Americans within their circle of acquaintances?

COMMUNICATING THROUGH WORDS

We seem driven by some mysterious force to explain ourselves and, in so doing, clarify who we are and what may be the meaning of our existence. "For human beings there is evidently something more important than to win," writes Paul Goodman. "They must explain themselves and have company."[3] When excited we insist upon infecting others with our excitement. When angry, we must vent our hostility. When deeply moved, we want others to feel our passions. When in love, we insist upon announcing it. When hurt it helps if our pain can be shared.

Words are a way of gaining a sort of mastery over experience, of objectifying it so it can be looked at, thought about, and finally assimilated. Rarely do we think before we speak, giving voice to already formed ideas; more often the act of speaking creates the thought. Through words we expose a confusing inner state to others who, from their perspective, may provoke fresh understanding in us. The words of St. Paul, though framed for a relationship more sacred than mundane, might well describe this search for comprehensibility: "For now we see through a glass darkly; but then face to face: Now I know in part; but then I shall know even as I am known."

Perhaps for these reasons many have proclaimed the capacity for conversation to be one of the highest attainments of human beings. Four hundred years ago the great French essayist Michel Montaigne wrote: "The most fruitful and natural exercise of our minds is, in my opinion, conversation. I find the practice of it pleasanter than anything else in life; and that is the reason if I were at this moment forced to choose, I would, I believe, rather consent to lose my sight than my hearing or speech."[4]

Yet the poverty of human conversation is, especially in this age, proclaimed with equal eloquence. The existentialists announced the sterility of language, the vacuity of talk, the impossibility of any real communion through words. Jerry, Edward Albee's protagonist in *The Zoo Story*, remarks: "I don't talk to many people except to say like: give me a beer, or where's the john, or what time does the feature go on, or keep your hands to yourself, buddy. You know—things like that."[5] But he also confesses to a desperate hunger for genuine conversation: "every once in a while I like to talk to somebody, really 'talk': like to get to know somebody, know all about him."

If we can learn more about what people talk about, how frequently, and in what depth, we may gain some understanding about how people develop close or lasting ties with one another. The quality of conversation is not only a fair barometer of closeness, reflecting how deeply people are involved with one another, but at the same time is the means by which such closeness is created.

Small Talk

So far we have said nothing about the place of "small talk," verbal exchanges that are without much substance and that contribute little to promoting intimacy (and may even serve as an escape from intimacy). As a form of communication it consists of highly predictable verbal routines, greetings, salutations, witticisms, gossip, and comments on the weather. It is a way of passing time but reveals little of the unique personalities of either party. Some estimate that over 90 percent of all human utterances are of this type. The figure, though exaggerated, suggests the extent to which communication in congested and fast-paced societies is reduced to mere contact. But it is a contact that may give way to fuller and more personal sharing of thought or feeling. At any rate, more extended conversations, where something more spontaneous and authentic is expressed, constitute the most valued moments spent with close companions. Something is said that "breaks through" the social roles and personal facades that monopolize a great many social encounters. People suddenly see themselves in a new light, share a significant experience, or realize more deeply their commitment to each other.

Communicating Through Silence

Silence, too, deserves some preliminary comment. It is more than the mere absence of speech; it is an equally potent form of expression. There is no way, as Paul Watzlawick, Janet Beavin, and Don Jackson point out, for people not to communicate; the unanswered question, the uncompleted sentence may be not less, but more, meaningful than a complete reply.[6] There is the silence that surrounds the experience of the overwhelming, the unexplainable, the ineffable, the inner state that is unnameable. Some of the deepest experiences of life cannot be captured in a skein of words; language diminishes them. But there are other, more numerous times, when people choose to be silent as the best or only way of symbolizing their feelings. "The need—or choice—not to speak or to speak is one of the most interesting things about us," writes Paul Goodman:

> There is the dumb silence of slumber or apathy. The sober silence
> that goes with a solemn animal face. The fertile silence of
> awareness, pasturing the soul, whence emerge new thoughts. The
> alive silence of alert perception, ready to say, "This . . . this." The
> musical silence that accompanies absorbed activity. The silence of
> listening to another speak, catching the drift and helping him to be
> clear. The noisy silence of resentment and self-recrimination, loud
> with subvocal speech but sullen to say it. Baffled silence. The silence of peaceful accord with other persons or communion with the
> cosmos.[7]

There is, as well, the silence that punctuates speech, that frames the words we utter. In a dialogue entitled "Why Do Frenchman?" Gregory Bateson and his young daughter probe the question of why the French wave their arms about so much when they talk.[8] In this delightful excursion into the epistemology of coversation, they conclude that people wave their arms about so that when they do not wave them it will mean something different from when they do. The same holds for the relation of silence and speech; each gives context to and enriches the meaning of the other. But our concern here is with the character of the thoughts and feelings shared through words.

SYMBOL AND SELF

The role communication plays in the forming of personality and the capacity to relate to others has become a subject of inquiry only recently. Sociologists such as Georg Simmel, Charles Cooley, and George Herbert Mead were among the first wave of scholars to explore the vital role communication plays in the emergence of a mature personality and in the ability to relate to others.

In his metaphor of the "looking-glass self," Cooley stressed that it is impossible to know one's self except through interaction: A self only comes into being through its relation to some thing or to some one.[9] From the responses of others we gain an impression of who we are and what we are like. Mead placed the process of communication in the center of his theory of personality and of culture: The newborn infant, he argued, has no sense of a separate identity, a physical or psychic self separate from the rest of the world. Through her parents the child begins to interact through simple signs at first, imitating the laughing, growling, purring, or winking of those around her. Mead called this primitive form of communication an "interaction of gestures" in which sequences of turn taking occur but they are without meaning beyond merely sharing in a common activity. As infants begin to notice consistencies in the actions of others they gain insight into the motives that prompt their behavior. Now the child can begin to communicate through symbols, deliberately employing certain signals to express her own needs while simultaneously taking into account probable reactions to her sounds and gestures. This double capacity to give appropriate form to one's own intentions combined with the capacity to project how others may interpret them constitutes mature communication. An "interaction of gestures" has become an "interaction of symbols." With added social experience the capacity to articulate one's inner meanings accurately and to interpret the behavior of others with sensitivity should grow.[10]

As people share their experience, making public what is inherently private, they are likely to understand one another better and, for this reason, respect each other more. Simmel noted, however, that disclosure may induce greater closeness or greater distance.[11] Complete disclosure may simply deplete the resources of meanings, leaving a vacuum of boredom: Close friends and married couples, having exhausted their past, sometimes have little or nothing more to say to one another, and the relationship dies for lack of nourishment. Yet if two people are continually expanding their experience or insight, disclosure may stimulate growth in each person and in their relationship. Another danger is that unlimited or indiscriminate disclosure could constitute a denial of the self. Without some sense of privacy, of a boundary between what is known to the self and known to others, there may be a loss of identity. Total accessibility, as Irwin Altman and Dalmas Taylor note, may deny the worth and integrity of the individual.[12] (A coercive instance of this is found in brainwashing.)

Disclosing the Self

These preliminary forays into a heretofore unexplored area of human activity stimulated a number of social psychologists and psychiatrists to pursue disclosure more systematically. The first to address this issue was the social psychologist Kurt Lewin. In 1948 in *Resolving Social Conflicts* he proposed a model of the personality that enabled him to contrast the disclosure patterns of Germans and Americans. The outer region of the personality, involving essentially public features of the person, was easily shared; the next region, consisting of more personal information, was more difficult to disclose to others; the inner core, intimate information, was the most difficult to reveal. Lewin thought Germans had less permeable outer regions, making it difficult to know them at first but easy to know well after the outer region had been revealed. Americans, on the other hand, had more permeable outer regions; one could get to know them quickly, but they resisted forming deeper attachments. A recent cross-cultural comparison of Japanese and American disclosure patterns found Japanese to be less disclosing to close associates and Americans more disclosing. [13]

Shortly after Lewin's pioneering efforts the structure of the personality and its bearing on personal relationships was explored more objectively. Arguing that we spend our lives trying to learn who we are and who our companions are, Sidney Jourard suggested this occurred through a gradual process of disclosure: "It is not until I am my real self and I act my real self that my real self is in a position to grow." [14] Only by expressing what one feels or thinks can one gain a sense of one's own uniqueness. Closing off awareness of inner meanings through denial or repression contributes to impoverishment of experience: Unhealthy personalities, it was argued, are engaged in a constant struggle to keep from knowing themselves or being known by others. To say we believe things we do not believe, or to say we feel things we do not feel, is to alienate ourselves from ourselves. It is a sentiment shared in some form by nearly every Western school of therapy; most approach their clients with a view toward opening up areas of the self that have been repressed or censored.

The extent of our disclosure appears to affect the depth of our relations with other people as well. Sharing of the inner self is believed essential to the achievement of intimacy. One can hardly value or love someone who is not really known. To the extent that a person conceals who he or she is, or presents a false self, there is little basis for, or substance to, companionship. Concealment not only complicates communication but also actively encourages misunderstanding.

Disclosure and Intimacy

Why, then, is authentic sharing of inner selves so rare in human encounters? Two reasons have been suggested: One is that in revealing who one is, what one truly feels or thinks, others may disapprove or dislike what is presented. It is often safer—or appears safer—to present a public image that is less likely to be ridiculed or criticized by conforming to the expectations of others. A second reason is that the person who reveals his ideas or feelings may not only hurt others but also may make himself more vulnerable by such disclosure; there is always the risk that others may take advantage of such confidences and exploit them. In view of the unpredictability of the consequences of disclosing oneself, we feel safer maintaining a certain distance, a core of privacy, to prevent such abuse. "Seeming" takes the place of "being." Perhaps for these reasons, disclosure is both a cause of growing intimacy and a consequence of it.

These assumptions became the basis of a widely used measuring instrument, the Jourard-Lasakow Self-Disclosure questionnaire. Ten questions clustered around six topics explore how much of the inner self is shared with a variety of partners. Despite occasional inconsistent results, the findings have suggested the following: Disclosure is greater with respect to topics such as tastes, interests, and social issues than money, personality, or one's body; people disclose more to those who are close than to distant companions; increased liking tends to be reflected in increased disclosure; the amount of disclosure by one person tends to induce an equivalent disclosure from the other. Three further conclusions have been less consistently confirmed: that the young disclose more than the old; that females disclose at higher levels than males; that mothers are disclosed to more than fathers. If younger people reveal more it may be due to the intensity of adjustments they face or to lowered defensiveness because of fewer risks perceived in social disclosure. Although the trend in early studies was to show females more disclosing than males, this has been unconfirmed and even reversed more recently; one suspects there may be some differences between the sexes but it may be more in what is disclosed than how much and to whom it is disclosed.

Getting in touch with others, and in touch with ourselves, according to Jourard, is indivisibly linked: "Transparency before another seems to be a condition for transparency to oneself."[15] Revealing past disappointments, current needs or confusions, and emerging fears or hopes is a way of clarifying them so they may be thought about and resolved. And both discloser and listener appear to benefit: the discloser from obtaining a clearer view of his or her situation and the person disclosed to through a deepening appreciation of the uniqueness of his or her companion. There are parallels between communicating with a friend and with a therapist: Both can produce insight by exposing the inner world of a person that in being shielded from others may be equally hidden from the person experiencing it.

More recently Altman and Taylor have linked patterns of self-disclosure to the evolution of friendship. They have argued that there is an orderly and systematic increase in what people disclose as they move from strangership to acquaintanceship to intimacy. As they see it, disclosure has two dimensions. One has to do with the *breadth* of disclosure, the topics one can discuss with strangers, parents, and peers: religion, money, past failures, politics, sexual behavior, the relationship itself. Another has to do with the *depth* of disclosure on each topic. With some people one might feel comfortable discussing a topic in a general way, as an abstract idea, but with others one might be willing to talk about it more concretely and personally.

Such collaborative sharing of highly personal information is thought to promote deeper concern and closer attachment. As long as such disclosure proves rewarding—is valued and respected rather than rejected or ridiculed—it contributes to deeper involvement. This process of widening and deepening the areas of shared meanings tends to stay at an optimal level that allows both partners to reveal as much as they wish without forcing them to discuss topics that make them anxious or defensive.

VERBAL DISCLOSURE: STEPS TOWARD INTIMACY

There are a number of provocative hypotheses concerning the role of disclosure in the creation of friendships. Some have been tested and confirmed; others await more conclusive proof. The most important of these hypotheses helped to frame the questions and interpret the data on the self-disclosure patterns of Japanese and Americans.

To begin with, individuals apparently have relatively stable levels of disclosure, varying somewhat from partner to partner and setting to setting, but fairly consistent over time. Some people are "high revealers" and others "low revealers." As Maria Rickers-Ovsiankina and Arnold Kusmin note, "Social accessibility is a fairly stable but not rigidly fixed feature of the individual personality."[16] What is talked about, and how personally it is discussed, is apparently largely under unconscious control so that people are seldom aware of the norms they observe in talking with strangers and intimates.

Also, people rarely talk about their private lives during initial encounters; most talk is highly impersonal, revealing little of the unique motives and feelings of the communicants. The formalities of greeting, the routine of introductions, such commonplace exchanges help to ensure that the first encounter will be as harmonious as possible. A social etiquette discourages remarks that might cause the relationship to flounder before it is strong enough to weather possible friction. Michael Argyle has described such initial contacts well:

> When two people first meet they do not at once reveal their innermost secrets, their deepest beliefs or their highest aspirations. Nor do they reveal much about themselves as social persons: their social techniques are restrained and subdued, so that a very poor sample of their behaviour is shown to each other. The reason is similar—if too much is revealed, there is a risk that the other may not like it; if too much of the social person is shown, there is a danger that it

may not be possible to synchronize with the other. More intimate information is revealed when it is felt that the other will not reject. There are certain standard, and safe, topics of conversation—the weather, cricket scores—for which the conversation is virtually scripted, and very little is revealed about the speakers—at any rate by the verbal aspects of the encounter.[17]

Like the captured soldier who reveals only "name, rank, and serial number," strangers tend to reveal little of themselves beyond their name, occupation, marital status, and place of residence, along with such demographic details as age, height, weight, and sex that can be observed directly. Cultures actively promote techniques for avoiding too hasty penetration: "There are norms about invasions of privacy, rules of decorum, implicit guides to avoid noticing the foibles of others, extended courtship concepts, socially approved modes of response which protect the individual from exposure, and sanctions against those who violate the norms of gradual interpersonal exploration. All these may be designed to pace the process of interpersonal exchange. Were there no such controls, interpersonal relationships would be unpredictable and volatile."[18]

Over time the breadth and depth of disclosure tend to expand. If at first communication concerns relatively insignificant features of the self, it tends to spread to more emotionally significant ones. Altman and Taylor, using an Intimacy Scale, found substantial agreement on the amount of disclosure reflected in six hundred typical remarks.[19] Not only are less personal statements more likely to be made at the outset but also positive disclosures are favored over negative ones, according to Shirley Gilbert.[20] Even more relevant, she found the likelihood of personal disclosure varied with the closeness of one's partner: 31 percent for strangers, 42 percent for acquaintances, 64 percent for parents, 89 percent for friends, and 91 percent for spouses, leaving what she called a "9 percent privacy margin."

Pushing this inquiry one step further, Charles Berger and his associates asked randomly selected residents of a Chicago suburb to order a set of one hundred and fifty statements according to when they might make such statements during an initial two-hour conversation. The remarks, varying from "I'm from New York" to "I am a Republican" to "I make $13,000 a year" were to be placed along a time continuum. They found a high degree of consensus on when such remarks should be made and a pronounced tendency to place low intimacy statements earlier than those of higher intimacy. No connection was found between the ordering of statements and economic status, self-esteem, birth order, or the number of their close friends. Of the features that did correlate, age had the most pronounced effect: Younger people placed more intimate items earlier than older people did. Those who desired more friends also tended to place intimate remarks earlier in conversations, leading to speculation that deviation from social norms may account for their alienating others and hence seeking more friends.[21]

Later studies in which people placed statements into appropriate intervals of two, five, and ten minutes demonstrated that early conversation focuses on demographic information such as name, hometown, and occupation—information unlikely to spark disagreement. Exchange of such superficial information then declines rapidly and is replaced by questions and answers about attitudes, interests, and opinions.[22] The function of this gradual revealing of the self appears to be complex: It reduces uncertainty about the personalities of one's companions; it enables one to estimate the extent of similarity and compatibility; it helps one to predict with greater accuracy the reactions of others.

Pacing of Disclosure

Yet the gradient of disclosure should be neither too large nor too small: If too large, there is risk of overwhelming one's partner and arousing his or her defenses; if too small, the lack of willingness to share one's experience may distance the two people and discourage involvement. Changes in disclosure patterns tend to take place gradually, without conscious thought. Each person awaits confirmation from the other that it is agreeable to share more private feelings or thoughts. Without such approval, companions are likely to retreat to norms previously accepted as appropriate for their conversations.

As with any social activity, conversation requires some matching of the behavior of one person by the other: Disclosure tends to be reciprocated. Everyone has a "comfort range" with regard to disclosing themselves to others, preferring to share little or much of themselves, disclosing to many or only a few of their closest companions. High disclosers tend to attract and to be attracted to high disclosers; low disclosers are more comfortable with and cultivate relationships with low disclosers. When one person asks a companion about a previously undiscussed topic, he or she is, in effect, announcing a willingness to share experience on that same topic. And if one volunteers a confidence, it is an invitation to the other to reciprocate the openness. To maintain one's conversational balance is difficult unless there is some matching of communicative behavior.

Disclosure also tends to intensify in periods of personal crisis. Although therapy is an extreme case, where a person seeks someone to disclose to even at great financial cost, it also occurs between friends at critical turning points in life—leaving home, a first love affair, entering or leaving a job, getting married or divorced, the birth of a child, the death of someone close. The pressure to explore such experiences in order to comprehend and assimilate them overcomes whatever resistance people may ordinarily have to sharing such private reactions. Such occasions temporarily violate existing communicative norms, but they often move relationships permanently to a new level of trust and intimacy.

Even the condition of loneliness may be linked to the capacity for disclosure. It appears to be less a matter of being physically alone, or of lacking companions, than it is of lacking a particular kind of companion, a partner with whom one can be more completely open, can talk freely about things that really matter, can be confident of being valued in spite of, or because of, sharing private feelings. The fact that people often report intense feelings of loneliness when surrounded by acquaintances, even husbands and wives, suggests it is a qualitative rather than a quantitative deprivation. Poverty of inner experience, or an inability to share it with others, may deprive human relationships of the satisfaction people seek in them.

It is not clear whether disclosure spreads first from a topic of lesser to one of greater intimacy, or to deeper levels of disclosure on topics usually discussed superficially. And do such changes occur abruptly or gradually? The latter has the support of common sense: It would seem that acquaintances, to avoid disrupting a relationship, would move cautiously in sharing confidences. But in some instances people have moved very rapidly from strangership to intimacy, apparently finding such compatibility at lower levels of disclosure that they short-circuit this gradual process. Perhaps both exist but apply to different friendships. Premature disclosure that violates one partner's comfort level usually forces both to retreat to shallower levels to prevent exchanges that may threaten the survival of the friendship. Finally, in some long-term relationships people declare certain topics off limits, or undiscussable, such as religion and politics, in order to preserve an otherwise satisfying relationship.

Disclosure and Vulnerability

"People are afraid of people at least as much as people need people," Joseph Luft has written. "Perhaps it is because people need people that they are afraid."[23] If disclosure is so essential to defining the self, to insight and growth, to attachment to others, why should people be reluctant to share their inner life with friends? The reasons are stated in an illuminating paper by Peter Kelvin, who suggests that "protection" and "exploitation" are closely linked to "vulnerability" and hence to decisions whether to disclose or not: "Very simply: in becoming and being attracted, the attracted makes himself vulnerable."[24]

To preserve our independence and integrity we maintain a certain degree of privacy. The less we are known, the less others can control us and the more we are in command of our own acts. (The parallel with the self-confessionals of totalitarian regimes is obvious here; to the degree that people have no private thoughts, or are forced to adopt the thoughts of others, they have relinquished control of their own lives.) Yet the growth of friendship depends on a progressive sharing of such areas of privacy, one hopes with sensitivity and respect for their personal significance.

Paradoxically, the shared secret carries a double potential: "The very same factors which enable one individual to exploit another are also the factors which enable him to protect the other: for in order to protect someone it is necessary to understand him, to be able to explain and predict where he is vulnerable: protection is, after all, forward looking."[25] To admit to weakness or guilt, or to special skill or knowledge, may be turned to advantage by an acquaintance, but it is also the only way a companion can help to keep others from hurting or embarrassing one. Revealing our motives gives others the power to understand us on our own terms, but equally to exploit us. Perhaps this explains why disclosure tends to be reciprocal. Through what people disclose to one another they attempt to control how they are seen by others, balancing the need to be accepted as one is against the risk of being hurt or losing the friendship.

Discussing emotionally significant topics is risky business. The inner core of the personality is well protected by a variety of defenses—from avoidance of sensitive topics, detours around emotionally charged issues and concealment behind ambiguous remarks to outright deception. But in protecting the inner self and reducing our vulnerability to abuse we surrender the special kind of rapport and validation that only close companions can provide. This "tolerance of vulnerability," says Kelvin, is linked directly to the capacity for love: "Love as a *relationship*," he writes, "entails the mutual opening of 'private' selves. This may lead to exploitation and to hurt; but it is also the basis of the ability to meet one another's needs, and the source of the power to protect."[26]

Culture and Disclosure

Very little has been done to explore the relation between culture and disclosure. The concept itself is a Western one, reflective of *self*-centered cosmologies, and measurement of it, unsurprisingly, has been carried out largely in the United States and Great Britain. An initial effort to study Japanese and American communicative behavior revealed cultural agreement on preferred topics of conversation, but great divergence with respect to the depth of disclosure on these topics.[27] This work has been confirmed and extended in further studies of Korean, Japanese, and American behavior. Consistent with these findings is the view of many observers of Japan that friendships there rarely involve intimate disclosure. "There is a degree of intimacy and sharing central to real friendship that Japanese traditionally reserve only for family," writes Maureen D'Honnau.[28]

Through acculturation every culture teaches its members distinctive norms to follow in what should be talked about and what should not, when it should be discussed, and with whom and at what rate one should share confidences with a companion. If the American image suggests substantial disclosure to close acquaintances because of an equality of status, an emphasis on verbal expression, and greater social spontaneity, the Japanese image suggests somewhat less disclosure due to more formal relationships, the higher value placed on harmony, and the lesser importance attached to purely verbal forms of disclosure.

DESIGN OF THE VERBAL COMMUNICATION SCALE

Since conversation is the commonest way people have of sharing their subjective experiences, it figures critically in creating and maintaining ties with others. With regard to conversation, however, a number of questions arise at once: How broad a set of topics is explored? Which are talked about easily and often, and which are rarely or only tangentially discussed? How deeply are people willing to share ideas and feelings with one another? Are insignificant topics discussed in depth, or intimate topics discussed superficially? Are conversations similar with distant and close friends? If not, do they differ mainly in the topics covered or the depth of exploration? Does disclosing oneself promote a feeling of closeness, or does a feeling of closeness make intimate disclosure possible?

The original form of the Self-Disclosure Inventory was subject to a number of limitations. The scale measured willingness to talk about a range of topics with unspecified others; in later forms, when companions were indicated, they consisted of broad categories of people (opposite-sex friend, same-sex friend) rather than specific friends. Finally, hypothetical rather than actual behavior (future rather than past behavior) was described.

The Verbal Communication Scale that we used counteracted these shortcomings in several ways. Topics were selected, as on the original scale, ranging from the less to the more sensitive areas of experience:

General: (The level and quality of my education; my family background and circumstances)

Tastes: (My preferences in clothing, cars, housing; my preferences in plays, films, television)

Feelings: (My intensity of affection for this person; things about this person that annoy me)

Public issues: (My views of the roles of men and women; my views on what should be censored)

Work: (My occupational goals and ambitions; my limitations and handicaps in my work)

Finances: (How much money I earn or receive; pressing financial problems I have now)

Physical: (What I like best about my face or body; my history of diseases, injuries, operations)

Personality: (The personal qualities I dislike in myself; my sexual adequacy or problems in my sexual relations)

Respondents were then asked not to speculate but to report what had actually been discussed with companions and in what depth:[29]

0 = I have *not expressed* my views on this topic.

1 = I have expressed my views, but have *misrepresented* them in part.

2 = I have expressed my views on this topic in a *limited way*.

3 = I have expressed my views on this topic in *considerable detail*.

4 = I have expressed my views on this topic in *great detail*.

Finally, the *specific* companions named as the people they felt closest to (one and two), the person occupying the middle of their circle of acquaintances (eight) and those named as least close (fourteen and fifteen) were identified. (All questions on this subscale and all subsequent subscales were answered with respect to these five companions.)

WHAT WE TALK ABOUT: JAPANESE AND AMERICANS

The descriptions obtained from the Verbal Communication Scale show a significant cultural disparity in the conversational behavior of Japanese and Americans. The presence of a cultural contrast in patterns of talk in the two countries, although significant, is less interesting than the locus of such differences. Is it to be found in what is talked about, with whom these topics are discussed, or in the depth to which thoughts are shared? There is some contrast in the ranking of topics of conversation, but the difference lies more in the topics avoided than in those favored. They indicate, as shown below, that people in both countries rank five of the topics similarly, but they agree more on preferred topics (the first four) than on those avoided (the last four). Although Japanese and Americans are less attracted to conversations about finances, public issues, their physical self, and their personality, they approach them with differing degrees of reticence. The similarity of topical orientations bears out earlier findings in the *Public and Private Self in Japan and United States.*

Preferred Conversational Topics

Rank	Japan	United States
1	Tastes	Tastes
2	General	General
3	Work/School	Work/School
4	Feelings	Feelings
5	Financial	Public issues
6	Personality	Financial
7	Physical self	Physical self
8	Public issues	Personality

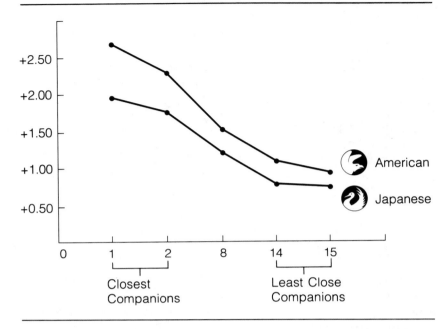

FIGURE 6.1   Levels of Disclosure to Closest (1, 2), Middle (8), and Least Close (14, 15) Companions

Japanese and Americans also both distinguish sharply between talking with people closest to them, those who occupy the middle, and those at the perimeter of their circle of companions. Figure 6.1 provides graphic illustration of the significant difference in what is disclosed to one's closest and distant companions.

The widest cultural contrast appears in the depth of disclosure. The average depth of disclosure of the self is 1.33 for the Japanese, or roughly between "misrepresenting" and "limited disclosure" of themselves. Among Americans the average level of disclosure was 1.73, or close to expressing one's views in "considerable detail." The contrast between the cultures is greatest with the two closest companions and decreases in size, but remains significantly different with even the least close companions. Thus disclosure is greater on all topics and with all partners for Americans, although the overall pattern of topics is similar in both cultures. (See Figure 6.2.)

No consistent difference appeared, however, with respect to male and female conversations in either culture; the sex factor, as found in recent studies, does not seem as powerful a determinant of the content of conversation as does culture.

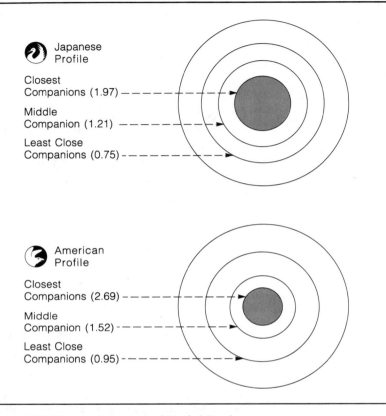

FIGURE 6.2   Intimacy and Verbal Disclosure

The Cultural Dimension: American Style

The disclosure profiles of the two cultures confirm those obtained in an earlier study, *Public and Private Self in Japan and United States*. There is similarity in preferred topics of conversation and in disclosing more fully to friends than acquaintances, and both studies found a significant disparity in the level of disclosure for all topics and all companions.

Clues to the sources of the contrast in levels of disclosure must be sought in the values promoted by the two cultures. From the moment of birth the American infant is enveloped in words, surrounded by an almost uninterrupted flow of speech even before it can be comprehended. In social situations the child is not merely the center of attention, but encouraged to express itself orally and rewarded when it does so. Almost immediately the child is disciplined at a distance through words. Formal education emphasizes this preoccupation with self-expression: There is competition in the classroom over who can speak first; individual assignments are often displayed for the approval of others; special awards are given to those with a flair for eloquence. The maturing child is given endless opportunity at school and at home to discuss, to debate, to persuade others. The oral tradition of the West has always emphasized the significance of the spoken word—"in the beginning was the word"—and continues to this day to emphasize its importance. All of these experiences create a heightened sense of self, the value of one's personal experience, and the desirability of communicating it to others.

The role models of American society are people gifted in articulating their ideas clearly and powerfully. The popularity of encounter groups during the past three decades reflects an unfulfilled hunger for more occasions for deeper levels of disclosure; preoccupation with baring one's soul, even to complete strangers, reflects the value attached to uninhibited spontaneity. In the United States, words like *genuine, authentic,* and *sincere* are used to refer to the consistency between what a person says and what he or she does; they imply that the public person is an accurate reflection of the private person.

To be accused of hypocrisy is one of the more devastating criticisms of an American, for whom there should be no separation between "being" and "seeming." Further, the maintenance of a public facade is thought ultimately to destroy the real self. Underlying the encouragement of self-expression is a deep-seated assumption that each person is different and that to confront such differences is the best way to respect and integrate them. It is not surprising, then, if the Japanese and many other cultures see Americans as "self-assertive," "talkative," "analytical," and "spontaneous."

There is something to be said, as Americans might argue, for promoting more honest communicative behavior. Does not the suppressing of feelings reduce the capacity for feeling? Does not the censoring of thoughts inhibit the capacity to think? Is not the opportunity to express an opinion often the stimulus for forming an opinion?

Although born as individuals we become persons only through involvement with other people. As the art critic Harold Rosenberg wrote, "In order to get any truth about myself, I must have contact with another person." The reason for becoming involved with other people is to share thoughts and feelings, to know and to become known, and in this way to extend the boundaries of our experience. "To fall back, to live on oneself, to withdraw, is sterility," Picasso once said.[30] To be forced to live apart from others is destructive psychically and, ultimately, physically as well.

But are there not equal risks in preoccupation with disclosing oneself? May it not encourage an oververbalization that is itself a kind of inarticulateness, forcing people to express themselves when they have little or nothing to express? Or could it lead to such an exhaustion of resources that they fall back on repeating themselves like a broken record? Human relations sometimes seem to wither because the inner experience of the two people has been so completely shared there is nothing more to share. Yet Joseph Luft, in response to the question "Shouldn't one keep a part to himself?" has given this blunt reply:

> The answer is no, quite the contrary. I say this unequivocally even though there must be times when everyone regrets having been too transparent. I cannot recall a single group of persons who came together to learn about people, about themselves, and about groups who did not discover that they were too closed off from people in everyday life in their families, on their jobs, and with friends.[31]

There is equal risk that in concealing ourselves we not only fail to understand one another but cultivate a deliberate misunderstanding of each other. The satisfaction of sharing a significant facet of our life with a close companion is deflected into sharing pseudoselves, fictitious selves. The wider the discrepancy between what one is and what one pretends to be, the more unfulfilling and precarious the relationship. Perhaps all human relationships involve some features of a performance, a certain editing of inner impulses in the presence of others, but Americans seem to regard this as a handicap in achieving an ideal relationship with intimates.

Having said this, it is still clear that Americans do not bare all, or even a great proportion, of their private lives to their most intimate companions. Although the culture may promote respect for the self and the value of expressing one's inner experience, this ideal is rarely attained. Americans may be somewhat more prone to disclose their thoughts and feelings with close companions than Japanese are, but both actually fall far short of what is possible.

The Cultural Dimension: Japanese Style

The Japanese culture, with its distinctive premises and values, frames the experience of its people differently in a number of respects, and these differences help to elucidate their communicative behavior. Here the infant is almost constantly in the immediate presence of its mother, talked to less but looked at more. The child sleeps with its mother in early infancy and with other family members during most of its childhood and early adolescence. (This pattern appears to be changing somewhat and with uncertain psychic and social consequences.) Even the architecture of the home, the confining space and absence of privacy, cultivates an awareness of how every act affects the lives of others.

There is less emphasis on external discipline until the child reaches school age. More importantly, parents discipline less through words and at a distance and more through example and indirect suggestions that deflect infractions of etiquette. In the family, as in the classroom, few issues are subjected to prolonged analysis or argument: Discussion, debate, and advocacy are rare in both settings; the emphasis is on making decisions quietly, fairly, and as undramatically as possible. Few academic courses or activities are designed to promote eloquence or skill in argument. Both at home and at school there is pressure to make the child appreciate the way every act impinges on the lives of others. The Japanese child is encouraged to take the role of others, viewing himself or herself from an external rather than internal locus. Interdependence, rather than independence, is cultivated: Individuals are taught to see how sensitively they can mesh their lives with those around them, particularly within the primary groups to which they belong. The same words Americans use so often to describe the virtues of the individual—*genuine, authentic, sincere*—in Japan tend to refer to the capacity of the person to subordinate his or her egotistic needs to the desires of others.

What all of this requires, Lebra writes, "is a formally impeccable presentation of the self" and this is best realized through formal relationships, routine exchanges, occasion-appropriate and status-appropriate disclosure.[32] Motivation for what one says or does arises from its suitability for a particular setting rather than from the impulses of the ego. The self, in many cases, is supposed to remain hidden; impulsive acts, blunt statements of opinion, and uncontrolled feelings threaten the harmony of the group and of the state. Negative feelings in particular, because they are likely to depress others, are rarely shared.

Artistic, rather than logical, principles regulate social encounters with words such as *form, proportion, harmony, balance,* and *beauty* dominating descriptions of Japanese communicative style over the centuries. "Aestheticism," notes the critic Robert Guillain, "rules social relations: It demands that disagreement and enmity remain unexpressed, hidden under the flowered veil of remarkable politeness."[33]

Japanese role models also contrast sharply with those in the United States: Admired people are, for the most part, distinguished by their modest demeanor, lack of eloquence, their public modesty. Edward Seidensticker, long a scholar of their culture, describes Japanese conversation in these terms: "There are subjects on which the Japanese can be extremely voluble, but one is struck at how very parochial they are. Eavesdropping on this or that conversation singled out from the enormous babble of a drinking place, one notices of how little interest the contents are to the outsider and to the world in general . . . It is all shop talk."[34] Even the samurai tradition, whose legacy lingers on and shapes contemporary behavior in some ways, warns against the inadvertent remark that might expose one's nature to the exploitation of others. Leaders in Japan are usually male, elderly, and, in Western terms, inarticulate.

Even the sheer quantity of verbal communication differentiates social life in Japan and the United States. Nearly a thousand daily logs of the communicative activities of Japanese and Americans were scrutinized by Ishii Satoshi and Donald Klopf.[35] They found the average Japanese spent roughly three and a half hours a day in conversation while Americans spent nearly seven hours, or twice as long, talking with their acquaintances. While the quantity of conversation is no index of topical breadth or depth, it does create a wider opportunity for self-expression.

If the culture of the United States rests squarely on the assumption of an individual, separate self, the culture of Japan rests on the assumption that one exists only in relation. As Harold Laski once observed, people lead "hyphenated lives," relating to one another through a plurality of selves. Nowhere is this gap so evident as in Western efforts to explore the "self-concept" of the Japanese. When Japanese are asked to answer questions about how they see themselves, confusion arises at once: How is someone who sees himself only as a brother to his sister, a son to his father, a subordinate to his section chief, and husband to his wife supposed to interpret such questions?

Perhaps the closest approximation to the idea of a self would be to regard the Japanese as having a "contextualized self," the ego incorporating within it all other members of the primary groups to whom one owes allegiance. One has a unique relation—hence a unique self—with each companion. The longer the relationship and the deeper the degree of incorporation, the less the need for verbal disclosure. In an ideal family the husband understands the wife's needs and pleasures, the wife equally the husband's. If they have such rapport, what is there to disclose or explain? As Robert Ozaki put it, "What is the worth of love if it cannot be felt without verbalizing it? The need to use words implies a lack of understanding."[36] A similar feeling permeates many, if not most, Japanese relationships. As Eto Jun summarizes the difference between West and East, "In other words, whereas Westerners base their lives on the premise that others naturally feel differently about things and view things according to different principles, the Japanese take it for granted in their daily lives that other people feel and think the way they do themselves."[37]

To the Western argument that self-expression is valuable, the Japanese might reply that this is true only if there is first sufficient inner reflection: The quality of outer dialogue can rise no higher than the quality of an inner monologue. Experience does not carry its own meaning; its meaning must be created. And this requires time to reflect on it, to consider its relation to one's past and to explore its future consequences, before a meaning is clear enough to articulate. Intrapersonal communication must precede—and may even supercede—interpersonal communication. The thrust of Japanese tradition and of Confucian, Buddhist, and Shinto thought regards reflection and meditation as more significant ways of becoming than through noisy argument with others. The introspectionist emphasis found in Eastern religions is more highly regarded by and seems more congenial to the Japanese than the expressionist emphasis found in Western religions and philosophy.

Linked to this elevation of inner dialogue is the lower status accorded to words. There is a sense that reality cannot be captured in words, that any statement about one's inner experience inevitably will distort and over-simplify it. The unique form of Japanese communication known as *haragei* suggests that truth resides not in the mind but in the belly. Hence efforts to intellectualize, to break experience up analytically in the effort to be precise, corrupt reality. The Western prefatory cliché, "Let me be perfectly clear about this," instead of heralding a special truth is seen by many Japanese as the childish claim of the verbally naive. Constitutions, contracts, regula-tions, and rules have always been viewed with a certain skepticism by the Japanese. The record of litigation, of dependence upon lawyers and courts to settle conflicts, contrasts sharply in the two countries.

In part this attitude toward verbal disclosure may be linked to language, especially the way it is used by Japanese. Kurt Singer argues that "the Japanese language is admirably equipped for such a style of life. Rich in ambiguities, elusive terms, indefinite constructions, it is a tool more for withholding and eluding than for expressing and stating."[38] One hesitates to blame language, for every language has its ambiguities, but patterns of usage among the Japanese seem to exploit these possibilities more than in other cultures. If not overstated it is accurate to say the Japanese prefer poetry to prose, metaphoric richness to precise description. Nevertheless, a language rich in ambiguity lends itself to concealment, to obscuring where one stands, and to protecting the speaker against complete disclosure of his or her meaning.

In interpersonal relations, Singer observes, the Japanese "knows how to draw around himself a wall of inscrutability and silence which allows him to live the life he likes best, shy, reserved, self-centered." Permanently secure within the primary group, supported without qualification at every transition in life, a Japanese has little need to extend himself socially, to seek and cultivate an endless series of friends to replenish those who make up his social circle. Yet how close, and how satisfying, are these primary relationships? The data here fail to support either the greater significance of family rela-tionships in Japanese social life or a greater depth of disclosure to family members or close friends.

In a recent work, Doi Takeo offers another explanation of Japanese verbal reticence, arguing that the mature Japanese is one who learns to compartmentalize outer and inner self, balancing the need to present an acceptable exterior that conforms to social conventions (*kao* as in "face") against the need to preserve an inner privacy (*kokoro* or "heart").[39] The issue, as he sees it, is not one simply of disclosing or not disclosing (as viewed in the United States), but of not pretending, deceiving, falsifying through outward behavior what lies inside. There is a position, then, midway between disclosing and not disclosing that consists of remaining silent. For a sensitive Japanese it should be possible to sense another's inner self (*ura*) through an empathic reading of the outer self that is presented (*omote*). Yet Doi's illustrations from Japanese literature frequently reflect an explicit disclosure of the inner self at least with intimates.

CULTURAL CONVERGENCE
AND DIVERGENCE

Clearly conversation is a significant feature of social life and differences in disclosure reflect the quality of personal relationships. The content of conversation between people who are close and those who are distant differs dramatically in both Japan and the United States. The level of personal disclosure changes with every degree of intimacy. The difference in such disclosure is so consistent that one could predict the closeness of relationships from knowing only what two people talk about and, conversely, could estimate what they might talk about from knowing the depth of their attachment.

There is also substantial confirmation here of the major theoretical hypotheses concerning disclosure: The breadth as well as the depth of topics explored varies with intimacy; the closer two people are the wider the topics they discuss and the more deeply they reveal their personal feelings. The idea that disclosure is a slow and gradual process, however, does not seem to fit the facts; close companions disclosed more than distant ones, but closeness, as revealed on the Acquaintance Inventory, is not highly correlated with how long two people have known each other. While some friendships evolve slowly, many move quickly from a superficial to a deep attachment in weeks or months, while it takes years, or never occurs, in other relationships. Relationships may move from plateau to plateau, advancing quickly or retreating quickly to congenial levels of disclosure, with periods of transition followed by periods of consolidation at a new level of intimacy.

What we confront here are two sets of norms that rest on different conceptions of human relationships, that converge in some respects and diverge in others. Japanese and Americans prefer to talk about similar topics and prefer to avoid similar topics. In both countries people differentiate conversationally among intimates, friends, and acquaintances. But the evidence also confirms that the Japanese tend to be more formal and restrained, less talkative and revealing of themselves; the evidence indicates equally that Americans are less formal and more assertive, more talkative and expressive of themselves. Perhaps this difference is what prompted the observation that Americans tend to meet one another in the realm of ideas while Japanese meet each other in the realm of people. In an essay entitled "Getting to Know You," Edith Ching Hayama noted how her American friends upon meeting a Japanese immediately wanted to know if the person was married, how many children she had, how the marriage was arranged, and so on. When she suggested this might appear forward and impertinent, an American friend replied, "But how else can I get to know them?"[40] Two Japanese meeting for the first time would choose less personal topics, ask fewer questions, and reply in less precise ways.

The consequences for cross-cultural encounters of Japanese and Americans are fairly apparent: The Japanese are likely to feel embarrassed with what appears to be invasions of their privacy, the Americans equally embarrassed by the indirectness and formality of the Japanese. One is put off by an intimacy that is imposed, the other by a subjective distance that is maintained.

In a number of respects the survey data do not confirm existing cultural images. When the behaviors reported on the Acquaintance Inventory and the Verbal Communication Scale are combined, it is not clear that the Japanese differentiate so sharply between their family group and those outside it; their closest personal ties are not limited to family members, and family members are not disclosed to any more deeply than peers are. Disclosure is a function of intimacy rather than of inheritance. And Americans cite family members among their intimates at least as often as the Japanese do and disclose to them also on the basis of their closeness rather than because of the accident of birth. Thus it is the special status a friend enjoys on a continuum of intimacy that influences the content of conversation in both countries, not whether partners are relatives or peers. Earlier research, which first categorized companions and then secured information on the conduct of these relationships, may have been self-fulfilling, producing a specious correlation between the type of associates and level of behavior. Here, where acquaintances were ordered simply on the basis of closeness, it appears there are fewer differences between relatives and nonrelatives, males and females, older and younger companions. And where differences in behavior occur, they are more traceable to the intensity of involvement than to the category of one's associates.

Yet the fact that in both cultures there is greater verbal accessibility with increasing depth of attachment suggests that disclosure does constitute a goal in many or all close relationships. The need to share subjective experience with others, despite the limitations of language, and to have that experience acknowledged and understood by another human being, seems to constitute more than a culturally unique phenomenon. Although disclosure to others makes us vulnerable to exploitation, it is also the major means to protect and confirm one another. It returns us to a point posed by Edward Albee: "We are all lonely at times, fearful at others, pained most of the time. Why we do not make use of such kinship rather than ignoring it, is a question worth answering."[41]

Although the verbal styles of Japanese and Americans are clearly distinctive, each may contribute to the enrichment of the other. As noted in an earlier study of the communicative styles of Japanese and Americans, perhaps these two cultural perspectives help to define the pathological extremes on a continuum of disclosure. Both the person who rarely discloses and the person who is preoccupied with disclosure appear maladjusted and unable to maintain close relationships. Private reflection and public disclosure thus combine in a communicatively mature person. Such a person has a capacity for private contemplation that is neither a product of repression nor a defensive retreat and a capacity for disclosure that is neither an aggressive exploitation nor a compulsive drive for attention.[42]

CHAPTER 7

Intimacy:
Its Nonverbal Dimensions

*The impersonality of life in our modern
world has become such that we have in
effect produced a new race of
Untouchables. We have become strangers
to one another, not merely avoiding but
actively warding off all forms of
"unnecessary" physical contact. The ability
of Western man to relate to his fellow
humans has lagged far behind his ability to
converse with computers, commune with
cars, and talk with toys. He can reach out
to the planets and meticulously monitor the
blips of deep space, yearning for a close
encounter of an alien kind, but too often
he will not reach out to his neighbor.* [1]
ASHLEY MONTAGU and FLOYD MATSON

Although some knowledge of our companions derives
from what they tell us, there are a multitude of other ways of gaining insight
into their personalities. Words are only one of many ways of knowing and
becoming known. The actions of other persons—the way they drive a car,
care for possessions, play an instrument, relate to children—may reveal as
much or more than does their speech. It is also true that such physical clues

121

may be more reliable indicators of their attitudes than what they tell us are their attitudes. Physical clues may be more reliable indicators because actions may be less capable of manipulation than words. In addition, some physical acts can evoke greater emotional impact. As Julius Fast reminds us, "The touch of a hand, or an arm around someone's shoulder, can spell a more vivid and direct meaning than dozens of words."[2]

There are startling estimates of the relative importance of verbal and nonverbal communication: Some experts contend that only 35 percent of our communication is verbal, 65 percent of it nonverbal; others argue that the proportion of information carried nonverbally is grossly underestimated by these figures. Albert Mehrabian contends that where feelings are concerned only 7 percent is conveyed verbally and 93 percent through physical cues.[3] If such estimates reflect the entire span of a day they may be believable, since we talk with people only a few hours each day. If, instead, they are intended to suggest that within any conversation most of what is said is of little consequence, such estimates must be viewed with skepticism. People talk about so many topics, for such different reasons, on so many occasions that it would be wise to suspend belief in any such neat estimate of the precise roles of verbal and nonverbal forms of communication. The value of such estimates lies, instead, in their directing attention to a long neglected but significant facet of social behavior.

LIMITS OF LANGUAGE

Preliminary to exploring these nonverbal forms, consider some of the limitations of language. Words are often an unreliable guide to meaning because they constitute an abstraction of any experience; they are once removed from the event they report. They distill and summarize an experience. To tell an acquaintance that you feel sad or frightened is an interpretation of an inner state and subject to the same errors of perception as any other observed event. But your sluggish walk and slumped posture, or your pale skin and mumbled replies are a direct reflection and part of that inner state. The physician not only listens to what people describe about their physical condition but also looks for direct evidence from the body that will confirm or contradict such claims. Words are a secondary rather than primary manifestation of our meanings.

In addition, our talk is usually about the past. What we report of the past is limited by our ability to recall it accurately and is shaped by our desire to have it promote a particular image of ourselves in the eyes of others. Talk of the future suffers from the same limitations plus the tendency to overestimate our commitment to future goals. That we often say we will feel and think and do certain things that others suspect we will not feel, think, or do may be less a matter of hypocrisy than of wishful thinking or underestimation of the complexities of that future.

The viability of the verbal code suffers one further limitation: Every language imposes its structure on the events it represents. Languages are systems of categories. Words are discrete, they have definitive boundaries. Every language also has a structure, a grammar that must be respected if one is to make sense. The flow of experience must be cut to fit the terms available and must be ordered according to the rules of grammar. Verbal codes are said to be "digital systems of communication," suited particularly to conveying distinctive bits of information that can be linearly ordered.[4] Obviously, many of the things people talk about are handled well, or with tolerable distortion, through words.

But not all: If language were sufficiently capable of representing the entire spectrum of meanings, it would never have been necessary to devise wordless alternatives. Painting, sculpture, mathematics, music, and dance each arose from the necessity of finding better ways of representing the nuances and complexities of human experience. No one has ever proposed that there is a sculptural equivalent of a poem, a mathematical equivalent of a painting, or an architectural equivalent of a song. Every code offers a unique vocabulary and alternative grammar for giving symbolic form to inner states.

THE NONVERBAL CODE

The human body is, as well, an expressive instrument. What we call the nonverbal code consists simply of the physical acts by which a person discloses his or her inner moods and motives. Many physical acts, from gesture to vocalization, seem to operate as "analogic" rather than "digital" forms of symbolization.* They represent meanings holistically without breaking them into component parts and presenting them sequentially. They seem particularly suited for conveying changing emotional states and for representing complex inner feelings. And much of the experience of life, perhaps most of it, is of this sort.

No clear boundary marks the beginning or ending of most nonverbal statements. It is difficult if not impossible to decide when a smile begins or fades away, people lean toward or away from each other, or a hostile gesture turns into a caress. Nonverbal acts not only lack clear boundaries but also accompany one another, elaborating, reinforcing, contradicting each other.

---

* Meanings coded in language are digital in the sense that a word is said or not said, but meanings are also coded analogically in the way the word is stressed, inflexed, accompanied by a slight or a broad smile. Language is an excellent tool for expressing information (though not exclusively so) while nonverbal codes tend to be excellent ways of expressing feelings and attitudes (though not exclusively so).

(Humor and satire are nearly impossible without such conflicting signals.) Finally, much of the meaning of any nonverbal act lies not in the act itself but in the way it is executed: The same gesture acquires different meanings when displayed rapidly or slowly, weakly or vigorously.

One distinction that tends to be overlooked in the expanding writing about nonverbal behavior is which physical acts constitute a symbolic code and which do not. As Desmond Morris reminds us:

> Many of our body actions are basically nonsocial, having to do with problems of personal body care, body comfort and body transportation; we clean and groom ourselves with a variety of scratchings, rubbings, and wipings; we cough, yawn and stretch our limbs; we eat and drink; we prop ourselves up in restful postures, folding our arms and crossing our legs; we sit, stand, squat and recline, in a whole range of different positions; we crawl, walk and run in varying gaits and styles.[5]

Many physical changes in an organism such as blushing, blinking, and enlarging or contracting the pupil of the eye do not constitute a code: They are symptoms rather than signals; they are expressive but do not stand for something else. As with temperature, pulse, and blood-sugar level, they are part of the state of the organism rather than a comment on the state of the organism. They *are* something rather than standing for something (even though they may be informative).

But other physical acts, such as approaching another person, waving a greeting, winking, or touching someone on the shoulder, do constitute a symbolic code. They are efforts to represent the attitudes of the actor and are displayed to exert some sort of influence. They may be accurate or misleading (as words may be), but they function symbolically.

It is a curious myopia that leads people to believe we become known only through what we tell others about ourselves. "At work or play," writes Frank Trippet, "everybody emits wordless signals of infinite variety."[6] The way one performs the tea ceremony, selects and gives a gift, competes in sports, responds to music, or orders a meal provides a constant flow of clues to the interior world of acquaintances. Broken friendships and broken marriages seem more often the consequence of what the two parties do rather than of what they say to one another. Arnold Shapiro and Clifford Swenson, for example, found in studying married couples that husbands and wives had accurate information about each other but "most knowledge of spouse's personality is apparently obtained from observation of behavior rather than self-disclosure."[7] There is no way to exist—to stand or sit, laugh or frown, bow or embrace, make or keep an appointment—that does not expose one to the judgment of others. The less conscious such acts are, the more they may reveal. Those that are consciously displayed are, of course, capable of the same deceits that appear in verbal disclosure.

Perhaps the research on "first impressions" needs to be reevaluated from this perspective. In many studies strangers have been found to form distinct impressions of one another before any exchange of words has taken place. Many of these impressions, favorable and unfavorable, are found to persist for months and survive intact in spite of numerous conversations. That talking with each other does little to change such impressions appreciably may only confirm that postures, alertness, grace of movement, and style of clothing are fairly reliable clues to the character of a person—more so, in some instances, than the words they exchange. In a study of somewhat flawed design, John Bardeen found that people who could only touch the other person (no talking, blindfolded), could only see the other person (no touching, no talking), or could only talk with their partner (no touching, blindfolded) formed different views of their personality. Although no way was found to check the accuracy of their perceptions, each channel provoked a description that was complex and coherent.[8] The presumption that a single channel is inherently superior remains doubtful until there is much more careful testing of the hypothesis.

A number of therapists also feel that in diagnosing patients it is as critical to pay attention to the way they keep appointments, where and how they sit during therapy, and their gestures and facial expressions as to attend to their remarks. Even among the so-called verbal therapies, Freud acknowledged that when patients were silent they maintained a stream of commentary through their bodies, their fingertips, their eyes, with significant clues oozing out of every pore.

SOME PRELIMINARY CONSIDERATIONS OF NONVERBAL COMMUNICATION

The field of nonverbal communication, one of the newest topics of inquiry among behavioral scientists, has produced an almost indigestible body of data during the past two decades. It was only a hundred years ago that the first work on the subject appeared: Charles Darwin's The Expression of Emotions in Man and Animals. The next major work did not appear until seventy years later with publication in 1941 of David Efron's Gesture and Environment, a work that described the gestural characteristics of Eastern Jews and Southern Italians in New York City. Ten years later Nonverbal Communication by Jurgen Ruesch and Weldon Kees distinguished among sign language (primarily gestures), action language (grosser aspects of physical style), and object language (manipulated artifacts).[9] None of these classic works prompted much response at the time of their publication, but interest has grown since then among psychologists, sociologists, and communicologists. In the past two decades that interest has spread by contagion into almost every discipline concerned with human affairs. The number of studies continues to multiply exponentially; there are over two hundred studies of eye movements alone. Still, a number of broad generalizations about nonverbal modes of interacting frame the research to be reported here.

One feature of physical style is its consistency; each of us has an identifiable way of behaving: The way we walk, the way we stand or sit, the way we smile and gesture are even more easily recognized than the topics we like to discuss or the opinions we hold. Although our manner changes from one occasion to another, and from one companion to another, it is still recognizably us. People do not, as a rule, suddenly change from being lethargic to animated, from rarely gesturing to constantly doing so, from avoiding the touch of others to seeking constant physical reassurances. Miles Patterson, for example, had people conduct a series of interviews in which they were able to position themselves as they chose; the distance at which people placed their chairs, the angle of address, the amount of eye contact, and the degree to which they leaned toward their partners were very similar over various occasions.[10] It is the uniqueness of each person's physical style and its consistency that makes it possible to use it as a way of gaining insight into individuals and cultures.

Another feature of nonverbal communication that makes it of more than usual interest is that it seems less subject to conscious control and hence more revealing of the true inner state of the person. We have the option of speaking or not speaking, of disclosing little or a great deal about ourselves, of phrasing our remarks so they provoke or please others. But that we are present or absent, dressed conservatively or flamboyantly, have a pleasant or unpleasant voice is something that may be beyond our control. Our manner of relating to people, because it was acquired so early in life, and at such great cost, may seem entirely natural to us as adults. But, as Erving Goffman reminds us, what seems "natural" now was acquired with great conscious effort and even pain:

> It should be nearly as evident that almost every activity that any in-
> dividual easily performs now was at some time for him something
> that required anxious mobilization of effort. To walk, to cross a
> road, to utter a complete sentence, to wear long pants, to tie one's
> shoes, to add a column of figures—all these routines that allow an
> individual unthinking, competent performance were attained
> through an acquisition process whose early stages were negotiated in
> a cold sweat.[11]

It is only when our manner of behaving disrupts a relationship that we suddenly are aware of its compulsive power. Attempts to modify our physical manner seem not only "unnatural" but as if we were being untrue to our real selves, as if we were putting on an act.

Just as verbal disclosure tends to deepen with growing closeness, nonverbal intimacy similarly increases over time. A respectful distance may be maintained at the first meeting; as time passes, formal greetings give way to friendly embraces. Entertaining a new friend is likely to be done somewhat formally; later the two people may share fish and chips out of the same newspaper. Anxiety over periods of silence early in a friendship give way to contentment as people get to know each other better. Over time there is less physical distance between companions and the frequency of physical contact also increases. Playful acts from teasing to roughhousing become less inhibited as confidence grows in the strength of the relationship.

There is another respect in which verbal and nonverbal communication parallel each other. In verbal disclosure the principle of reciprocity seems to operate: What one partner reveals tends to obligate an equal disclosure from the other; in nonverbal interaction the principle of synchrony similarly holds that the habits of posture, gesture, and touch of one person tend to prompt similar acts from the other. The principle of reciprocity and of synchrony may measure the potential for effective bonding of two people: Whether the empathy is a verbal one (the sharing of ideas) or a nonverbal one (from parallel ways of expressing emotional states), each seems to reflect the potential for rapport between the communicants. The absence of verbal or nonverbal rapport (or particularly, of both) would seem to guarantee an awkward and uncongenial encounter. Physical compatibility seems at least as important as intellectual compatibility in predicting success or failure in interpersonal relations.

All of this would seem to justify more serious consideration of physical styles of communication as a factor influencing the outcome of cross-cultural encounters. Yet such comparisons are as rare as comparative studies of the content of conversation. This gap is particularly serious in the case of Japan and the United States, where differences in nonverbal manner are so often emphasized and so rarely investigated.

PHYSICAL STYLE OF COMMUNICATING IN JAPAN

If Japanese and Americans prefer different levels of verbal disclosure with intimates, we might suspect even greater differences in their management of time, space, silence, and touch—toward many forms of nonverbal communication.

There is no lack of anecdotal description or of speculation on the physical styles of Japanese and Americans. With one notable exception, there is almost complete agreement on the distinctive physical manner of members of these two cultures. There are speculations, but sparse evidence.

With the Japanese one can start with their widely shared assumption of similarity. As Edwin Reischauer and others have noted, "the Japanese today are the most thoroughly unified and culturally homogeneous large bloc of people in the world."[12] Isolated by an accident of geography and equally by deliberate policies of exclusion, Japan has had no significant immigration by outsiders throughout its history. The nation has little ethnic diversity. Despite a population half that of the United States, and seventh largest in the world, outsiders constitute less than 1 percent of the population. Few, if any, truly sharp differences divide the population or culturally alienate one group from another. Writers often refer to the nation as resembling an extended family more than a corporate state. And, as is the case with families, it is thought that less needs to be communicated through words: Thoughts and feelings can be more cryptically conveyed through subtle physical cues.

Further, a large proportion of communication, it is said, takes place within primary groups with whom one shares a lifelong relationship. The central place of the household is challenged today by growing attachment to occupational groups, but both promote greater ease of understanding. Whenever people interact out of a common background of similar values and congruent goals—where people tend to see the world in similar ways—communicants can take a lot for granted. A greater proportion of communication is possible without words; more of the intended meanings are conveyed through a sigh, a puzzled look, the character of a gift, a sharp intake of breath. Differences may be expressed, but they are identified from subtle changes in manner rather than elaborate verbal explanations. Hence meanings are often communicated without resort to words.

Another, less explored, feature of Japanese social behavior is found in the extent to which communication operates indirectly through mediating agents of one kind or another. The most obvious example is the go-between (nakōdo) who arranges marriages, but go-betweens also pave the way for encounters with almost everyone: government officials, corporation executives, political leaders, employers and employees. A more subtle and culturally unique form of indirection lies in the extent to which objects serve as instruments of communication, a tradition more richly elaborated in Japan than in the rest of the world. It occurs when two people wish to comment on their relationship or their lives, but instead of discussing their feelings in so many words do so through some external object or action: The tea ceremony (cha-no-yu), flower arrangements (ikebana), writing of poetry (haiku), and calligraphic representation (shodo) all become vehicles for revealing one's thoughts as powerfully, but less explicitly, than through verbalization. A remark about a feature of nature—reflections in the water, the shape of a stone, the changing of the seasons—becomes a way of revealing oneself to a close friend but via the agency of a mediating object or event. It is not that such indirect forms of expression play no part in Western societies but that they are thought to play a smaller and less critical role in the maintenance of personal relations. Many of these replace words as a vehicle for sharing attitudes, and they may be one of the most distinctive features of the communicative style of Japanese.

As noted earlier, the Japanese seem to hold words in lower esteem than do members of other cultures. If true, one might expect this to also heighten respect for nonverbal ways of managing social life. The emphasis is on listening rather than speaking, on intuition rather than explanation, on synthesis over analysis. The Japanese seem to prefer to regard human relations as proceeding better through heart-to-heart than through mind-to-mind exchanges. In societies where understanding is thought to require analysis and argument, words are critical; in societies where it evolves out of an intuitive sensitivity to total behavior, words may be less informative. When and where and how often two people meet, where they sit and how well they listen, their poise under stress, and their responsiveness to the needs of others may seem more informative of what they are like than what they say about their attitudes and intentions.

Differences in emphasis upon nonverbal channels of communication may also arise from cultural attitudes toward conflict. Although there is a communicative etiquette in Japan that disapproves of noisy argument, critical rebuttals, and blunt disagreements, one suspects that behind this sense of propriety lies a deep concern for the destructive potential of conflict. Among the Japanese, it is said, the preservation of harmonious relations is more highly valued than pursuit of the "truth," particularly if such a pursuit might irreparably damage relations with people on whom one depends. Since it is almost impossible for Japanese to restore a relationship once it is broken, outright disagreement carries far more serious social consequences than in the West. Confrontation is risky business. The special appeal of nonverbal forms of communication lies in their less explicit meanings, greater ambiguity, and lower potential for provoking hostility. It is difficult, if not impossible, to present an ultimatum, articulate a line of argument, or draw firm conclusions through posture, facial expression, or gesture. Advocacy requires verbalization; to forsake it forces greater reliance on other modes of communicating.

Further, Japanese respect for consensus, for seeking agreement rather than disagreement, may also discourage verbalization. To build such a consensus, one is likely to be more attentive to similarities than differences, alert to signs of assent rather than dissent. Signs of affirmation may be more readily conveyed nonverbally, whereas disagreement is likely to require explicit verbal justification. Living on islands surrounded by strangers, living and working in quarters that provide little privacy, according to Reischauer, discourages public displays of emotion. "In fact," he writes, "the Japanese have a strong aversion to most open displays of feelings, whether of anger or of love, though like most rules this has its exceptions in their maudlin drunkenness and their unabashed sentimentality."[13]

Finally, there is the well-advertised Japanese attraction to silence. Silence, we are told, is not viewed by the Japanese as the absence of meaning, the empty space that surrounds words, but as itself a reflection of meanings no less profound than those expressed through speech. There are silences as damning, eloquent, reassuring or confirming as any remark one might make. Indeed there is growing appreciation of the communicative import of silence in both countries.

Recently Roy Miller has argued that the communicative behavior of the Japanese is confounded by a myth of the uniqueness of their language and an equally misleading antimyth (sic) of silence:

> We are a nation, the antimyth teaches, not of language, but of silence. Our forte is nonverbal communication. And if you thought our language was difficult to learn and impossible to master, then, how, the antimyth taunts, can you ever hope to succeed in becoming fluent in our silence?[14]

What passes for silent communication, he argues, is no more unique or incomprehensible in Japan than in the United States. Does Japanese homogeneity, group centeredness, and preference for harmony and consensus reveal itself in more intense reliance upon physical forms of communication? Is this myth or reality, fiction or fact?

PHYSICAL STYLE OF COMMUNICATING IN THE UNITED STATES

What features of the American scene frame Americans' attitudes toward and reliance upon nonverbal forms of communication? To begin with there is a presumption of difference rather than similarity; individual uniqueness is compounded by ethnic diversity. Homogeneity seems contradicted at every street corner. Americans daily, even hourly, confront myriad life-styles: a multitude of nationalities, a variety of religions, interacting in a variety of tongues and accents. Increasing heterogeneity is still the rule. An Urban Institute economist suggests that "the United States may, in fact, be riding its biggest immigration wave ever."[15] He has estimated that as many as eight million people entered the United States in the past decade. Another estimate claims the United States now takes in twice as many people from abroad as does the rest of the world combined. That so diverse a population with such contrasting verbal and nonverbal styles can communicate at all continues to surprise visitors.

Perhaps because of this diversity, combined with the necessity of shaping a new nation, Americans developed profound respect for the right of each person to express himself or herself in distinctive ways. A nation of rugged individuals, unfettered by a sense of social responsibility, however, seems a contradiction in terms. Perhaps that accounts for an almost equal passion for voluntary collaboration through an infinite number of groups and associations. But such collaboration tends to be temporary, lasting so long as it serves the transient needs of its collaborators: There is little sense of lifelong attachment to a closed group of permanent friends. "Instant friendships" are said to be characteristic of the culture, dissolving as quickly as they materialize, reflecting short-term commitments. A society constantly on the move, taking advantage of every opportunity for advancement, may require skill in accelerated intimacy. This mobility might dictate the use of all channels of possible communication, nonverbal as well as verbal.

Americans' predilection for direct rather than indirect confrontation may also affect their nonverbal manner. American resistance to formal, status-conscious, routine exchanges is at least as strong as Japanese resistance to their opposites. The excessive informality of American social behavior may be its most noted feature of communicative behavior. And this informality is not simply a matter of first names, casual dress, uninhibited gestures, or animated facial expression. There is a mistrust of social proprieties, a feeling that restraint in any form only serves to deceive or mask from others what one is really thinking or feeling. The more spontaneous the acts of companions, the more truly they can be trusted. For this reason Americans might be expected to be as expressive nonverbally as they are verbally disclosing.

An "expressive culture" such as the United States and a "receptive culture" such as Japan may regard nonverbal forms of communication in distinctive ways: the former seeking constantly to expand opportunities for self-expression, the latter feeling less need to display feelings before others. Where the Japanese may be comfortable with periods of silence, and even value them, Americans are thought to be uncomfortable at such times: Silence may be seen as a breakdown in communicative rapport or, more seriously, as a sign of a deteriorating relationship. Silence must, or should be, filled with more words as soon as possible.

CULTURAL CONTRADICTIONS

Cultures, however, rarely can be characterized so simply; they are, more often, marked by complexity and contradiction. And this is the case with regard to prevailing attitudes toward nonverbal forms of expression.

In a majority of encounters, people have to be able to figure out what their companions want or don't want, like or don't like, will or won't do. It is impossible to carry on any cooperative activity in the absence of such information. Meanings have to be shared if a friendship is to begin and to survive, if not in one channel, then in another.

The Japanese in their search for consensus, dislike of verbal argument, and preference for visceral over cerebral forms of empathy might be expected to make greater use of physical rather than verbal modes of communication. Such silent languages as posture, facial expression, glances, and pregnant pauses should play a larger role in relating to companions. But Japanese emphasis on situational formalities, dislike of public displays of emotion, and disapproval of physical demonstrativeness would predict the opposite. Remnants of the samurai tradition with its emphasis on strength through silence—a silence not only of speech but also of any physical slip that might expose inner weakness—remain alive today. Such contradictory impulses within the Japanese psyche might inhibit the grosser forms of nonverbalization such as facial expressiveness, gestures, and touching, but emphasize the use of space, time, and silence as appropriate ways of conveying feelings.

Such contradictory impulses can be found, as well, within American cultural values. The desire for widening outlets for spontaneous expression, an aversion to proprieties, a confidence that honesty will promote intimacy suggests that nonverbal channels will be fully exploited. Yet American emphasis on rationality, objectivity, and dialogue suggests less reliance upon the more ambiguous and more emotional meanings carried in the nonverbal code. Again such contradictory tendencies might be resolved by selectivity in the silent languages employed: greater use of grosser forms of nonverbalization through posture, gesture, and facial expression but less reliance upon the more subtle forms of physical expression such as space, time, and intonation.

DESIGN OF THE PHYSICAL COMMUNICATION SCALE

Fighting and loving, the two most extreme forms of interpersonal involvement, are both primarily realized through physical means of communicating. Nonverbal acts are, as with words, a way of achieving intimacy and a reliable barometer of the changing intensity of personal relationships.

Since the forms of nonverbal communication are almost without limit, which physical acts are most significant and feasible to measure? Several criteria were employed in making these decisions. What was sought was a reasonably representative set of physical behaviors that both Japanese and Americans might employ in interacting with companions of varying degrees of closeness. To make measurement feasible, nine forms of nonverbal behavior were included on the Physical Communication Scale.

Some guidance in selecting the nine areas of investigation was obtained from earlier theoretical and empirical research on nonverbal behavior. A clarification introduced by Erving Goffman distinguished between the physical cues one "gives"—presented more or less deliberately to influence people around us—and those one "gives off"—that are accessible to others simply because of our presence and less subject to manipulation.[16] Our appearance, for example, permits others to learn something of our sex, age, height, weight, and race by merely observing us; a number of other more dynamic and subtler cues such as skin color, pupil size, blinking rate, sweating, or yawning are also visible and largely beyond our control. The cues one "gives off" tend to be relatively stable attributes of a person and, therefore, less significant in comparing the way people communicate with close or distant partners.

Another useful distinction is between "microacts" and "macroacts." The literature abounds with studies of small, almost imperceptible, changes in facial expression, visual glances, body angles, and the pacing, pitch, and stress patterns of speech. Although such physical features are undoubtedly interpreted, they are so subtle that they are nearly impossible to report with any accuracy, or even to recall. Instead, it is larger units of nonverbal behavior that are more easily noted and remembered that became the focus. Our inquiry lay in that middle ground somewhere between minute descriptions of finger or eye movements and broad descriptions of posture, gait, and gesture. Some features of nonverbal communication have attracted the attention of social scientists, but a number of them—such as time patterning, entertaining, gift giving, and playing—have not been given the serious attention they deserve.

The nine types of communicative acts singled out for investigation included (1) "scheduling behavior," the extent to which a person modified his or her activities to spend time with a companion; (2) "entertaining," the extent to which a person entertained a partner away from or within his or her home; (3) "spacing," the distance one maintained between oneself and one's associates; (4) "greeting behavior," preferred ways of initiating contact with close associates; (5) "playing," the frequency of engaging in forms of play with various partners; (6) "touching," the frequency and areas of the body that are touched during interaction with companions; (7) "feeling," preferences for ways of expressing positive feelings from embracing to sexual intercourse; (8) "silence," the length of comfortable or empathic silences experienced with close associates; and (9) "gift giving," how often objects are given to express affection or fulfill obligations.

Within each of the topical areas five questions, of increasing intimacy, sampled the frequency of such physical acts. The format of the questionnaire is illustrated here:[17]

Activity	1	2	8	14	15

Scheduling
1. I have used scheduled activities as an excuse not to be with this person.
2. I have seen this person when my schedule permitted it.
3. I have rearranged my schedule to be with this person.
4. I have postponed projects to be with this person.
5. I have failed to meet critical deadlines to be with this person.

As with the other subscales, respondents were asked to indicate the frequency of each pattern of behavior with respect to their two closest companions, one from the middle of their circle of acquaintances, and their two least close acquaintances.

THE SILENT LANGUAGES:
OVERALL CULTURAL PROFILES

The patterns of physical communication for Japanese and Americans yielded a number of surprises. Not only was there a highly significant difference in various forms of nonverbal communication but Japanese and Americans also differed consistently on nearly all physical acts and differentiated among all five companions. As with verbal disclosure—where the cultural difference lay in the depth of disclosure rather than topic—the difference in physical communication revealed a higher frequency of more intimate behavior of all types by Americans. The overall average difference in the scores of the two cultures on reliance upon physical forms of communication was very large: The American average score of 144 was nearly twice the Japanese score of 88. Both verbal and nonverbal channels of expression appear to be more heavily employed by Americans. Sex differences, as one might expect, were somewhat greater in Japan, but in neither country was the difference reliably greater than chance.

Both cultures agree on the *importance* of certain modes of nonverbal communication, but disagree on others: Japanese and Americans both scored highest on their handling of space, sharing of routine activities, and management of time. The widest cultural discrepancy appeared in the higher ranking of playing and silence by the Japanese and touching, entertaining, and feeling among Americans.

When it comes to how people relate to their companions, the widest difference between the cultures occurs with the two closest companions and tends to diminish as the emotional distance increases; nonverbal behavior in the two cultures is more similar with respect to acquaintances at the periphery of the circle of intimates.

Time

As Edward Hall suggests, "Time talks. It speaks more plainly than words. The message it conveys comes through loud and clear. Because it is manipulated less consciously, it is subject to less distortion than the spoken language."[18] It should not be lightly dismissed, then, as a factor in friendship. How frequently two people meet, and for how long, depends on the time each has or can make available for the other. The decision each person makes with respect to competing claims on his or her time comments on the relative importance attached to each relationship. For someone to meet an acquaintance only when it cannot be avoided, or to meet no matter what sacrifice is involved, is a powerful statement about the attractiveness of various companions. By regulating accessibility to other people, time alone may limit how deeply two people may become involved.

It is not surprising, then, that members of both cultures score so high on this mode of communicating nonverbally. In neither were scheduled activities often used to avoid being with their closest partners; to do so would apparently raise instant doubts concerning the commitment to each other. Postponing or neglecting other responsibilities to be with highly valued companions occurred significantly more often with close rather than distant acquaintances. The relatively higher scores of Americans suggest the higher value attached to personal as compared to public commitments. Or the lower scores of Japanese may reflect greater Japanese sensitivity to public responsibilities and the more severe consequences of putting personal needs ahead of obligations to others. The social consequences of rearranging schedules or of failing to complete tasks on schedule may be less severe in the United States. Although the data suggest such speculations, further research is needed to confirm whether the Japanese pattern results from a more restrictive social milieu or the American pattern from a stronger need to affiliate with people.

Entertaining

People everywhere have invented ways to consummate and celebrate their affection for one another. Such occasions permit friends to eat and drink together, laugh and chat informally, to shed their public persona and behave more spontaneously. Another way in which we display our feeling about others, therefore, is by our effort to provide pleasurable experiences for them. The distance traveled and the effort or cost involved in entertaining others comments on our attachment to them. A formal banquet, picnic lunch, barbecue, or home-cooked dinner all create and reflect a different level of intimacy. The most revealing of such entertainments is probably found in the home. To invite an acquaintance to one's home displays a willingness to expose one's private life. The interior of an apartment or home is without equal in providing clues to the interests, attitudes, temperament, and values of its owner. (It may be why therapists rank the decorating of one's home among the most anxiety-creating challenges of life.) Limiting access to one's home is a way of controlling how much others are able to learn about how one really lives when free of the need to maintain a role or image in the eyes of others.

Here respondents were asked to indicate how frequently they had entertained friends "away from home" or invited them to their home for "a meal," "to stay overnight," "to stay for an extended period," or had "lived together." The difference between the scores of Japanese and Americans on entertaining was the second largest obtained. For each level of entertainment and for each partner from close to distant Americans scored significantly higher than the Japanese; Americans entertained even their most distant companions more frequently at home than the Japanese did their most intimate friends.

The findings confirm what observers of both countries would predict; interpreting the source of this difference is more problematical. Americans are among the best housed people in the world, the Japanese among the poorest housed of any industrial nation. It would not be surprising, therefore, if patterns of entertaining reflected pride or embarrassment over the material level of one's life. Yet a sample of college students should reduce somewhat these wide discrepancies in housing conditions. And, no matter what the standard of living, the willingness to expose one's closest friends to how one has adapted to his or her environment is unquestionably revealing. Between close companions the material conditions of life should not matter so much, and reluctance to share one's residence may reflect more a reluctance to be so deeply exposed.

Gift Giving

In the potlatch ceremonies of the Northwest Native American cultures chiefs competed to see who could give away the most possessions. It is one of the most dramatic instances we have of societies governed by the ritual exchange of presents. The role of gifts—so often trivialized in contemporary society—may be a moral one that binds giver and receiver together. In his essay on "Gifts and Presents," Ralph Waldo Emerson was struck by their mystical power to hold members of a society together.[19] The gift, it seems, is more than a gift. As Marcel Mauss, the first and only writer to give serious attention to the role of gifts, notes: "It expresses intimacy and distance, commemorates rites of passage, is involved in reunions and reconciliations, combines obligations and feelings."[20] Why do friends give wine or candy or flowers, gifts of little economic value, to their friends? They do so, writes Robert Brain, "to express, cement, and create alliances."[21] Equally, the failure to accept a gift, or to acknowledge or repay it, implies hostility. The gift not only expresses affection but through the selection or creation of it reflects the rapport that exists between giver and receiver as well. For these reasons it is a valuable sign of the depth of understanding and strength of attachment between people. Yet almost nothing is known about the role gifts play in friendships.

Most observers have noted the almost constant exchange of gifts among Japanese and the relative absence of such exchanges among Americans. Yet gift giving as a form of nonverbal communication enjoys the same relatively low status on the scale of importance in both countries. And, surprisingly, the overall frequency of gift giving is nearly twice as high among Americans as among Japanese. As before, the widest difference appears with respect to intimates and again disappears with companions who are the least close. The Japanese more often reported giving a gift "because this person needed something" or "as a remembrance," but Americans much more often reported giving gifts "as a token of appreciation" or "as a symbol of my affection." The evidence here fails to confirm a greater reliance upon gifts as a form of communication among the Japanese—just the opposite is the case—although they may employ gifts far more often with people outside their circle of intimates than Americans do.

Greetings and Goodbyes

Greetings and partings might seem to be among the least informative features of social life, but they are not without significance. As Goffman notes: "When unacquainted people enter each other's presence there are numerous ways they indicate that they do not know one another; similarly, when acquainted people enter each other's presence, there are ways they display to others signs of the fact that they are acquainted and *even the intensity of that relationship*" (italics added).[22] Ethnographers in studying animal and human societies have consistently found that the manner of greeting expresses, confirms, and predicts the nature of relationships. Anyone who visits an airport or train station will not find this difficult to accept. Recognizing or failing to recognize someone is a way of opening or closing a channel of communication. A number of the features of salutations—length of greeting, physical distance observed, form of contact, intensity of involvement—reflect the length of separation and degree of intimacy that exist.

Greetings and partings, however, are regulated by different cultural norms in various parts of the world. (For this reason comparing individuals within a culture may be more fruitful than comparing cultures.) Although routine acts were engaged in similarly by Japanese and Americans, there were wide variations in the forms of greeting. The scale measured degrees of physical intimacy from mere "recognition" to "kissing," so a wide difference was expected and found. There was little cultural contrast in "recognizing" or "waving or bowing" but a much greater difference in "putting my arm around" or "kissing this person." Americans employed more intimate forms of physical contact more frequently, and the difference was most pronounced with the two closest partners. It was particularly true of the way the closest friend was greeted.

Space

The communicative implications of space were first noted in animal communities. Scientists learned that territorial boundaries and proximity were such powerful factors that they could affect food consumption, reproductive rates, nurturance behavior, and aggression. Only recently have we taken seriously the impact of spatial norms on human beings. The immense power of this variable, according to Desmond Morris, derives from its potent role in infancy:

> All through childhood we will have been held to be loved and held to be hurt, and anyone who invades our Personal Space when we are adults is, in effect, threatening to extend his behaviour into one of these highly charged areas of human interaction. Even if his motives are clearly neither hostile nor sexual, we still find it hard to suppress our reactions to his close approach. Unfortunately, different countries have different ideas about exactly how close is close.[23]

Edward Hall, who first introduced the concept of proxemics, has suggested dividing interpersonal distance into four zones, each of which signals a unique type of communicative involvement: (1) "intimate distance," from actual contact to roughly eighteen inches, a distance that ensures maximum sensory exposure; (2) "personal distance," from eighteen to forty-eight inches, a distance that reduces sensory involvement and widens the field of interaction; (3) "social distance," from four to twelve feet, where one can still perceive details of behavior but at a distance more appropriate for impersonal encounters; (4) "public distance," from twelve to twenty-five feet and beyond, a distance suitable for public performances and public meetings.[24]

There is good reason to believe that the management of space constitutes a language of sorts, perhaps less conscious but more potent than words themselves. (Two dimensions of space have drawn attention: *territoriality*, identification with a bounded and permanent area, and *personal space*, or proximity, in interaction. The focus here is on personal space.) The earliest studies confirmed that physical distance reflects psychological distance. People sit and stand closer to intimates than friends, closer to friends than acquaintances, closer to acquaintances than strangers. When people dislike one another they tend to stay out of "each other's territory" or keep their distance when in each other's presence. As intimacy increases people move closer to one another; they face each other more directly, there is greater eye contact and a leaning toward one another. As dissatisfaction increases there is a leaning back, turning at an angle, and glancing away. Individual norms with regard to closeness have been found to identify others as having "warm" or "cold" personalities.

In a carefully designed experiment on how culture, language, and sex influence conversational distance Nan Sussman and Howard Rosenfeld compared the spatial norms of Japanese, Venezuelans, and Americans during conversations in their own language with members of their own culture and sex. They found Japanese sat at a significantly greater distance (40.2 inches) than did Americans (35.4 inches) or Venezuelans (32.2 inches). The experimenters concluded that distance was a way of controlling sensory accessibility, with decreased stimulation at greater conversational distance.[25] In an interesting sidelight on cultural relativity they note that "The Venezuelans argued that the Americans were too withdrawn, whereas the Japanese argued that the Americans were too intimate."[26]

Here Japanese and American respondents were asked to indicate the frequency with which they had "avoided" their companions, had visited places "they were likely to meet," had "stood or sat close enough for our bodies to touch" in public or private settings. Somewhat surprisingly the two cultures disagreed least on this facet of nonverbal communication, but this may be an artifact of sampling a college-age population where there is a greater need for physical intimacy and less conformity to cultural norms.

Rarely did members of either culture "avoid" their closest companions, and the slightly higher score of Americans is almost entirely traceable to greater physical proximity with their two closest partners.

Although the data suggest some cultural similarity in the management of space, the findings should be viewed with caution. Other studies, using a variety of approaches from observation and interviews to projective tests and controlled experiments, consistently have shown wider differences in the spatial norms of Japanese and Americans.

Touch

Touch is undoubtedly the most primitive form of communication. It is the first channel to mature and operates even before birth: "The child begins to respond to vibrations of the mother's heart beat which impinge on his entire body and are magnified by the amniotic fluid. In one sense, our first input about what 'life' is going to be like comes from the sense of touch."[27] Touch retains its influence in subsequent encounters with the world.

Its potency lies not only in its primacy but also in the immense sensory capacity of the skin for processing information. As J. L. Taylor emphasizes, the skin is the largest and most sensitive of all our receptors. A single square inch of skin contains millions of cells, glands, nerve endings, and blood vessels. The skin picks up the slightest change of temperature, humidity, and pressure, providing a constant flow of news about the warmth, texture, and form of our surroundings.[28]

Communication with mother and father provides the prototype of all future human relationships. Yet these bonds are formed almost exclusively at first through the way the infant is handled, played with, comforted, and loved. The child relies heavily during the first year or two of life on exploring the world by reaching out, picking up, manipulating, and hitting objects in his environment.

As with so many of the other channels of physical communication, touch was mastered so early in life that it remains largely out of conscious awareness and control, yet it is no less profound in its effects for that reason. Rarely does anyone remember receiving explicit instructions about how to touch, when to touch, whom to touch, or where to touch other people.

Touch is not only a way of conveying affection and love, but a way of expressing hostility; it is a way of comforting and encouraging another person, but also a way of torturing and violating them. Reciprocated touch, Nancy Henley has observed, is a powerful sign of solidarity; when unreciprocated, it is a way of asserting superior power or status.[29]

Not surprisingly, so potent a means of communication has restrictions placed on it, limiting such contact to certain places, certain times, certain people, and certain areas of the body. Japan and the United States offer an interesting contrast in the cultural norms that surround touching as a communicative act. Studies by William Caudill and his associates demonstrate that physical contact is sustained longer and plays a larger role in the bonding of mother and infant in Japan.[30] In the United States such contact is more rapidly and more completely replaced by words. Traditional bathing practices and sleeping arrangements also point to greater physical closeness among Japanese than Americans. Yet the difference between the two countries in child-rearing practices is reversed in adult life: Greater distance and lower incidence of touching among the Japanese contrasts with greater closeness and frequency of contact among Americans. Although Michael Watson, in a very broad regional comparison, places both Japan and the United States among the noncontact cultures, a finer comparison would suggest that Japan would rank comparatively as a lower-contact and America as a higher-contact culture.[31]

Sidney Jourard, a pioneer in studying communication through touch, measured the extent of visual and physical contact with twenty-four regions of such target persons as mother, father, and same-sex and opposite-sex friends with a Body Accessibility questionnaire.[32] Later in the *Public and Private Self in Japan and United States,* this instrument was adapted for comparing touching patterns of Japanese and Americans.[33] Although residents of the two countries touched and avoided the same areas of the body, they differed sharply on the extent to which they touched parents and peers. Shortly after, a study by Rob Elzinga confirmed the greater tactility of Americans and found, as I did, that physical accessibility was greater between same-sex friends among Japanese and between opposite-sex friends among Americans.[34]

Backed by the consistency of such findings, we focused here on the five areas of increasing resistance to physical contact found in previous work: hand, arm and shoulder; head, neck, and upper chest; mouth, nose, and cheek; chest and abdomen; the pelvic region. The responses confirmed again that Japanese and American tactile communication differs significantly: Americans reported nearly twice as much contact with their close companions as Japanese did. The contrast was smallest with regard to the most accessible area (the touching of hand, arm, or shoulder) and was widest with respect to the least accessible area (the pelvic region). Members of both societies were most alike in touching more distant companions and were most different in touching their closest partners. Clearly the two cultures subscribe to different communicative norms with regard to physical contact.

Is there a connection between patterns of verbal disclosure and physical accessibility? Do both expand or contract together? Or does one increase as the other decreases? The data reported here, and in earlier research, confirm that they correlate highly. Darhl Pedersen's study to test the relation among verbal disclosure, physical contact, and personal space confirmed this connection. The two modes of communicating tend to increase or decrease together.[35] Thus touch not only plays a communicative role in early infancy, shaping the child's image of the world in which he lives but also remains a potent channel for sharing a wide range of feelings throughout life.

Sensual and Sexual Expression

There is a common assumption, writes Peter Kelvin, "that we only open our bodies to those to whom we have already safely opened our minds."[36] While numerous exceptions come to mind, people generally express their growing involvement with one another through a progressive series of physical acts. The sexual act may constitute the ultimate form of human empathy, but many stages short of sexual intercourse express affection for other people.

Even sexuality as J. LaPlanche and J. Pontanlis point out, "does not mean only the activities and pleasures which depend on the functioning of the genital apparatus: it also embraces the whole range of excitations and activities which may be observed from infancy onwards and which produce pleasure that cannot be explained in terms of satisfaction of basic physiological needs."[37]

"The path to passion," writes Harry Harlow, "is paved with play."[38] Pointing out the close connection between attitudes toward physical contact and sensuality, he writes: "Play in all its complex forms is impossible if bodily contact is looked upon as undesirable or loathsome. Just as there is seldom fun without feeling, there is seldom feeling without fun."[39] Displays of feeling, in one form or another, seem not only unavoidable but even imperative if two people are to confirm their attachment to each other and to enjoy the relationship.

Accordingly, a wide range of adult "playing activities" and "affect displays" were tapped to measure this facet of communication. Japanese and Americans indicated, in two different series of questions, the extent to which they had engaged in such activities as "tickling, teasing, wrestling, roughhousing, dancing" and had expressed their feelings through "hugging, kissing, caressing, or sexual relations." The widest cultural difference on the Physical Communication Scale appeared with respect to the more intimate forms of sensual communication: The frequency of such acts was roughly five times higher among Americans than Japanese. And, again, the widest discrepancy is in encounters with the two closest companions, but a large contrast appears with respect to all five partners. Since these activities have sexual connotations, the wide difference may reflect the somewhat higher Japanese comfort with same-sex companions and American comfort with opposite-sex companions. But the contrast is large enough to demonstrate sharp differences in cultural norms regarding displays of affection.

Silence

Moments of silence in human encounters do not signal the interruption of communication any more than a rest in music or a pause in dance is devoid of meaning. Speech and silence are complementary forms of communication; each acquires significance from the other. Silence is often as eloquent as speech. Silence can signal apathy, confusion, repressed hostility, thoughtfulness, sadness, or awe; it can voice an infinity of meanings.

Ambiguity endows silence with immense power. Thoughts and feelings occur within a silent companion, but remain inaccessible and undisclosed. A phrase or even a gesture offers some clues to meaning, but silence is often lacking in such clues, depending entirely on the interpreter's sensitivity to ascertain its significance. Not to speak to someone has long been used as an extreme form of punishment, but silence is equally seen as evidence of extreme empathy. The capacity of silence to provoke such diverse interpretations makes it one of the highest forms of communication and one of the greatest sources of misunderstanding. It also makes it one of the most elusive of all communicative behaviors to describe and measure.

Prevailing opinion holds that Japan and the United States hold radically different attitudes toward and make distinctive use of silence as a form of communication. Each nation's heritage seems to nourish this contrast. Although Zen Buddhism has never attracted a large following, its influence on Japanese aesthetics and personal relationships has been disproportionate to its number of adherents. One of its tenets is that words are deceptive and silent intuition a truer way to confront the world; mind-to-mind communication through words is less reliable than heart-to-heart communion through an intuitive grasp of things. Such Japanese art forms and social activities as calligraphy and the tea ceremony encourage a dialogue of silence. Even the dominant form of learning—apprenticeship, in which one learns through imitation rather than explanation—cultivates respect for silence. Many sayings—"A flower does not speak," "The mouth is to eat with, not to speak with," "He is like a carp in May" (referring to the empty paper banners shaped like fish that celebrate Boy's Day in Japan)—reinforce the notion that the truly important things are shared in silence. Enryo—the attribute of humility, modesty, reticence—is admired in the silent communicator.

There is little evidence to prove or disprove such claims; silence does not lend itself to systematic study. An exploratory study by Milton Wayne used a series of sketches, showing expressionless faces in various social settings, to see how Japanese and Americans would interpret silences of various lengths. He concluded that where Americans interpreted them as signs of worry, criticism, regret, or embarrassment, Japanese saw them more often as a neutral waiting period or evidence of agreement.[40] Edward Seidensticker, long a student of Japanese culture, appears to agree, noting that it is not that the Japanese do not like to talk but "that they do not have the distrust of silence that Americans have."[41]

Roy Miller objects to the idea that silence plays a distinctive role in the social life of Japanese. In *Japan's Modern Myth* he argues that Japanese use silence no more positively, or with any greater sensitivity, than do any other people. The myth of a nation that communicates silently, he contends, only promotes their image of themselves as a mysterious, undecipherable, and hence profound culture.[42]

The American heritage also includes its disciples of silence. Puritan America nurtured the humbler forms of speech and made a virtue out of silence. Westward expansion, which isolated people, contributed also to respect for the "strong, silent" personality. Yet Alexis de Tocqueville, one of the first critics of American culture, concluded that democratic societies hold meditation in low esteem and promote an active life over a contemplative one. And contemporary anthropologists such as Edward Hall feel Americans emphasize doing over being, activity over inactivity, talking over thinking.[43] Silence is considered neutral at best and, at worst, as a symptom of social inadequacy or even emotional illness. What research has been undertaken in the United States treats silence more as a symptom of pathology or form of resistance than as a sign of growth. The contemporary American myth of silence, if myth it is, would view silence as a communicative failure or evidence of a deteriorating relationship. Yet after reviewing the literature on silence, Thomas Bruneau warns that its role in American culture is "complex and profound."[44]

Although one researcher has called for a "theory of silence," no such theory yet exists. Silences, he suggests, are of two types: that which occurs when the flow of words stops because of inner fear, anxiety, or anger and that which occurs because of immense psychic comfort—where two people identify so fully they need no words to confirm their rapport. Silence is so inaccessible to traditional forms of inquiry that it is easy to claim almost anything for it that one wishes.

In a plea for more serious study of the role of silence R. Johannsen suggests starting with two basic questions: (1) How *frequently* do close companions experience silence when they are together? (2) How *comfortable* are acquaintances with silences of short and long duration?[45] Accordingly, a series of questions on the Physical Communication Scale asked Japanese and Americans to describe the frequency and duration of silences shared with their close or more distant companions.

Although silence, along with space and time, was one of the three aspects of physical communication that showed the least cultural divergence, the difference was significant. Americans scored higher on comfort and frequency in nearly every category: "less than five minutes," "six to fifteen minutes," "sixteen to thirty minutes," "one to two hours," "more than two hours." The frequency of intervals of silence declines, as one would expect, with diminishing involvement with identified companions. Again the widest cultural difference is concentrated among the closer rather than more distant acquaintances. These findings lend some support to Miller's contention that Japanese use of silence as a communicative strategy is more myth than reality.

EXTRAPOLATION: WHAT THE FINDINGS SUGGEST

The nonverbal styles of the two cultures confirm some, but fail to confirm many other, characteristics attributed to Japanese and Americans.

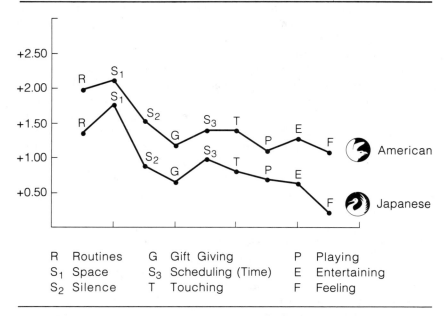

FIGURE 7.1 Nine Dimensions of Physical Intimacy: Japanese and Americans

There is at least indirect evidence here that verbal accessibility and physical accessibility parallel one another: Those who are verbally more expressive tend to be nonverbally more expressive. In comparison with Japanese— though not with more demonstrative cultures—Americans communicate their affection for close companions more through their use of greetings, gift giving, touching, silences, and sensual expression, indeed via all channels of nonverbal interaction. The largest cultural difference in modes of physical expression is found with respect to the two closest partners; cultural similarity increases with more distant companions. A comparison of the overall non-verbal communicative styles of Japanese and Americans is illustrated in Figure 7.1. The two profiles show how nonverbal patterns of interacting with companions converge and diverge with respect to the nine dimensions reported.

Why should nonverbal acts be taken so seriously? As the prototypic ways of relating to people in infancy, they retain a potency that may be unequalled by other forms of symbolic behavior, particularly words. In addition, physical acts are less conscious and less subject to deceptive manipulation, thereby giving them an authority that verbal statements often lack. But the power of physical acts may lie even more in their capacity to convey meanings that cannot be expressed, or cannot be so sensitively expressed, in words. An embrace cannot be translated into a sentence without losing most of its impact. To limit our communication with others to a single code seems to impoverish human relationships and to limit our capacity to satisfy a full range of human needs.

CHAPTER 8

Commitment,
Conflict, Integration

Every human being, whether child or adult,
seems to require significance, that is, a
place in another person's world. [1]
RONALD LAING

Three features of intimate relationships that have received little attention from behavioral scientists are among the most
important qualities of such relationships. One is the extent to which attachment involves a commitment to provide assistance and to promote the
welfare of the other. A second is the way in which people who care about
each other manage the inevitable differences that arise when people share a
significant part of their lives. And third, the most serious of all, is the extent
to which each person is changed by involvement in the affairs of another. An
Accommodation Scale, a Difference Scale, and an Affiliation Scale were
designed to explore patterns of commitment, decision making, and ego
incorporation among Japanese and Americans.

TIES THAT BIND:
INTERPERSONAL COMMITMENT

In "The Anatomy of Loving," Richard Sutherland reminds us of four
basic attitudes one can take toward objects or people: One can ignore them,

147

flee from them, attack them, or join them. He notes that these correspond to the classic emotions of indifference, fear, anger, and love. In exploring love, he distinguishes three stages in maturing personal relationships: the first in which one does something *to* others, a second in which one does something *for* others, and a last one in which one does something *with* others.[2] All involve some personal sacrifice, but the last stage, he argues, is found in the deepest forms of attachment.

When people are asked to name the qualities they value most in their closest friends, they frequently cite "commitment," "trust," and "empathy." The first, commitment, refers to confidence that each will assist the other in time of need, trust implies that the relationship will survive any crises encountered, and empathy is the capacity to share the experience of the other. In systematically exploring the attributes of close relationships, John LaGaipa found "authenticity," "acceptance," "empathy," and "helping behavior" were the most consistent qualities. His "Helping Scale," which focused on sacrifices for one another, turned out to be the best single measure of the strength of friendships.[3] Vance Packard, comparing friendships in East and West Coast towns of the United States, found residents valued most those acquaintances on whom they could rely in an emergency, when they needed money, or when they were hospitalized.[4]

Personal sacrifice takes two forms, both tangible and measurable, for expressing our commitment to others. The first is through the sharing of possessions. At first, this appears puzzling. What is there about material objects that endows them with emotional significance? Partly it may be their value; to loan or give someone a possession of great monetary value, or to withhold it from them, is a comment not only on the value of the object but also on the value of the friendship. In addition, a possession is, in a sense, just that, a part of the person. For most of human history possessions have been buried with a person because they were regarded as belonging to and being part of them. In some cultures this involved killing survivors who were related or close to the deceased so they might not be separated even in death. Later when survivors were no longer sacrificed, symbolic objects, often of great beauty and value, continued to accompany the deceased. Burial practices have changed radically in the past few centuries, but many possessions, from pets and paintings to sports cars and souvenirs, evoke powerful meanings for their owners; their abuse or loss provokes a strong feeling of sadness, even the loss of an intrinsic part of the self.

Sharing Possessions

Allowing certain people to use one's office or clothing or hi-fi while not permitting others to do so is a way of displaying regard for them. As Altman and Taylor point out, "There is a maintenance of privacy, possessiveness, and territoriality in many areas, areas which are never violated or at least not without caution and/or conflict. Thus certain objects (for example, a wallet, a drawer in a bureau, a desk and its contents, a purse, a certain article of clothing) become wholly attached to one person and are inviolate, except under very special circumstances."[5]

The particular objects with such meanings tend, of course, to vary from person to person: In answering a newspaper's "Question Man" people nominated as most valued "my good clothes," "my sleeping bag," "my car," "my albums," "my cheerleading outfit," and "my tent"; the list is probably very long.[6] That possessions vary in their latent meanings for their owners suggests they may be a tangible counterpart of levels of verbal disclosure and degrees of physical accessibility examined earlier. The more people incorporate certain possessions as part of their identity, include them within the boundaries of their ego so to speak, the more sharing them with companions creates another channel of communication through which to express or reflect the depth of their attachment.

Providing Assistance

Another expression of personal commitment is displayed not in the objects given or shared but in the services provided an acquaintance. "Responsibility," Arthur Miller once said, "is a kind of love."[7] People often require assistance of one kind or another: Groceries are borrowed, accidents occur, children need supervision, advice is sought, plants or animals require attention, illness strikes. Who one calls in such emergencies and to whom one will respond is likely to depend on relational priorities. Thus to loan material possessions and to provide personal care constitute major ways of communicating the extent of one's commitment to others.

Giving and Receiving Help

Although research is limited, a substantial body of theory explores the connection between intimacy and commitment. Social exchange theory holds that people form relationships and sustain them on the basis of the costs they involve (time, energy, expense) and the rewards they provide (support, status, affection). "Every relationship," writes LaGaipa, "has an aspect of exchange insofar as the acts of one person are predicated on the expectation that some kind of reward will flow from the act—if nothing more than an expression of warmth or gratitude."[8] The more valued the act and the more it is rewarded, the more often such acts tend to be performed. Similarly, acts that prompt no reaction, or some form of punishment, tend to weaken a relationship. But exchange theory requires two extensions: One, the "satiation effect," which holds that the same act repeated tends to provide diminishing reward; the other, the "equity principle," which holds that the supportive acts of one partner tend to be reciprocated by the other. It is not clear whether the help is reciprocated out of a sense of indebtedness or because giving assistance is as satisfying as receiving it.

One of the most successful efforts to probe the connection among giving and receiving help, inducement to reciprocate, and growing attachment to acquaintances is found in experiments by Alan Gross and Julie

Latané. Although subject to the limitations of all laboratory experiments, the data confirm that people "feel more positively toward people who help them *and* more positively toward people they help."[9] We help those we like and like those we help; giving and receiving appear nearly equally rewarding and influential in cementing human relationships.

But what constitutes a reward or punishment is far from clear. Early work by U. G. Foa suggested six categories of rewarding acts: love, status, information, money, goods, services. He found these varied along two dimensions: their concreteness (or tangibility) and their appropriateness for a particular friend. Foa also found that friends tended to repay each other in the same way they were rewarded.[10] Lee Beach and William Carter did not find this to be true. Instead, "givers" rated the help they had given higher than receivers did, receivers tended not to repay fully the amount of their indebtedness, and the form of repayment was determined more by its appropriateness for the recipient than by the category into which the original assistance fell.[11]

Personal Sacrifice and Intimacy

Finally there are grounds for assuming a linkage between the value of the object or assistance given and the intensity of the relationship. The more intimate and valued an object is in the eyes of the giver, the more selectively it may be shared with others. Similarly, the greater the sacrifice involved in time and effort, and less attractive the service is, the more selectively it may be offered. Closer companions are more likely to be the recipients of both types of sacrifice. Gerald Chasin reported some evidence of this; he found the degree of intimacy (casual, good, and best friends) influenced the extent to which people were willing to aid their acquaintances.[12]

CULTURE AND COMMITMENT: JAPAN AND THE UNITED STATES

Since there are distinctive social values in Japan and the United States, the precise way exchange theory might operate in the two settings is uncertain. From Ruth Benedict's *Chrysanthemum and the Sword* to Nakane Chie's *Japanese Society* and Doi Takeo's *Anatomy of Dependence* there is a consistent emphasis on the large role obligation plays in regulating social intercourse among Japanese. A host of terms—*gimu* (duty), *on* (obligation), *giri* (indebtedness)—reflects the complexity of commitments to family, work group, and nation. But the closeness of attachment, according to Benedict, also has a direct bearing on the extent of interpersonal commitment:

> Casual favors from relative strangers are the ones most resented,
> for with neighbors and old established hierarchical relationships a
> man knows and has accepted the complications of *on*. But with mere

acquaintances and near-equals . . . they would prefer to avoid getting entangled in all the consequences of *on*. The passivity of a street crowd in Japan when an accident occurs is not just lack of initiative. It is recognition that any non-official interference would make the recipient wear an *on*. [13]

One reason, then, for Japanese reluctance to form casual friendships is thought to be the responsibilities one assumes with respect to friends. Such debts are considered both permanent and virtually unpayable in full. Mutual obligations, therefore, may play a larger role than mutual affection in mediating personal relations in Japan. All of this would suggest the Japanese might be more highly sensitive to their commitments and be more self-sacrificing in giving assistance to acquaintances on whom they depend.

In contrast, American culture emphasizes individual autonomy, spontaneity, and freedom from responsibility, and these qualities would seem to lessen the depth and duration of commitments to associates. Americans, though highly approachable, might be less willing to give assistance or repay assistance. The emphasis on contractual agreements, even between close companions, may reflect a lack of concern for the welfare of others. Growing resort to lawyers and the courts for resolving the respective obligations of husband and wife, employer and employee, or parent and child is dramatic evidence of lack of interpersonal responsiveness. If societies are held together by intersecting sets of "rights" and "obligations," Japan may emphasize the latter over the former, while the United States stresses rights over obligations. To what extent do these images of the two cultures hold true at the level of commitment to intimates?

THE ACCOMMODATION SCALE

Because the measurement of interpersonal commitment is still in its infancy, it was necessary to create a scale that would sample the extent to which Japanese and Americans actually sacrificed for the benefit of their companions. Such sacrifices seemed to fall rather naturally into two classes: (1) the extent to which people were willing to loan or share their material possessions and (2) the extent to which people were willing to provide services for close or distant companions. While love is an equivocal term, and an even more elusive standard of measurement, acts prompted by feelings of affection are concrete enough to be identified and measured.

The format of the Accommodation Scale reflected a central assumption that the fifteen items that made up the Scale of Shared Possessions and the Scale of Personal Care could be ordered with respect to the degree of sacrifice involved. For example, it was assumed that sharing stamps or cigarettes was evidence of less commitment than sharing clothing or loaning a large amount of money. Similarly, to care for plants and to nurse a person during an illness also reflects different levels of personal sacrifice. The ordering of the items in the two subscales, therefore, incorporated not only the size of the sacrifice but also the degree to which it was a more intimate, or more revealing, kind of behavior.

The extent to which each respondent accommodated the needs of their companions was based on the following scale of frequency:

0 = I have *not* done this (in the past year).

1 = I have *rarely* done this (in the past year).

2 = I have *occasionally* done this (in the past year).

3 = I have *frequently* done this (in the past year).

4 = I have *very often* done this (in the past year).

Surprisingly, the levels of sacrifice for close companions were not high for either culture (Japanese = .69; Americans = .98), but were significantly greater among Americans. Again the two cultures differ most in the way they relate to their closest companions and least with respect to distant ones. There is also a more pronounced difference in the level of commitment to the closest and second closest partner, suggesting this may be one of the best indicators of intimacy.

In the rank ordering of "articles shared" and "care provided" the two cultural profiles show both some agreement and some contrast. Japanese and Americans agreed on four out of five of the most frequently shared articles (sundries, food, small amounts of money, household equipment), but agreed on only two of the least frequently shared (sports equipment, large amounts of money). With respect to the care provided, the two cultures agreed again on four of the five most common forms of services (emotional support, maintaining contact at a distance, giving advice, and personal evaluations), but agreed in the rank ordering of only two of the least common (emergency care, child care).

Scores on the lower ranked items, however, probably reflect the rarity of such emergencies and of limited needs for child care within a university population rather than their inadequacy as indexes of commitment. It is surprising, however, given the images of the two cultures, that the Japanese score lower on the frequency with which they share possessions and on all forms of personal care provided for close companions.

The Accommodation Scale's results also confirm a sharp drop in behavioral commitment to close and more distant companions in both societies, making the scale another reliable index of the depth of involvement. The sequencing of the fifteen items on each subscale, however, did not confirm that each of the listed acts showed a significantly greater degree of sacrifice. This may be an artifact of the particular sample used here. But since the significance of any object or act resides in the "eye of the beholder," it is more likely that sacrifices cannot be objectively ordered in terms of their meaning for the giver and receiver. Clearly, we have a lot more to learn about the nature and ranking of objects and services provided for the people who make up our circles of acquaintances.

INTIMACY: THE CHALLENGE
OF DIFFERENCES

"The course of true love," it is said, "never runs smooth." Nor, we might add, does the course of long-term friendships. Despite a similar genetic inheritance and shared environment, each person's experience of life is unavoidably unique. Even two people growing up in the same family and in the same place will mature into persons with distinctive needs, skills, and ways of relating to people. In forming close ties, no matter how close they may become, we do not discard our own ways of seeing the world, interpreting events, or relating to others. Every personal bond of any significance is subject to the stresses and strains arising from the necessity of accommodating such differences.

Whatever the nature of such differences, whether they lie in the content or manner of communicating, they arise within the larger framework of a mutual commitment to each other. This commitment is to growth and enrichment of the lives of each other and to the life of the relationship itself. As we have seen, considerable evidence shows that similarity plays a major role in the selection of a circle of companions. When serious differences surface that challenge the strength of bonds based on similarity, how are they managed to avoid permanently damaging or terminating such relationships?

One way of reducing the threat of differences is to avoid communicating with people with whom we expect to strongly and consistently disagree. Racial and religious segregation have their counterpart in the interpersonal world in simple avoidance. Few people have not, on some occasion, failed to keep an appointment, refused an invitation, or crossed the street to avoid a confrontation. Or when avoidance is impossible, kept the relationship from getting into sensitive topics. Encounters are formalized, based on defined roles and duties, and limited to an exchange of commonplaces. As Michael Argyle notes, "People present a somewhat improved, idealized and censored version of themselves for public inspection, so that there is likely to be some discrepancy between the presented self and the real self."[14] To the extent that people avoid truly meeting as persons, they neutralize the threat of potential differences.

But the more deeply we get to know another person, the greater the likelihood of exposing differences. We are more alike in our public selves than in our private selves. In public we cultivate a greater similarity of dress, posture, and manner than we do in private. The moment we begin to know our companions not as representatives of a culture, class, company, age, or sex, but as individuals, the more uniqueness we encounter. As relationships become closer and our commitment to them increases, there is a growing disclosure of real thoughts and feelings. Intimacy, no matter what its rewards, is not achieved without risk. One risk is that the real differences that are gradually revealed may prove more powerful than the forces that bind the two people together.

An added complication is that as people invest more of themselves the relationship becomes increasingly important to them and the possibility of failure takes on a more frightening aspect. Many relationships have a paradoxical quality: As people get to know one another better, the chances of discovering painful differences increase, yet as the relationship deepens, the consequences of failure to integrate such differences also rise. Thus within every significant relationship it is essential to create or adopt strategies for addressing differences. Conflict always has the potential for undoing the bonds that connect two people. "Discord," writes Leslie Miller, "is threatening to togetherness because togetherness is a voluntary involvement, a seeking of harmony."[15]

Coping with Conflict

In studying the principal ways people cope with conflicts in close relationships, Michael Roloff identified forty specific reactions. When these were clustered on the basis of their similarity, five generic strategies emerged: regression, revenge, physical aggression, verbal aggression, and prosocial efforts. Regression involves a retreat to infantile reactions; revenge uses control of information to harm associates; physical attack hurts companions physically; verbal aggression attacks the status and image of the person; prosocial modes involve exploring differences through rational discussion. Roloff notes that prosocial modes promote deeper involvement and even accelerate the process of bonding; the other four responses slow or disrupt the formation of such bonds. Prosocial modes, of course, do not guarantee that people will become closer companions, only that they will come to know each other better. As he notes, "It is entirely possible that two people may learn enough about each other to realize that they are totally incompatible."[16] A constructive approach does not guarantee anything, but limits the conflict's destructive potential while people gain a clearer understanding of themselves, of each other, and of the possibilities of integrating such differences. The way two people fight is significant.

Probing further into the forms of prosocial strategies, Leslie Baxter and Tara Shepherd posed five major ways of coping constructively with differences: avoidance, accommodation, compromise, collaboration, and competition.[17] Each reflects a balancing of one's own goals against those of a companion: Avoidance indicates a low concern for both one's own and one's companion's goals, collaboration shows a high concern for the goals of both, competition means a high regard for one's own goals but low concern for one's partner's goals, accommodation reflects a willingness to sacrifice personal goals for those of the other, and compromise incorporates respect for the positions of both parties. Figure 8.1 illustrates these five alternatives.

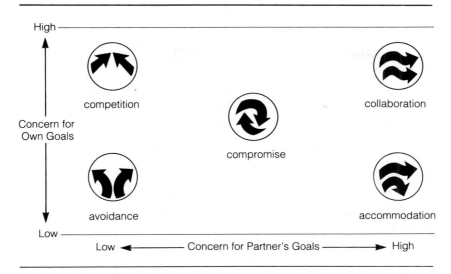

High

Concern for
Own Goals

competition

compromise

collaboration

avoidance

accommodation

Low

Low ◄——— Concern for Partner's Goals ———► High

FIGURE 8.1   Five Coping Strategies in Interpersonal Conflict

Preferred modes of approaching conflict seem to reflect positive or negative attitudes toward associates: Accommodation and collaboration were more often used with liked than disliked companions; even compromise was associated with liked people. There was evidence that people possess limited strategies for dealing with differences and that the manner of coping with conflict tends to be consistent for any individual from one setting to another.

Conflict and Culture: The Case of Japan

Decision making, as Fred Kerlinger reminds us, is one of the most revealing artifacts of culture: "It may be regarded as a synthesis of a society's beliefs, an epitome of its ideology, the action product of its thinking."[18] And Japan and the United States appear to employ distinctive ways of managing conflict and sharply different views of its role in human relations.

"The Japanese," writes Robert Ozaki, "are not fond of solving their disputes in court. They do everything possible to dissolve their conflicts extralegally."[19] They appear more inclined to view disputes from a larger frame in which everyone involved is assumed to be at least partly to blame; proving who is right and who is wrong, particularly in public, is regarded as displaying a lack of compassion for human imperfections. Promises and contracts are eschewed because of the explicitness with which details must be spelled out; ultimatums that force people to take positions are rarely employed.

But even within more personal encounters a similar view prevails. In a chapter entitled "We the Japanese," Richard Halloran tries to crystallize the behavioral consequences of underlying Japanese values. With respect to disagreement he writes: "It is true that we Japanese try diligently to prevent any situation from becoming what we call *tairitsu*, a confrontation, whether in our personal lives or in business or politics."[20] The pressures to avoid disagreement are so great, adds Harumi Befu, that "you have to develop ways of saying one thing while meaning another."[21]

The motive prompting such behavior derives from the value attached to congeniality and consensus, the importance of preserving and promoting a harmony of feeling. The reluctance to confront differences directly is a consequence of Japanese sensitivity to the feelings of others and the risk of hurting them: "They do not say what they want to say because they sincerely hope not to hurt others' feelings, and they say what they do not want to say, believing that their discomfort is less important than the happiness of others."[22] In this pursuit, Ozaki warns, harmony can become a form of tyranny, limiting the free flow of ideas on even the most vital personal and public issues.

This other-focused approach requires a slow and careful articulation of positions and a highly sensitive search for an emerging consensus. The consensus should enclose everyone; no one should be exposed to the embarrassment of remaining apart or opposed to the final decision. This requires immense sensitivity to the process of communication itself. In such a strategy, attention is on areas of agreement rather than on areas of disagreement; logic is less influential and facts less important. As Nakane has observed:

> For the Japanese, logic exists in books and lectures, the scholar's study and the lawyer's work; it does not belong to the salon and the coffee shop or the dining table and the banquet. If someone brings logic to such an occasion, the topic will be dropped as being argumentative, and this type of person will be shunned.[23]

Words play a larger role as a social lubricant than as a tool for sharply defining and distinguishing competing points of view. And, finally, there is the sense of *shi-kataganai*, a sense of fatalism and the futility of seeking the truth through argument. There is perhaps, as well, a lowered concern with differences.

Although there has been little direct investigation of the management of conflict with close friends, a pilot study by Shirono Itsuo is highly provocative in its findings. Through analysis of the typescripts of the interviews of five Japanese and five American couples he sought to identify who initiated decision making, who made decisions, how thoroughly the matter was discussed, and how the decision was reached. He found that Japanese husbands were more often the initiators and more often the final decision makers, while in American couples both spouses were initiators and both contributed to the final decision. Japanese couples discussed the decision less than American couples did. With regard to the manner of reaching agreements he writes, "The particular way of the Japanese couples was either by acceptance of the situation, or with one party deciding and the other agreeing. . . . The way of agreement of the American couples was based on their rational discussions in which both individuals exchanged opinions."[24]

For these reasons, one might expect the Japanese to manage differences more often through avoidance or rely more on accommodation. Collaboration, too, might be found, although collaborators usually express different views before arriving at some integration of them. Exploratory work cited earlier suggests that rarely are Japanese relationships repaired or restored once they have been broken. If true, then confronting differences directly would be an extremely hazardous way of addressing differences in Japan.

Conflict and Culture:
The Case of the United States

American culture, with its emphasis on the individual and self-expression, its tradition of freedom of speech, and its commitment to decisions through argument, stands in sharp contrast to Japan. Differences are seen as not only inescapable but also of great positive value. Confrontation between divergent views is regarded as the only way to test their relative merits. The major documents of the society articulate a commitment to the unrestricted exchange of ideas. Contracts and regulations, arrived at through hours of negotiation and made as explicit as possible, are relied upon to evaluate performance and adjudicate disputes. Where such contracts were once confined to regulating public affairs, they now intrude into many aspects of social and private life.

The pervasiveness of conflict in American life has forced the cultivation of skill in managing such conflicts. The eloquent articulation of convictions is among the most valued virtues of its citizens, and the arts of argument and debate are encouraged in the home, school, and marketplace. A greater ease in handling evidence, constructing arguments, and defending positions tends to reduce the destructive potential of such differences. Indeed there is even pleasure and excitement obtained from a stimulating clash of opinions. One of the most frequent shocks experienced by Japanese in coming to America is the resilience of friendships in the face of such strong clashes of opinion: Friends are able to confront each other, to vigorously argue contradictory views, and to continue to be close friends in spite of their differences. Even when arguments disrupt a relationship, Americans are able to revive them; sometimes such conflicts even nourish deeper involvement and commitment.

In view of these characteristics, we might expect a contrasting cultural preference for ways of approaching conflict. Avoidance and accommodation may be less attractive to Americans and competition and compromise more attractive ways of making decisions. Collaboration might prove equally or more attractive to Americans when faced with different points of view.

THE DIFFERENCE SCALE

Although the potential areas of conflict in friendships may be infinite—from what movie to attend to going into debt—it is possible to sample critical areas in which differences are likely to arise between close friends. A representative sample of such issues can throw light on dominant cultural modes of handling such differences. Accordingly, eight areas of potential conflict were included on the Difference Scale: (1) personal taste (what to eat, wear, or purchase); (2) leisure time (how much time to spend on activities, vacations, choice of entertainment); (3) everyday tasks (how to prepare foods, use equipment, treat relatives); (4) personal (habits of dress, grooming, tactful or tactless behavior); (5) financial (how much to spend, save, or go into debt); (6) public issues (political or economic views, candidates to support); (7) relational (how to help or criticize each other, show affection); (8) personal philosophy (personal goals, roles of men and women, religious or philosophical values).

Next we considered the alternative ways of addressing such differences. Two separate issues to consider here are a person's "orientation toward conflict" (whether it is seen as threat or opportunity) and "preferred modes of coping with conflict" (the range of strategies open to two people who wish to negotiate a decision). Accordingly, the first set of possible responses had to do with whether or not an area of conflict was actually confronted: "We did *not* discuss this: (1) because it has *not come up*; (2) because we *agree* on it; (3) because we *disagree* on it." Answers to these questions measured the extent to which differences were perceived and whether or not they were addressed. (The difference might be suppressed for a variety of reasons; it might destroy an otherwise satisfying relationship or it may have been explored and proven unresolvable.)

The second set of questions explored the manner in which such differences, if talked about, were resolved (temporarily or permanently): "We did discuss this: (1) and decided to follow our *individual* preferences; (2) and adopted *one* of our preferences; (3) and *compromised* on our preferences; (4) and found a *new approach* to the issue." The frequency with which each tactic was relied upon provided an estimate of the relative proportion of decisions that employed independence, accommodation, compromise, and collaboration as ways of arriving at a decision.

Decision Making:
Japanese and American Style

The overall profile of decision-making preferences, surprisingly, showed no significant difference in the strategies employed with close companions among Japanese and Americans. The lack of cultural contrast should be viewed with some skepticism for several reasons. The samples include only a few married students; marriage is probably the most prolonged and most intensive partnership that people experience and one in which differences are likely to be faced on a daily, even hourly, basis. However, both samples included mothers, fathers, sisters, and brothers with whom there is also frequent contact. Perhaps a more serious limitation is that this was the last subscale to be administered and there is some evidence of a "response set" in completing this scale. This is the tendency, under prolonged testing, for people to give similar answers to questions that are superficially similar but not really alike. Fatigue is likely to be a factor when instruments such as this one require over a thousand answers. It is also possible that the format of the Difference Scale encouraged people to identify issues as "undiscussed" rather than having to answer "how they were settled."

Still the patterns of Japanese and American responses if not definitive were highly suggestive. There was a striking difference in the frequency with which differences "did not come up at all." Potential areas of conflict surfaced at a rate one third lower in Japanese friendships, supporting the speculation that Japanese prefer to avoid outright conflict. And Americans scored twice as high on the extent to which potential differences were not discussed "because we agree," perhaps reflecting the greater disclosure found to be characteristic of Americans.

When differences were talked about, however, both cultures relied most on decisions based on independence (following individual preferences) and on compromise. The Japanese seemed to show somewhat greater sensitivity to status differences in their greater reliance upon dominance (adopting one person's preference). But on the management of differences through collaboration (finding a new approach), Japanese and American scores were virtually identical.

The intensity of involvement with companions also played a role in attitudes toward differences and the manner of making decisions. In both countries conflict is increasingly avoided as relationships become more distant. Among Japanese, for example, 50 percent of the conflictful issues "did not come up" with one's closest partner but 80 percent failed to do so with the most distant partner. Among Americans 27 percent of potential conflicts "did not come up" with the closest companion but 70 percent did not surface with the most distant companion. And Japanese and Americans handle conflictful situations more similarly in this case with close than with distant acquaintances.

The topics on which people might disagree, however, carry different implications. Some topics are virtually unavoidable if two people spend much time together; others are easily avoided if either person wants to. Some differences provoke no more than a lively conversation, but others are so consequential that they may destroy a relationship. Interestingly the areas of avoidance in both countries are in the area of personal philosophy (religious values, life goals, personal rights, and responsibilities) and financial decisions. Decisions based on independence were favored by the Japanese on matters of money and by Americans on matters of personal philosophy.

Differences, it appears, are a ubiquitous and inescapable feature of human relationships, and their role in strengthening or shattering such relationships has been neglected too long. The frequency with which differences are expressed is clearly related to the strength of attachment; the closer the bond between two people, the more they reveal their uniqueness. Growing awareness of this singularity, when it combines with a growing commitment to the relationship, leads to willingness to discuss rather than avoid such differences. Apparently financial and philosophical differences—and especially the relationship itself—are among the least openly confronted differences. And the limited reliance upon collaboration suggests that all of us have more to learn about how to accommodate differences more creatively.

Robert Kaplan has contrasted the two major styles of coping with differences as "maintenance-by-suppression" and "maintenance-by-expression." In the former a superficial congeniality is preferred to risking loss of the relationship; in the latter there is a more hazardous effort to obtain insight into and integrate differences. Yet Kaplan warns wisely against too strict a dichotomy: Avoidance of conflict need not prevent insight and growth in a relationship, and probing such differences openly does not guarantee that confronting them will resolve them.[25]

THE CONSEQUENCES OF INTIMACY: EGO INCORPORATION

Every living organism is enclosed in some boundary that gives it a separate identity. For symbolizing forms of life, such as human beings, there is also a psychic boundary that separates us from one another. What each of us has experienced in the past and is experiencing at the moment is known only by us; we share experience with others only through the medium of symbols.

This self may include a veritable storehouse of experiences. In the words of William James, "A man's *Me* is the sum total of all that he *can* call his, not only body and his psychic powers, but his clothes and his house, his wife and children, his ancestors and friends, his reputation and works, his lands and horses, and yacht and bank account."[26] Virtually anything may be endowed with sufficient emotional significance to influence one's thoughts, motives, feelings, and actions. When any aspect of the symbolic self is threatened or demeaned, we become angry or depressed; when some feature is respected and valued, we are filled with euphoria and pride.

The psychological identity of a person tends to vary from culture to culture. In some cultures, one's ancestors are a part of the self and influence how one lives; in another, material possessions heavily influence the decisions one makes; in still others, family members or close friends are part of the self and influence behavior. The nature of this attachment to other people may have a profound effect on the people we once were, now are, or are becoming.

Boundaries of the Ego

Thus to explore the consequences of bonding with other people, we are forced to confront a boundary problem: As attraction increases *between* two people, what happens *within* each person? What happens as an *I* becomes a *we*? How is the *other* accommodated within the *self*? In *Member of the Wedding*, Frankie's plea—"Where is the 'We' in 'Me'?"—attests to the damage to one's sense of one's own identity when attachment fails or abruptly ends.[27] Where does the border of one self stop and the border of the other begin?

Surprisingly little is known of the changes in the concept of the self brought on by deep involvement with another human being. According to the ancients, durable friendships produced a merging of the two personalities, each complementing and completing the other. In this century George Santayana saw it similarly: "Friendship is almost always the union of one part of one mind with the part of another."[28] More recently Wilson Van Dusen has remarked that "it is as though the self and the loved one are a one which cannot easily be separated."[29] George Herbert Mead created the term *significant others* to identify the key role of parents and siblings in shaping the identity of the newborn infant. But, in fact, an entire cast of significant others makes entrances and exits during the course of a lifetime, with each leaving some trace on the selves we become.

Some assessment of the impact of involvement with other people upon the scope and configuration of the symbolic self seems overdue. Robert Katz has offered a four-part evolutionary model for describing the replacement of self-consciousness with other-consciousness: "detachment" (changes in the person's pattern of perception because of another's presence), "reverberation" (awareness of both your own experience and that of the other), 'incorporation" (including the other's experience as part of your own), and "identification" (absorbing the self of the other).[30]

Types of Ego Incorporation

Here we shall attempt to simplify and extend the possible ways in which affection between two people may affect the way they see themselves. At one extreme lies "domination" in which the needs and motives of one person are imposed upon the other; there is little responsiveness to their unique meanings or perspectives. In the case of psychological "independence" each person acts on the basis of his or her own self-interest without regard for the consequences for the other. In the case of "sympathy" and closely related "altruism" there is concern for the fate of the other but a concern based on how the sympathizer would feel if he or she were in the shoes of the other. The Golden Rule of Christianity embodies this ideal: "Do unto others as you would have them do unto *you.*"

Farther along the continuum of identification lies "empathy." As defined by Rosalind Dymond it is "the imaginative transposing of oneself into the thinking, feeling, and acting of another and of structuring the world the way he does."[31] There is a temporary suspension of self-consciousness and self-interest in favor of participating in the experience of a companion without imposing judgment on it. Empathy reflects, as Milton Bennett has suggested, an extension of the Golden Rule: "Do unto others as *they* would have you do unto them."[32] Empathy, however, tends to be a fleeting phenomenon, fluctuating from moment to moment and from situation to situation while incorporation reflects a more or less constant presence of the other within the borders of the self.

When our every act takes into account the consequences for others— even when they are not present—one can say the self now *includes* the other. In empathy one is still conscious that the self and other are separate though simultaneously experienced; in incorporation it is not clear where the personality of one person stops and the other begins. One acts to serve two selves at the same time. Risking one's life to save a valued possession or valued companion is prompted not by seeing the object or person as something apart from the self, but as an intrinsic and essential component of the self. (Even those who give their lives for a cause or a country may be seen not as acting *unselfishly* but in their own larger self-interest.) To promote the welfare of a partner involves no sacrifice because the self and the other overlap. This may account for why so many lovers and marriage partners feel they give less than they get, for what is given to the other is also rewarding to the self. As Harry Stack Sullivan remarked, "When the satisfaction or the security of another person becomes as significant as one's own satisfaction or security, then the state of love exists."[33]

Finally, there is "introjection" where one becomes so absorbed with the other that no sense of having a separate self remains. One becomes the other, lives only through the other, one's children, parents, heroes, or through some all-absorbing cause or institution. This may be an essential state in the maturation of a child when the boundary that divides outside and inside are still forming. Parental introjection, for example, may contribute to the formation of a child's superego and to the emergence of a unique identity. In adulthood it constitutes an abandonment of the self in favor of experiencing the world only through others. The person is, in a sense, "possessed" by the other; something or someone becomes so internalized that the person is no longer aware of having unique feelings and impulses of his own. The actress Carrie Snodgrass, speaking of her broken marriage, commented that "I became Neil, wanting so much to please him that it was like living with two of himself. I always considered him first."[34] There is, in short, a psychological denial of the existence of a separate self and of the distinctive meanings that are, or should be, the most human thing about us.

Concepts of the Self:
Japanese and American

There are good reasons to expect some contrast in the character of the social involvements of Japanese and Americans. Social life in the two countries flows from different premises. In Japan, attention is focused on the group as the measure of all things. From infancy children are encouraged to recognize their obligations to others—family members, schoolmates, work associates—and this may result in a less sharp boundary of the self. The Japanese tend not to think of the self as something constant and immutable that lies between one's shoes and one's hat, but as a constantly changing set of relationships, a multitude of selves rather than a singular self.

Irwin Mahler, one of the few to complete comparative studies of the self-image of the Japanese, found his data confirmed the view of a Japanese psychoanalyst, Tatara, who suggested that the ego boundary tends to be "diffuse," leading to a "blurring of the separate identity of the individual."[35] Edwin Reischauer, too, sees strong group ties requiring the Japanese to "subordinate their individualism" to the welfare of others.[36] Even the notion of being an individualist suggests an egotistical and insensitive person. The relation of infant to mother in which there is scarcely a sense of being a separate self is regarded as the highest form of relatedness (and the happiest time of life), a model of how adults should strive to relate to one another. But this idea of self-sacrifice is not always realized: "Saints and the selfless do not represent mankind."[37] Like other people the Japanese face the dilemma of accommodating the conflicting impulses of the self and the needs of others. It is simply that the choice for them appears to be slanted more sharply in favor of others: Obligations have a higher priority than rights. A person lacking in concern for the consequences of her own acts upon others is often despised and shunned.

The isolation of Japan over a period of centuries is also thought to make identification with others easier. On the other hand, the hierarchical social structure, where status distinctions mediate nearly all personal encounters, would seem to discourage such identification. On the whole, however, a heightened sense of obligation to others may encourage greater incorporation between close companions in Japan.

In Western cultures in general, and American culture in particular, the individual is the measure and arbiter of all things. Here the process of acculturation encourages the cultivation of a unique self. People belong to a multitude of groups, far greater in number than their Japanese counterparts, but they are for the most part organized to carry out specific tasks and exist only as long as they satisfy the needs of the participants. Rights—property and personal—are emphasized over duties. Relationships that require constant subordination of one's own interests are viewed as demeaning and destructive. Maturity resides in the capacity of each individual to be self-sufficient, to see that one's needs are respected and fulfilled while avoiding any interference in the pursuits of others. Although the great ethnic heterogeneity of the United States might make communicative rapport harder to achieve, emphasis on equality would seem to encourage empathy and attachment to close companions. The American cultural dynamic, thus, by cultivating a sharper sense of self, may favor independence or empathy while discouraging dominance, submission, or incorporation. If saints and the selfless are rare in Japan, hermits and sociopathic individualists are equally rare in the United States. As there are few human beings who are totally self-sufficient, rejecting any emotional attachment to others, so are there few who can be said to be so possessed by their obligations to others that they have no sense of a separate personal identity. Friendships not based on some capacity to experience the world of another person probably rest on a shallow and very fragile foundation.

THE AFFILIATION SCALE

In close human relationships there are likely to be varying proportions of concern for the self and for others. This balance of self-other concern may shift from topic to topic and activity to activity: One might be willing to choose some activities that benefit the other more than the self, but not other activities; one might feel right in interfering in some critical decisions a friend was to make, but unwilling to do so in other instances. Consequently, we sampled ten potential areas of involvement to explore the relative emphasis placed on the balance between concern for one's self and for one's companions: (1) recalling, (2) supporting, (3) anticipating, (4) assimilating, (5) temporal, (6) physical, (7) comprehension, (8) feelings, (9) privacy, and (10) decisions.

Although it was not feasible to construct items that corresponded strictly to such abstract psychological concepts as "independent" and "introjective," we did create a continuum of questions reflecting various degrees of communicative preoccupation with oneself or partner. The Affiliation Scale explored the balance of concern for self and others. At one extreme was *independence* (in thought and feeling, use of time, making decisions); at the other extreme was total *submission* to the thoughts, feelings, and needs of the partner. Between these two poles lay three other sets of ego boundaries: one in which there is *awareness* and some consideration of the interests of the other, a middle point where there is *mutuality* or a balancing of concerns for self and partner, and another where there is *incorporation* of the other and self. Figure 8.2 illustrates these relations.

A series of five questions in each of the topical areas probed the frequency with which respondents acted with regard to the balancing of self-other priorities. The five statements probing "supportive" behavior are illustrative:

1. I have chosen activities for us that benefit me alone.
2. I have chosen activities that would have some benefit for this person.

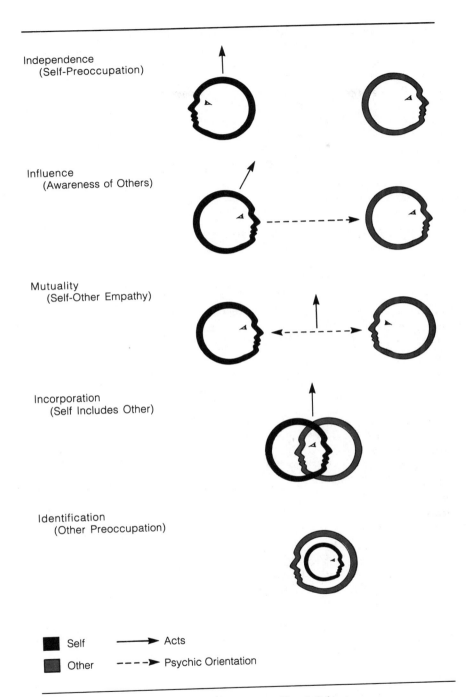

FIGURE 8.2 Potential Relations of Self and Other

3. I have chosen activities that would benefit us both.
4. I have chosen activities that would benefit this person more than me.
5. I have sacrificed activities I preferred to do things that would benefit this person.[38]

As was the case throughout the testing, these questions were asked of Japanese and Americans with reference to their two closest companions, the person occupying the middle of their range of companions, and the two located at the outer edge of the social circle. This made it possible to study relationships of varying depth and intensity with respect to the balancing of focus on the self or other.

EGO BOUNDARIES: JAPANESE AND AMERICAN

The findings reveal a consistent overall difference in the forms of attachment and with all partners. In spite of some marked similarities, Americans reflect roughly 30 percent higher frequency of involvement. More provocative still are the details of these two cultural profiles. Both cultures prefer what many regard as the healthiest form of attachment—mutuality— where there is a balancing of concern for the self and equal concern for the needs of one's partners. The second most frequent pattern reported in both samples is one in which the person is aware of the needs of their companion but acts primarily on the basis of self-interest. Both Japanese and Americans are least often involved in encounters in which they subordinate or sacrifice their own interests to those of their partners. Despite these similarities there is a significant difference in the magnitude or frequency of all forms of involvement, with Americans showing higher scores across the scale.

When we compare the various topics, the Japanese show the highest degree of mutuality in the area of feelings (sharing a mood) and in sharing decisions. Both confirm existing images of the Japanese. Americans display the highest mutuality in the area of time (desire to be together) and privacy (willingness to share private thoughts). The former suggests, as some observers have, that Americans have strong needs to affiliate, and the latter parallels the findings with respect to American depth of self-disclosure.

Both cultures report preoccupation with the other primarily in the area of comprehension (expressing the thoughts of others for them) and privacy (knowing what others feel without asking them). Scores on independence were highest for both cultures on comprehension (preferring to think about myself) and on decisions (telling others what decisions they should make). Although "sacrificing the self" was least favored in both countries, the Japanese did report this frequently with respect to privacy.

There is a general preference for "mutual involvement" with all companions on all topics in both cultures. Where there was previously a sharp drop in activities, verbal disclosure, physical expressiveness, and commitment as one moved from the closest to most distant companions, here the decline was more gradual. Again, however, the widest cultural difference appears with respect to the two closest companions.

RECONSIDERING CULTURAL IMAGES

It is tempting once we have become attached to certain views of a culture for such images, through constant reiteration, to acquire the power of myth. And in regard to the depth of commitment and quality of involvement with companions, this may be the case with Japanese and Americans.

The Japanese are often alleged to be more deeply committed to their closest associates, while Americans are more cavalier about obligations to companions. Yet despite similarities in the objects shared and personal assistance provided close friends, Americans report higher levels of these kinds of support than do the Japanese. In both countries, however, commitment is a reliable index of intimacy; taking responsibility for acquaintances drops off rapidly as the strength of affiliation diminishes.

Existing cultural images also suggest that Americans, constantly reminded of their need to be self-sufficient, and Japanese, equally encouraged to respect their dependence on others, may differ in how they see the borders of the self. Again the data do not confirm these images. In both cultures, mutuality is the dominant pattern of involvement, with needs of the self and partner taken equally into account. In both countries introjection, or sacrifice of the self, is the rarest form of involvement. Although the profiles of bonding are remarkably parallel, all forms of self-other involvement are reported more often by Americans.

Even in regard to conflict the data provide some surprises. There was no evidence of cultural difference in this area and much evidence of similarity in the way differences were managed with close associates. Japanese and Americans both relied most heavily on decisions that respected their differences or compromised them. Both were similar in their somewhat lower reliance upon collaboration as a creative way of integrating their desires. While both cultures often avoided discussing potential areas of conflict, the Japanese, as the stereotype suggests, reported that a greater proportion of their differences were never discussed.

Although there is abundant speculation about many facets of Japanese and American social behavior, there is a poverty of objective and descriptive data about such behavior. Exploratory studies, such as this, are by no means definitive—no single research study ever is—but the evidence is strong enough (encompassing large samples and extensive data) to suggest there may be a substantial gap between cultural clichés and cultural realities.

CHAPTER 9

The Vital Connection: Images and Realities

There are no noble people, or thrifty or harmless or evil or fierce people—only people, human beings, and that is enough of a problem. [1]
JOHN PFEIFFER

As we have seen, critics of life in the twentieth century are legion. And far from temperate in their denunciation of the quality of our personal relationships. Alienation from nature, from one another, even from ourselves echoes in our literature, poems, and plays, permeates our films, and is the dominant concern of contemporary philosophers. Even among the sciences that focus on human beings, people are portrayed as predominantly manipulative and exploitative.

Pessimism is no new phenomenon, but a feature of nearly every age. And apathy or impatience are far from helpful in addressing the situation. Even if the past were more humane than the present, it cannot be reconstructed. As William Barrett reminds us:

History has never allowed man to return to the past in any total sense. And our psychological problems cannot be resolved by a regression to a past state in which they had not yet been brought into being. On the other hand, enlightened and progressive thinkers are equally blind when they fail to recognize that every major step forward by mankind entails some loss, the sacrifice of an older security and the creation and heightening of new tensions. [2]

That we confront a new world is undeniable. But neither a romantic yearning for the past nor righteous indignation over the evils of the present is particularly useful in confronting it. The reason is two-fold: There is little evidence that the past more richly fulfilled human needs, and there is no possibility of going back, no real alternative to addressing the challenges this age poses.

When we speak of the past we envision a time when a strong sense of community prevailed, when people were rooted for generations to the same plot of land, where one knew who one was and where one stood and had permanent ties to kith and kin. But this is a one-sided portrait of the past. It was also monotonous, with little choice of destinies, and few material comforts or expressive outlets. When everyone knew everyone else, errors and indiscretions were rarely forgiven or forgotten and relationships endured out of necessity rather than choice. There may have been less overt aggression, because the lines that divided races, classes and nationalities were so impermeable. Oppression and exploitation coexisted with sensitivity and compassion. The world we have lost, suggests Abraham Kaplan, was no golden age of respect and affection:

> Many people who talk about the problems of our cities are victims of a myth of the Golden Age. They speak of the "breakdown of community," as though somewhere in the past, people really were together, and now we have lost it all; usually the loss is blamed on technology or science or numbers or something modern. All that, I think, is a myth; but I do think it is true that a great deal of our lives with other people is spent in collectivities and not in communities. [3]

Nor does the present age lend itself to global assessments. It is clearly one of rapid change, of abrupt transition to a new age and environment in which to realize human needs. "Nobody is at fault for our present plight," Paul Goodman writes. "We have not yet learned how. Modern conditions are too new."[4] We will be at fault—and suffer for it—only if we fail to address these conditions.

Periods of historical dislocation, when the institutions and practices of the past no longer provide security or satisfaction, are also periods of opportunity—opportunity to reflect on what should be preserved, what should be modified to better accommodate emerging conditions, and what new norms might enlarge human potential and enrich personal relationships. Whether the leap from wandering clans and farming villages to congested cities will succeed is not clear; it will, in all probability, turn less on our technological capacity than our talent in creating a new social structure and ways of communicating with our contemporaries. As John Gardner put it, "A generation doesn't have much choice in the problems that the forces of history throws in its lap. It does have a choice as to whether it will face those problems honestly."[5]

THE EMERGING PSYCHIC CHALLENGE

The study of ecology suggests that human nature and human conduct reflect the milieu in which they appear. If so, one can hardly imagine a more striking ecological transformation than has occurred in industrialized nations during the past hundred years. The contrast is most striking when one compares the daily lives of our relatives of only three generations ago. Then most people lived on farms, dying in the same home in which they were born, and living with a dozen family members of three different generations. Formal education was limited and there were few ways of learning much about the world beyond the horizon. At the same time, people were in constant touch with nature, knew its seasons and secrets. They walked to their fields, worked with their muscles, used simple tools. Their roles were few and well rehearsed through lifelong apprenticeship. Involvement with relatives from birth to death left little opportunity for meeting or experiencing alternative life-styles. Work and worship dominated life. Neighbors were always accessible and helped one another in periods of stress. Social activities consisted mainly of infrequent seasonal or religious celebrations. There were no films or broadcasts, few plays or concerts; people created their own recreation. Life proceeded at a pace governed by the rhythms of nature and of the body rather than by calendars or clocks. The past was familiar, the future predictable.

Then we were suddenly catapulted into a new age, with an explosive growth in population and a massive move into congested cities teeming with strangers. Impersonal institutions of immense scope and power arose to satisfy human needs. The size of the city, combined with its segregation of activities and segregation of people, made high-speed subways and freeways essential. Modern technology demanded extended occupational preparation and further segregated city dwellers. People now meet in the context of vast bureaucracies, their actions programmed by the roles they occupy and the regulations they apply. The pace of life has accelerated, enabling people to speed from place to place and activity to activity. Whatever leisure is gained is promptly filled by an unresponsive media that is a constant temptation and distraction for the senses.

Contemporary residents of Tokyo and New York now confront a physical environment that is remarkably alike. People are likely to live in a variety of places from rented room to dormitory to apartment to single dwelling. They will be raised in a family limited to two parents—and often only one—with only a single sibling. Formal education occupies nearly one third of their lives, preparing them for such technically sophisticated careers that periodic retraining will be imperative. Career choices are nearly incalculable but also unfamiliar. People speed to school, work, shops, recreation, and home insulated from one another by necessity or choice. Within vast bureaucracies, people still interact, but their conversations focus on routine and functionally appropriate topics. Outside they are surrounded by strangers who differ in interests, values, experiences and life-styles, affording a wide set of companions. Encounters with family and friends are likely to be more fleeting and periodic, requiring prior arrangements to make shared activities possible. Removed from nature, urbanites are likely to be informed about people and events a continent away, their lives more likely to be altered by distant crises than by local events. Leisure not devoted to public recreations such as attending concerts and sporting events is balanced by private recreations such as listening to the radio or records and watching television. Time is elaborately segmented to match the requirements of work deadlines, transport schedules, and daily appointments. A constantly increasing pace of changes makes the past seem irrelevant and the future unrecognizable.

THE INTERPERSONAL CHALLENGE

Among the assessments of the tragic consequences of this radical change in the material conditions of life is the notion that large urban populations leave the individual swallowed up in a crowd of strangers, unknown and powerless to control his or her destiny. Yet is it the number of our contemporaries that provokes dissatisfaction? "What makes mass society so difficult to bear," writes Hannah Arendt, is not the number of people involved, "but the fact that the world between them has lost its power to gather them together, to relate and to separate them."[6] Another complaint is that the sheer size of cities, combined with their deliberate partitioning of widely dispersed residential, work, shopping, and recreation districts, has isolated urbanites and turned the leisure time they might spend with friends into an endless dash from one place to another, leaving no time for the casual, informal contacts that once sustained friendships.

Yet we are also told that modern cities provide more contacts and opportunities for communication than has ever existed. More contacts, the critics say, but a larger proportion of them routine contacts of an impersonal sort providing less time or energy to cultivate deeper and more personal ties. The city is said to create more "single-strand," or fractional, relations in which companions share only a single facet of their lives (to attend class, play golf, or go to the theater) rather than the "multiple-strand" relationships of earlier times. Still, no one has offered proof that a number of unique relationships are necessarily more shallow or less rewarding than fewer, more comprehensive ones.

To other critics it is not the functional or fragmentary quality of social encounters in the city that robs them of emotional depth but that they are so fleeting and transitory. Intimacy, Christopher Alexander contends, involves "close contact between two people in which they reveal themselves in all their weakness, without fear."[7] He adds that modern life has robbed people of the constant "dropping-in" that is essential to cultivating trust and intimacy. But do more frequent meetings guarantee deeper relationships? Are less frequent contacts necessarily superficial? Finally, there is the charge that the larger and more congested the city, the greater the severity of the pathologies it breeds. The evidence here is also less clear than one might hope. The proportion of deaths due to disease, criminal assault, and severe mental illness does not vary with urban or rural settings. Indeed the evidence suggests a slightly higher incidence of social pathologies in rural areas. It is social deprivation, not the locus of that deficiency, that seems to be critical. Cities, at the very least, provide a wider field of social opportunity. "The crucial lack of our society," says Edgar Friedenberg, "is not opportunity, but intimacy. We must take time to use our affluence and our leisure to redefine our selves and reform our institutions—and, to some extent, the other way round."[8]

In assessing modern city life as a context for communication one should not discount its compensating forces. First, and most obvious, is the increase in the number of possible companions, thereby raising the odds of forming compatible relationships. People are drawn to cities not only for employment, but for the richer social and cultural outlets they provide. For most urban residents, cities are desirable places to live. No other setting provides the same level of excitement or range of activities that a large city provides. Historians have often, and quite rightly, seen cities as essential in promoting cultural achievement; they provide a setting in which creative people can meet and collaborate and an audience for their plays, paintings, music, dance, and inventions. The diversity of population does not force but encourages people to cross the barriers of race, religion, class, and nationality that so often inhibit communication between people of differing life-styles. The diminishing importance of the family has expanded the role of choice in personal attachments. Fewer of our companions are dictated by birth or geography. Shorter hours of work leave more time available to spend with friends and more collaborative occupations widen the access to people with common interests. City life, in short, may provide a more diverse social field, a wider scope of social activities, and a greater sense of equality and respect for differences, all attributes that contribute to empathy and affection in human relationships. As Alexander notes:

> Modern urban society has more contact and communication in it than any other society in human history. People who would never have been in contact in a preindustrial society are in contact today. There are more contacts per person, and there are more kinds of contact. Individuals are in touch with a wider world than they ever were before. As metropolitan areas grow, society will become more

differentiated, and the number and variety of contacts will increase even more so. This is something that has never happened before, in the whole of human history, and it is very beautiful.[9]

Whether we are entering a brave new world full of possibilities for enhancing human potentials or a frightening new world hostile to these potentials is not yet clear. In periods of rapid and radical change—and human history includes several such turbulent periods—it is difficult to know whether one is moving toward or away from something better. Reliable forecasting of the future eludes us; it is difficult even to get a reliable reading of the present.

COMMUNICATION: ITS PERSONAL FUNCTION

Against this backdrop of revolutionary change in the physical conditions of life there is the undeniable need for others to share our fate. "The longing for human intimacy stays with every human being from infancy through life," writes Frieda Fromm-Reichman. "There is no human being who is not threatened by its loss."[10] In his classic work on friendship, Robert Brain agrees: "We must in fact for our peace of mind either feel ourselves loved or in a position to be loved."[11] The data collected clearly confirm these observations: Failure to bond in infancy, the lack of friends in childhood, the effects of anomie in adult life and of rejection in old age demonstrate the tragic, even fatal consequences of being without close companions. It is not enough to exist; one needs to feel one has made a difference. There may be no outlet for realizing one's self as powerful as seeing that something one has said or done has made a difference in the eyes of another human being.

The critical place of relations with others seems to stem from the nature of the human organism; our social needs derive from our biology. We enter a world devoid of meaning, but are forced by the need to act into giving meaning to it. We are uniquely endowed to make such attributions; our senses provide continuous access to the shapes, colors, sounds, tastes, and textures around us; our brains select and organize sensory data into useful configurations; our memories provide a record of past efforts at interpreting events; our interpretations, in turn, arouse emotions that motivate our actions; we review these acts, from winking to embracing, to decide what we will do next.

These processes of sensing, organizing, comparing, and evaluating all take place within us; they involve a form of communication that is essentially intrapersonal. Language greatly enhances this process because its vocabulary supplies a set of categories into which to fit people and events, and an elaborate grammar suggests ways they may relate to one another. The capacity to think abstractly, and thereby create symbols that represent events, is the feature that most distinguishes the human species.

But the system is far from flawless. Our view of things is always incomplete; it fails to take into account the infinity of features that are present and observable. It is also highly selective, tending to focus myopically on features that serve our motives and moods of the moment. It is also a highly fallible process; we often fail to notice what is there and see what is not there. And we tend to interpret events according to an inner logic that is deeply wedded to serving our personal appetites. Finally, the decisions we reach are often beyond the ability of a solitary individual to carry out.

COMMUNICATION: ITS SOCIAL FUNCTION

Communication, however, is more than a private activity; it has a social function as well. "There may be truths beyond speech, and they may be of great relevance to man in the singular," Hannah Arendt has written, "but in so far as [people] live and move and act in this world, [they] can experience meaningfulness only because they can talk with and make sense to each other and to themselves."[12] People seek the company of others partly to escape the prison of their private meanings. It is a way of transcending an overwhelming sense of aloneness born of our physical separateness. Partly, too, communication affords a way of comparing experiences testing the reliability of our reactions. The incompleteness of our knowledge provokes curiosity about how others see the same events; through symbols we may be transported into the world others inhabit and incorporate their experience as part of our own. Further, there is the need to collaborate; most human enterprises from constructing buildings to space travel require diverse talents and exquisite coordination. Finally, talking with others is an end in itself; people need people not only when they lack information or need help but also when they are excited, inspired, hopeful. Everyone seeks a place of affection and respect in someone else's world.

COMMUNICATION: ITS CULTURAL FUNCTION

Communication has a cultural dimension as well. If two people are to understand one another they require some means to overcome their physical separateness. That means is nothing more substantial than the sounds and scratches people use to express themselves and the social norms that frame human encounters. What makes sharing experiences possible is an agreement to give similar form to inner meanings and to attribute similar meanings to similar forms of outer behavior. One person displays her thoughts or feelings and those who observe the flow of phrases, gestures, and hesitations employ similar rules in interpreting what they have seen. What the members of a community share is not the world, but the structure of their minds; to the extent they share a universe of discourse they share a universe of meaning. And as a consequence, they feel a sense of their common identity. Difficulties in communication still arise within a community because the rules of meaning and of interaction are never perfectly understood or perfectly applied. Between cultures—when neither the symbols nor the norms that govern social activity are shared—wider difficulties are likely to arise. Coping with such misunderstandings is further complicated because members of each culture resort to strategies for correcting such misunderstandings that are equally foreign to each other.

THE COMPREHENSIVE INVESTIGATION OF IMAGES AND REALITIES

In *The Republic* Plato suggests that if a group of prisoners were chained for years in a cave so that they could see only the shadows cast by objects placed behind them would they not, when released, argue that the shadows were real and the objects only an illusion?[13] It is to this interface between image and reality that we turn here. To what extent, and at what points, do our images and the realities of social life in Japan and the United States converge or diverge?

The aim of this exploration through the Dimensions of Interpersonal Relations study was, in an apt phrase of Erving Goffman's, "to uncover the normative order" found in social life. Our focus has been not on the individual, but on relationships, and not with what people think about their relationships, but their actual behavior with close companions. The approach has been multidimensional, examining a wide range of activities rather than concentrating on a single facet of such relationships.

It would be well to remember, as Gregory Bateson has written, that "science *probes;* it does not prove."[14] Research is just that, a "searching again" to seek patterns of behavior of which we are unaware, the discovery of which, as Freud pointed out long ago, is a step toward understanding ourselves better and thereby making it possible to choose those actions that are most fulfilling.

Few things seem as critical in determining the health or happiness of a human being as the quality of his or her relations with other people. Yet the conditions of life have changed so radically that those born today inhabit a world that would be unrecognizable, and probably intolerable, to an earlier generation. It is, we are told, a time of turmoil marked by a loss of a sense of community, of family disorganization and fragile friendships, of manipulative and crippled communication.

The poverty of factual evidence to confirm or disconfirm these often eloquent denunciations prompted this effort to obtain a more concrete description of the actual state of human relations in the contemporary world. Japan and the United States, two representative industrial cultures with distinctive styles of adaptation, seemed to afford a promising field of inquiry. Large samples of Japanese and Americans were asked to describe their lives with their closest companions: How did they meet? What do they talk about? How do they reach decisions? How do such bonds affect them? Looking first at the features of friendships common to both cultures may suggest hypotheses worthy of testing for their universality.

Despite all dire pronouncements to the contrary, there is little evidence in Japanese and American friendships of estrangement or alienation. Modern cities may lack the public life of earlier times and may favor a social order based on association rather than community, but people maintain circles of intimates with whom they communicate regularly and at length. There are cases of very superficial involvement (notably more in the Japanese than in the American sample) and of affiliations limited to a particular kind of partner—all relatives or no relatives, all the same sex or opposite sex, all the same age or older or younger acquaintances—but they represent a *very small* minority. Few in either country are without a circle of at least fifteen companions with whom they felt some closeness, that they felt understood them, and in whose company they felt comfortable. As in the only other recent survey of friendships (in the United States) people were found to be satisfied or enthusiastic about their closest friends. As Mary Parlee and her associates concluded from their survey of 40,000 Americans, "The results give cold comfort to social critics."[15]

Do relationships deepen gradually or do they progress through a series of stages, periods of consolidation followed by periods of transition to a new level of involvement? Japanese and American accounts consistently favor the notion that friendship progresses through a series of distinct stages. In both cultures, the patterns of behavior with people at the center and the periphery of the social circle are significantly different: Not only was this true of the closest and most distant companion but there also were consistent differences among each of the five companions studied in depth (one, two, eight, fourteen, fifteen). People periodically, and somewhat abruptly, move to levels of higher or lower intensity as the relationship matures. Some eligible partners get no farther than an exchange of greetings and pleasantries, some move to the deepest sharing of private confidences; some move toward intimacy slowly, others apparently precipitously; some gather momentum as they mature, while others retreat from a closeness they once achieved. Although an occasional respondent expressed some difficulty differentiating between involvement with the most distant two or three partners, none had difficulty ranking the others they identified.

A closely related issue concerns whether intensification of a relationship is signalled by change in a *particular mode* of behavior, for example, greater physical intimacy preceding deeper verbal disclosure, or is reflected simultaneously in *all modes* at about the same time. The evidence here indirectly favors the latter conclusion: Close relationships are marked by deeper verbal disclosure, greater physical intimacy, more collaborative activities, wider sharing and sacrifice, and greater psychological assimilation. More distant bonds show a fairly consistent reduction in all modes of intimacy. A person acts as a whole not only in singular activities but also in all relations with other people.

Most of the research on attraction shows similarity to be a powerful factor in the choice of friends. Although residential and occupational proximity create a field of eligible partners, demographic similarity (age, sex) and biographic similarity (education, occupation) act as a first filter. Similar personal traits and interests act as a second filter, similar opinions and values are a third filter, ways of interpreting events are a fourth, and, finally, complementary psychic drives make for the deepest and most durable attachments. If so, then the findings on the Acquaintance Inventory offer some surprises. In contrast to laboratory findings the actual companions named by Japanese and Americans as their most intimate partners show them to be a rather diverse set of people. True, there is evidence of similarity of age, education, and economic status but also evidence of immense variety in their choice of friends. They include newborn infants and people in their eighties, close and distant relatives, and supervisors, neighbors, teachers, and priests. And some of the similarity reported could be an artifact of location rather than an active search for someone similar. The social lives of people as they are actually lived appear more diversified and less narcissistic than laboratory findings indicate. Or it may be that the factors that provoke an initial *attraction* are not the same factors that determine *affiliation;* in more durable and deeper partnerships we may seek different qualities.

Allowing people to name their own partners without regard for the category they occupy (parents or acquaintances, for example) focused attention on the quality rather than the origin of the friendship. The results were highly provocative. Relatives and nonrelatives were both included within the social circles of Japanese and Americans and were found distributed almost randomly across the scale of intimacy. Although a few participants named no relatives among their closest companions and a few named mostly relatives, neither pattern is typical of the two countries. Only mothers were named on some lists, only fathers on others, and more rarely both or neither were named. When named, parents rarely occupied the same rank; sometimes they appeared among the four or five closest companions, but just as often were among the least close. A variety of relatives appear without discernible pattern: sometimes an aunt but not an uncle, a sister-in-law but not a brother, a nephew but no cousins. Relatives play a smaller role in both cultures than friendships with unrelated people (a finding that may confirm the declining influence of the nuclear family).

People have no control over the particular family into which they are born, but they still *choose* to become close even within inherited or enforced relationships. Whether one is close to a parent or sister is not ordained by the fact of sharing the same household but because of the empathy people create or fail to create out of that fact. Eastern and Western commandments to the contrary, family affection cannot be decreed; it must be created. If, as was found in previous research, fathers and mothers are more equally regarded in American families while fathers are more remote in Japanese families, it is a consequence of their behavior, not of their legal status; intimacy is an accomplishment.

Finally, there is convergence with regard to the connection between (1) closeness and (2) frequency and duration of contact between friends. The closest companions in both countries tended to see each other frequently and over somewhat longer periods of time. This confirms George Homans's hypothesis that there is a connection among opportunity to communicate, the activities shared, and the intensity of feeling that grows between two people.[16] While the closest partners saw each other frequently, more distant ones did not. In some cases there is evidence of "suspended relationships" in which people who could not communicate for long periods of time still felt closer to such partners than to those with whom they spent a lot more time. The evidence, thus, points in two directions: It is likely that close relationships will result in more time spent together, and more time spent together will tend to deepen relationships. And once a close bond is formed, it is capable of surviving long periods of absence.

IMAGES AND REALITIES:
THE CULTURAL CONTEXTS

It is not only what is common about human relationships in these two countries that is important but the patterns that distinguish them as well. The archaeologist tries to reconstruct the life of past cultures by scrutinizing a few fragments of broken pots, but we have the reports of actual behavior on which to construct profiles of contemporary social life in Japan and the United States.

Collecting such data is a complex and exhausting task but one never so risky as in interpreting what has been found. Still, data are worthless unless they are interpreted and can contribute to our understanding. And, in this case, the data can improve the quality of cross-cultural rapport that might obtain from improved understanding. In spite of the obvious importance of such intercultural understanding, Edward Norbeck and George DeVos conclude that "A conspicuous failing of both Japanese and American scholarship has been a scarcity of comparative studies in all aspects of personality and culture."[17] Nor has the situation changed radically since this challenge was issued.

There is no end of speculation, however, about the character of these two cultures, their styles of behavior, or their underlying dynamics. The images are nearly beyond enumeration: Japan and the United States have been characterized as "shame-oriented" and "guilt-oriented," as "intuitive" and "rational," as "reductionist" and "expansionist," as "group-oriented" and "individual-oriented," as "status-conscious" and "egalitarian," as "familial" and "contractual," as "introspective" and "expressive," as "compulsive" and "impulsive," as "harmonizing" and "confronting," as "dependent" and "independent," as "high-context" and "low-context," and as "feminine" and "masculine." The images differ in focus and emphasis, but all can make some claim to validity.

Yet in studying cultures one is repeatedly impressed with how complex they are, even how contradictory. While there are reasons to endorse each of these images, there are reasons for resisting them as well. Many, if not most, have yet to be tested empirically. Their seductive simplicity may deceive us by making the real world appear to be a simpler place than it really is. At any rate, many observers describe Japan as a culture that emphasizes status, group membership, harmony, modesty, obligations, and sensitivity to others. There is nearly as much agreement in seeing the American culture as emphasizing equality, independence, self-expression, competition, spontaneity, and confrontation. To what extent do these images match the actual behavior of Japanese and Americans as they communicate with one another?

Strangers

Some suggest that Japanese tend to be indifferent and even hostile toward strangers, while Americans are more open and receptive toward them. Here the data endorse these images convincingly: Americans are more likely to notice and approach strangers and to initiate conversations with them; Japanese are less likely to do so. The reports also show Americans communicating far more often with strangers than do Japanese. In both countries, however, people are attracted to strangers of one's own age, sex, education, income, and dress; religious, political, and personal values appear to play a more ambiguous or less critical role in approaching strangers. Although conversations with strangers tend to be brief, the Japanese learned more about the occupation and status of the stranger, confirming the image of the Japanese as more status conscious, while Americans learned more about the activities and interests of their new acquaintances. Where Americans learned details about their partners that might make it possible to continue such relationships, Japanese were less likely to do so and were inclined to prefer that this not happen. As their image suggests, the Japanese apparently are more reluctant to communicate with strangers partly because of the ambiguity of the status relation and partly because of the obligations that might accompany involvement in the personal life of such strangers.

Companions

When it comes to descriptions of their fifteen closest partners, Japanese and Americans display both similarities and differences; neither group is always consistent with expectations. There is great diversity in the selection of companions in both countries and preference for partners of the same age and same nationality (in spite of Americans' exposure to a culturally diverse population). Although similarity would also predict a preference for same-sex friends, members of both cultures included almost exactly the same number of males and females among their associates. Residential proximity contributes somewhat to the choice of acquaintances, but it plays a diminishing role in more durable relationships. "Physical accessibility" may be a more useful environmental variable since it takes into account not only where one sleeps but also where one works, studies, and plays; all these places were important settings for the initial and continuing contacts of Japanese and Americans.

The image of Japanese as having more lasting friendships and of Americans having more transitory ones was not confirmed: There was no difference in the durability of friendships in the two cultures. And despite all ominous speculations about the fragile and fleeting contacts of rootless urbanites, the facts do not support that notion. Nor do the findings show only brief and infrequent contact between close friends: In both countries people spent more than a hundred hours a month, more than a thousand hours a year, with their closest friends, with the frequency and length of contact decreasing, as one would expect, as intimacy decreases. Indeed, there is a greater amount of socializing between Americans than between Japanese.

Still more striking was the contrast between cultural predictions of the role of relatives in the lives of Japanese and Americans: In both cultures unrelated partners make up a far larger share of the circle of intimates. (It is a mistake to call them *peers* given the diversity of their ages.) Americans, again upsetting predictions, listed a significantly greater number of relatives as close companions than did Japanese. The findings, however, do lend support to the view of critics that the influence of the family is declining and being replaced by the growing influence of unrelated partners.

Shared Activities

No one has yet studied or linked the character of social activities to the dynamics of culture. Although a hierarchy of preferred ways of spending time with friends clearly exists, Japanese and Americans tend to rank the attractiveness of such activities similarly. More significantly, and not entirely in keeping with the images of either culture, there is agreement on the form of participation preferred; both cultures engaged primarily in activities that permitted each person to act independently, to observe some event together, and to collaborate on a common task. Only in the ranking of competitive and hierarchical settings did behavior conform to the image of Japan as a status-oriented and the United States as a competitive society. Yet the amount of social activity of all types is significantly greater for Americans.

Verbal Intimacy

The first specific feature of interpersonal communication examined was the content of conversation. We found, as expected, that the amount of talk, the topics discussed, and the depth of disclosure all increased as Japanese and Americans felt closer to their partners. Whether feelings of intimacy induce greater sharing of confidences, or greater sharing of confidences induces feelings of closeness, the two phenomena are clearly related. In general both Japanese and Americans prefer to talk about impersonal topics and avoid more personal ones; they share more of themselves with people close to them and less with those more distant. What they share, and how deeply they share, is sensitively adapted to the level of intimacy. But Americans disclose on all topics and with all partners at a significantly greater depth.

If the capacity to talk comfortably about a wide range of personal experiences is one measure of the bond that connects two people, the image of Japanese as more deeply involved in fewer but more durable relationships and of Americans as more superficially involved in more transient relationships is at odds with the reported behavior of members of the two societies. The patterns of verbal communication suggest the two cultures hold somewhat different views of the goals of communication: Among Americans disclosure tends to be viewed as an effort to build a more complete and authentic understanding of self and other; among Japanese communication seems to be viewed as a means of maintaining harmonious relationships in which deep disclosure appears too self-centered and too potentially disruptive to be undertaken. Clearly the two cultures have different conceptions of the role of verbal communication.

Nonverbal Intimacy

Although conversation is what most people associate with personal encounters, more is involved than an exchange of words no matter how concealing or revealing they are. The data on nonverbal communication also cast some doubt on existing images of the two cultures. Americans more often sacrificed other commitments to spend time with friends and they entertained them in more intimate and revealing settings. The data on greetings and farewells, on touching as a form of communication, and on sexual expressiveness fit existing expectations: The Japanese are less physically expressive in greetings and farewells, touch their companions far less, and less frequently engage in sensual-sexual behaviors.

But a number of nonverbal patterns contradict existing stereotypes: Americans give gifts more frequently than do Japanese and do so more spontaneously and as a symbol of affection rather than because it is appropriate or required. The greatest surprise, however, appeared with respect to silence. Among the Japanese silence is thought to be a highly cultivated, culturally distinctive form of communication. Or is it, as recently suggested, only a myth that persists because it is so often repeated and satisfies a need for cultural uniqueness? Despite its alleged importance, it is among the least investigated of Japanese cultural features. The data here suggest it is more fiction than fact. Americans experience periods of silence that are as long and as comfortable in the company of their closest friends as do the Japanese. A heightened sense of decorum may produce silence; a reticence about asserting oneself may produce silence. But that it is a highly developed means of generating understanding among the Japanese seems unsupported by the findings. It appears, in short, that words and acts complement rather than substitute for one another. Expressive cultures and individuals disclose more verbally and nonverbally; less expressive cultures and individuals are more verbally and nonverbally reticent.

Interpersonal Commitment

Associated with the idea of companionship is the notion of commitment, of willingness to share and to sacrifice for the benefit of one's friends. For most people, closeness implies taking responsibility for one another. In spite of this belief, neither Japanese nor Americans reported sharing objects or providing assistance "more than rarely in the past year" with close acquaintances. And although much has been made of Japanese emphasis on obligations to others and of American emphasis on the rights of the individual, Americans more frequently shared their possessions and provided more personal assistance than did the Japanese. Contemporary friendships do appear to involve shallower commitments than are thought to have existed in the less urban, less specialized, less independent societies of earlier ages. But the pattern may also reflect the greater material affluence of today.

Interpersonal Conflict

Because it affords a unique focus for cultural comparison, decision making was also studied. In respondents' descriptions of the "differences that came up" and "how they were managed" the findings suggest that existing images are overdrawn or in need of some qualification. As suggested by cultural observers, the two cultures do differ in their attitudes toward potentially disruptive encounters; differences in attitudes, beliefs, and behavior surfaced less often in Japanese than in American relationships but not significantly so. In both countries the closer the two people, the more likely they were to confront their differences directly. And, surprisingly, members of both societies resolve conflicts in similar ways, preferring to make independent decisions or to compromise. (They may, however, differ in the way these ends are approached.) Decision making is an aspect of communicative behavior that deserves closer attention, particularly since it is the arena in which so many encounters between the two countries take place.

Consequences of Attachment

One of the most intriguing features of friendships is the psychological consequence of affiliation. How are people affected by sharing their lives with others? Do they seek some integration of self and others? Do they become so absorbed with their partners they no longer see themselves as separate persons? Here members of both cultures preferred a balancing of the needs of self and other, a pattern that psychologists in both countries would probably endorse as the most healthy. The findings, however, fail to confirm either the other-centeredness and dependency often attributed to the Japanese or the self-centeredness and independence attributed to Americans. Also, in contrast to expectations, the extent of incorporation appears greater between American companions than between Japanese. Again the findings open up and identify an area of great complexity and of profound cultural and personal significance, one deserving of the most serious and extended study.

CONTEMPORARY SOCIAL LIFE: GENERAL SYMPTOMS OF MALAISE

Although the circumstances of life have changed beyond recognition in the past century, Japan and the United States, according to the evidence here, have adapted to the challenges of a congested, mobile, and impersonal urban existence surprisingly well. Is there any evidence of weakness or inadequacy in contemporary social life? There is. Three major areas of vulnerability emerge. Although the profiles of relationships demonstrate that people are maintaining a diverse and durable set of ties with other people, there remains an unsatisfied hunger for still deeper involvement. Although nearly all questions on the Dimensions of Interpersonal Relations instrument required descriptions of past actions, one question probed current satisfaction. People were asked whether they wanted more friends and/or acquaintances, fewer friends and/or acquaintances, or if they were satisfied with their circle of companions. Only 6 percent of the Japanese and 15 percent of the Americans were satisfied with the number of their friends and acquaintances. The overwhelming choice was for "more close friends" and "more acquaintances" among the Japanese (61 percent) and Americans (41 percent) sampled. Although a desire for a richer social life may have existed in all times and places, it is a figure that cannot be discounted.

Further, despite the evidence of shared activities, verbal disclosure, physical intimacy, and commitment to companions, the levels at which these occur might be seen as less than satisfactory in many eyes. The sharing of personal experience rarely extends beyond "limited disclosure," physical closeness is experienced "only occasionally," the extent of sacrifice for even the closest companions is very limited, and the bonds with friends are not strong enough to tolerate the discussion of many differences. There is no way of comparing the strength of affiliation today with previous ages, but there are scarcely grounds for celebration.

Finally, the averaging of scores often conceals symptoms of pathology at either extreme. A number of cases, usually five or ten out of a hundred, revealed how very fragile and shallow the social life of an individual can be in today's urban cultures: These people participated in social activities rarely, disclosed almost nothing to anyone, seldom experienced any form of physical intimacy and appeared, on every measure, to illustrate the most extreme forms of isolation. In both samples, though more frequently among the Japanese, there are clearly outsiders who lack ties of any depth with their contemporaries. The devastating pronouncements concerning modern urban life are not without foundation; instances of alienation exist. They simply are not characteristic of the general quality of human relationships found in these two societies.

CULTURE-SPECIFIC SYMPTOMS
OF INADEQUACY

According to Edwin Reischauer, Japanese young people rank the highest and Americans the lowest in dissatisfaction with how their respective cultures operate. While global estimates based on vague criteria must be viewed with skepticism, they encourage a search for the sources of dissatisfaction in the two countries. In Japan one of these sources may be found in the emphasis given to group identification, what Nakane has called the "we-they" problem, for it discourages exposure to people who lie outside the group. Outsiders are nonpersons she suggests.[18] As found here Japanese communication with strangers occurs rarely, was reciprocated less often, and was less likely to lead to continued contact than in the United States. In the increasingly congested environment of the city this strategy reduces distraction but also limits access to people who might prove compatible partners.

Perhaps the most provocative evidence has to do with the low level of social activity, the limited sharing of personal experience, and avoidance of physical intimacy among the Japanese. Although these behaviors may arise from preoccupation with the needs of others, the desirability of harmony, and the danger of breaking the fragile bonds formed with acquaintances, they severely limit opportunity to explore the meaning of one's own experiences and to learn from the insights of others. Doi Takeo in addressing this issue found that only through therapy did many of his patients come to realize the importance and meaning of their own lives: "I took this as a step toward the emergence of a new consciousness of self, inasmuch as the patient could then at least realize his previous state of 'no self.'"[19] An unwillingness to express one's inner thoughts and feelings may cripple the capacity to have such thoughts and feelings.

The findings also suggest that so strict an avoidance of differences may also impoverish relationships. One wrong phrase, one inappropriate gesture, Robert Ozaki notes, "may turn out to be a fatal mistake, the beginning of the end of a warm friendship. In Japan, no one can afford to take a chance. A Japanese is compelled to be polite and reserved."[20] Yet the denial of differences seems, in part at least, a denial of the humanity of another person. A feeling of harmony and of rapport may be an ideal sought in many human societies but a questionable one if it rests upon appearances alone.

It is noteworthy that when it comes to sharing and caring for close companions, the level of commitment is surprisingly shallow, and it does not confirm the greater interdependency of the Japanese. It should be emphasized that "obligations" to others (such as work associates) or "devotion" to others (such as family members) are not the same as feeling close, of being drawn to others because of understanding them or feeling understood.

The more restricted social opportunities, constraints against self-expression, and pressures to maintain pleasant, if superficial, relations appears to prompt the occasional outbreaks of resistance and rebellion found among young adults in contemporary Japan; such rebellion is less visible there than in the United States writes Reischauer only because it is "masked by the Japanese desire to maintain a show of harmony and to avoid confrontation."[21]

Although Japanese may suffer from too great restrictions on their individuality, Americans, it is claimed, suffer from individualism run rampant. Yet reports of their personal relationships suggest a depth and durability that hints this is, in part at least, a myth. As Roger Rosenblatt observes, "If you would win over a crowd of Americans, use the term rugged individualism; they will salute it like a flag," but he hastens to add, "of course, the picture is pure hokum, and everybody knows it. The West was won by wagon trains, the East by sailing ships, and they all had plenty of passengers aboard by necessity working together."[22] The impulse from the founding fathers to the present, he argues, has been a collective one. Collective, no doubt, but one based on shifting alliances that serve changing needs rather than on a permanent collectivity based on family or occupation providing security throughout a lifetime.

A provocative and critical view of the American social scene is obtained from examining it from the perspective of the theory of *amae* formulated by Doi Takeo.[23] The theory holds that Japanese experience their most fulfilling relationships in the infant-mother bond; that throughout their lives they seek to recreate this sort of affectionate and protective relation with their companions. It was often thought that this sort of "dependency" (the term *amae* does not translate into a simple English equivalent) resulted from the stifling of the infant's drive to become a separate and independent individual. The theory, as elaborated more recently, questions if it is not the West that encourages the stifling of a natural impulse to maintain bonds of interdependency and, in this way, prepares the child to participate as a separate entity in a competitive society.

The obvious excesses of the American society—juvenile delinquency, drug addiction, divorce, murder, and other crimes—do seem a pathology connected in some way with an uninhibited assertion of the self. Matsuyama Yukio in a "Candid Letter from Japan to America" writes that "the American love of freedom has exceeded all reasonable bounds and threatens to degenerate into self-centeredness."[24] The vices and virtues of society, as of every individual, tend to be one and the same. Strengths become weaknesses when carried to excess. "No country," says Henry Grunwald, "carries the belief in freedom so far or is so deeply committed to the notion of unrestrained self-expression: We have broken or bent all the traditional framework of rules, in religion, in family, in sex, in every kind of behavior," adding "yet we are surprised when the result is both public and personal disorder":

> We somehow believe that we can simultaneously have, to the fullest extent, various kinds of freedom: freedom from discipline, but also freedom from crime; freedom from community constraints, but also freedom from smog; freedom from economic controls, but also freedom from the inevitable ups and downs of a largely unhampered economy.[25]

It is doubtful, however, if the accounts of Americans who participated in this study provide any but the most tangential evidence of an unbridled egoism. Almost the contrary seems to be the case. There is evidence of a fairly broad tolerance in the choice of companions (though not as broad as expected), durable relationships with them, substantial sharing of personal confidences, willingness to explore differences, and efforts to resolve them equitably.

If there is an underlying malaise among younger Americans it may arise less from their personal relationships than from their relation to the larger society of which they are not yet a part. It may be anxiety over the lack of assistance in finding an occupation, of locating employment, of maintaining security in an unpredictable and complicated economic system. This feature stands in contrast to the orderliness and predictability of Japanese life, in which others can be trusted to provide a circle of companions, will intervene to promote one's interests both personal and professional, and will guarantee lifetime employment. Yet, as David MacEachron notes, "Americans would go mad if forced to live within the tight web which unites and controls Japanese through such institutions as family, social convention and large corporations or government bureaus."[26] The Japanese might be equally disturbed by the lack of such controls, personal or public competitiveness, or the constant confrontations and conflicts that characterize life in the United States.

De Tocqueville is always challenging, insightful, or both. In speaking of societies in which status is differentiated he notes that citizens are always attached to one another. There is someone above them to whom they owe allegiance and someone below from whom they receive allegiance. If the difference in status complicates communication between them, it also ensures they will never be isolated. The denial of status, as in the United States, makes for an easier and more natural communication between people but often leaves them with no secure connection to others. "Democracy," he writes, "does not attach men strongly to each other; but it places their habitual intercourse upon an easier footing."[27] While the findings here clearly confirm the ease with which Americans approach strangers and their fuller expression of themselves verbally and physically, they do not confirm the alienation de Tocqueville sees.

Japan and the United States seem to represent, in almost classic form, the clash between the respective claims of the individual and the society. Which is to come first, the person or the culture? No person can achieve his or her fullest development without the nurturance of a surrounding society; no society attains its full potential without the diverse and creative contributions of its members. Highly congested urban societies, their residents situated in specialized institutions, racing to keep pace with technological change and tomorrow's deadlines represent the latest challenge to the balancing of public and private needs. Never have people been so utterly dependent upon one another; never have they seemed so insistent on pursuing their own ways. Although Japan appears to tip the balance in favor of obligations to others and the United States in favor of obligations to self, both countries struggle to improve the balance. Perhaps this is why they have so much to learn from each other. In the mature human being and the mature social order the needs of individual and of the community seek equitable resolution.

TWO CAVEATS

There are two cautions to stress in interpreting the cultural profiles presented here. The first is that such profiles reflect what the statistician calls the "central tendencies" of the data. Hundreds of descriptions of specific acts performed with specific partners are reported. These are then averaged to obtain a single figure that best reflects these cultural-specific behaviors. Given a normal variety of such acts, some people showing more and some less of a particular behavior (giving gifts to friends or avoiding certain subjects), the mean is the best single figure for describing such behaviors. But remember that the range on any dimension may be broad; there are Japanese who disclose more or less and differ with their partners more or less, and Americans who disclose and differ more or less. When intercultural encounters go well, as they sometimes do, it is often because each person deviates from his or her own cultural norms in the direction of the norms of the other culture. A highly sociable, verbally revealing, and physically expressive Japanese meets a restrained, less talkative, and less confronting American. Although the central tendencies in the two cultures were so divergent as to pose no problem of interpreting the broad features of the two cultures, the range of personal styles should not be overlooked.

There is another, more serious, caveat. When one studies the patterns of communication in the two countries it is inevitable that they will differ in some respects. In this case, they differ in a number of respects. It is then difficult to resist concluding that one is superior and the other inferior with respect to this or that quality. To the Japanese eye the expressive individualism of the American looks self-centered, aggressive, and inhuman; to the American eye the group dependence of the Japanese looks repressive, suffocating, and inhuman. Cultures, like beauty, reflect the eye of the beholder.

This notion assumes there is some universal and objective standard on which to base such evaluations, that each society lies somewhere along a single evolutionary line. That this is *not* the case cannot be overemphasized. We are not occupants on a stable platform from which to observe a competition in cultural achievement. We are, instead, like passengers seated on a train unable to judge whether we are moving or the train beside us is moving. We are not dealing, in short, with cultural inferiority or cultural superiority but with simple difference. History may decide the relative viability of human cultures, but it cannot be demonstrated from within the value system of a single culture. We can do no more than describe similarities and differences in the behavior of Japanese and Americans and raise questions about their causes and consequences. There is, however, one final thing that can be done and that is to speculate about the difficulties that are likely to arise when Japanese and Americans meet each other and attempt to form friendships that are intercultural as well as interpersonal.

THE INTERCULTURAL ENCOUNTER

As the twentieth-century German novelist Hermann Hesse writes in *Steppenwolf:*

> Every age, every culture, every custom and tradition has its own character, its own weakness and its own strength, its beauties and cruelties; it accepts certain sufferings as matters of course, puts up patiently with certain evils. Human life is reduced to real suffering, to hell, only when two ages, two cultures and religions overlap.[28]

One need search no farther than the headlines of the morning newspaper or the marketplace of a modern metropolis to find evidence of such suffering. "One culture is always a potential menace to another," as Ernest Becker once wrote, "because it is a living example that life can go on within a value framework totally alien to one's own."[29]

In intercultural encounters, many people embrace the assumption of universality, convincing themselves that human beings are basically alike; if we are "truly ourselves" (honest), are "of goodwill" (well intentioned), or "try hard enough" (persistent), whatever differences that divide us will disappear. The assumption that everywhere men and women inhabit the same world and assign essentially the same meanings to events of their lives is perhaps the most pervasive and most intractable barrier to intercultural rapport. As Milton Bennett incisively puts it, "Assuming that others are like ourselves when we talk to them is tantamount to talking to ourselves."[30]

THE VITAL CONNECTION: IMAGES AND REALITIES   189

It is not simply that people speak in different tongues but also that they see differently, think differently, feel differently about their experience. "If, by some miracle, Americans and Japanese were to wake up one day and find ourselves talking the same language," observes George Packard, "we would still be faced with the problem of our massive ignorance about each other, we would still have difficulty in knowing what to communicate because we have so much to learn about what motivates the other."[31] The Japanese who masters English and the American who masters Japanese have acquired a remarkable tool for addressing their associates in each other's country, but they will not by that fact alone become immune to misunderstanding or being misunderstood.

Communication, as we have seen, is a multichanneled and multidimensional process for handling meanings. Meanings are implicit not only in the words one utters but also in who one speaks to, how they are approached, what one talks about, how one manages time and space, how differences are regarded, and myriad other bits and pieces of behavior. Where there is no consensus on the rules of meaning, communication falters or fails. Intended meanings elicit unintended conclusions. And "honesty," "goodwill," and "persistence" only exacerbate the difficulties for they, too, are displayed and interpreted differently across cultural borders. As Charles Krauthammer put it:

> To gloss over contradictory interests, incompatible ideologies, and opposing cultures as sources of conflict is more than antipolitical. It is dangerous. Those who have long held a mirror to the world and seen only themselves are apt to be shocked and panicked when the mirror is removed, as inevitably it must be. On the other hand, to accept the reality of otherness is not to be condemned to the war of all against all.[32]

The denial of differences only multiplies the difficulties by increasing the hostility differences engender; the maximizing of differences is equally misleading but may be less likely to disrupt the communicative process. In assuming the uniqueness of another person, or another culture, one need not deny that similarities as well as differences exist. But understanding, respect, and affection seem strongest when based on the reality of the other rather than on a distorted reflection of ourselves. Hesse addressed this issue in another of his novels when he wrote: "We were not separated from the majority of men by a boundary but simply by another mode of vision."[33]

What are some of the probable consequences of encounters between Japanese and Americans? The Japanese are likely to be startled at the ease with which Americans approach and enter into intense conversations with people they scarcely know. Americans' lack of sensitivity to protocol and to status differences, or their deliberate efforts to undermine them, may appear naive or downright insulting. Their constant questions and revealing disclosure may seem intrusive and overbearing, forcing the Japanese to discuss matters they regard as private. The extent to which Americans recount their experiences, failures, and successes may sound self-centered and pompous. Their informality and impulsiveness may deprive social occasions of their congenial predictability. The pace at which Americans move and talk, their verbal and physical flamboyance, may be unnerving. Their eagerness to contradict, even to argue bluntly, disturbs the harmony that should prevail. Equally astonishing is their ability to engage in such conflicts without it impairing their feeling for each other. Their endless analyzing, insistence on verbal precision, and binding agreements reveal an incredible trust in words over people. They are prone to error because they are always in such a hurry. They are an inscrutable people!

The Americans, in turn, confront Japanese who appear reluctant to meet strangers and slow to get to know them. The Japanese seem preoccupied with the relative status of people and are constantly deferring to those above them. They also are constantly apologizing. They seem to view conversation as some sort of formal ceremony rather than a real meeting of the minds. They are reticent about saying much about themselves, preferring to comment on superficial and irrelevant topics. When questions are put directly to them the answers are so vague that one has little idea of where they stand. They all repeat the same things as if fearful of disagreement. They are as physically opaque as they are verbally—except when drinking—and rarely show feelings of any kind, particularly negative ones. They are composed in the way they sit, the way they stand, the way they talk, as if some accidental and uncalculated act might expose them. There is a reluctance to dig into problems, analyze them step by step, and agree on specific solutions. And they seem oblivious to deadlines. A highly inscrutable people!

When difficulties arise, as they often do, the American approaches them by calling the misunderstanding to everyone's attention, explaining and justifying his or her behavior and asking others to be equally frank in explaining their position. Once the sources are identified and responsibility for them is admitted, some compromise course of action should be acceptable to everyone. A Japanese, equally sensitive to the fact that things are not going well, decides to postpone further conversation or propose some indirect way of defusing the situation without embarrassing anyone. Thus even the approaches to cross-cultural misunderstandings are culturally distinctive! It is helpful in such situations if Japanese can develop greater comfort in approaching difficulties more directly and analytically, or if Americans can develop greater patience and skill in ameliorating such difficulties less bluntly. In this connection Sheila Ramsey has offered an extremely helpful proposal for approaching such intercultural confusions, recommending what she calls "context-cracking": "Listening, watching, and participating in events are often more helpful in discovering the intricacies of context [culture] than asking 'why'."[34] The reason is fairly obvious: What each person otherwise does is to act naturally, that is, according to the dictates of his or her own cultural premises, and how does one explain acts that are so natural that they spring from sources of which the actors themselves may be unaware?

ONE CULTURE OR MANY?

The immensity and abruptness of the transition from hunter to farmer to technician and from village to supercity severely strain the capacity of the species to adapt to new conditions of life. How to live—alone and with others—in such a world remains an unsolved issue and one with interesting ramifications. One of these concerns the extent to which distinctive cultures will prevail in the future: Will industrialization, mobility, and the flow of information bring about a homogenization of cultures? William Caudill argues that as countries face similar technological changes they must inevitably become more alike, a sentiment shared by many who have traveled widely during the past few decades.[35] In addressing this issue some Japanese have questioned if primary group attachments, personal dependence, lifetime employment, and collective responsibility will work for the Japanese in the complex world of tomorrow. Similar doubts are raised by American observers. In earlier times human relationships endured as much out of environmental necessity as out of spontaneous affection. Today human beings find themselves capable of total independence, of never having to ask assistance of anyone for anything. But American commitment to independence, Slater argues, "is not a viable foundation for any society in a nuclear age."[36]

But cultures have always confronted somewhat similar material conditions and yet have always responded in highly distinctive ways. The spread of Buddhism, Islam, Christianity, and Confucianism did not homogenize the societies they enveloped. It was usually the other way round: Societies insisted on adapting the religions to their own cultural traditions. The same seems to be true of democracy and socialism, of free and managed economic philosophies. As a leading student of social change has observed:

> Countries have been absorbing the features of other cultures for as long as there have been different communities of human beings. While they have sometimes adopted nearly outright the tools and techniques of each other they have, far more often, filtered them through their own normative screen and generally adapted them to their cultural ethos.[37]

If outwardly there is little to distinguish what one sees on the streets of Osaka and Chicago—hurrying people, trolleys and buses, huge department stores, blatant billboards, skyscraper hotels, public monuments—beneath the surface there remains great distinctiveness. There is a different organization of industry, a different approach to education, a different role for labor unions, a contrasting pattern of family life, unique law enforcement and penal practices, contrasting forms of political activity, different sex and age roles. Indeed, most of what is thought of as culture shows as many differences as similarities.

And would one wish it otherwise? "The coming of a single world culture has grave dangers," Kenneth Boulding sagely warns. "It means that if anything goes wrong, everything goes wrong."[38] Cultural diversity, as with personal diversity, provides the species with endless and continuing experiments in survival; some individuals and some cultures inevitably fail due to inner flaws that make them vulnerable. Should all persons and all cultures become carbon copies of each other the world would not only be a far less interesting and creative place but also a far more dangerous place lest a fatal decision doom us all. Consider Boulding's view of the future:

> The problem of communicating across cultures therefore involves not merely the integration of cultures into a larger system, it involves the preservation of cultures across which communication takes place. It may be that the greatest problem of the human race in the next two hundred years will be the preservation of variety in the face of the enormous pressures of the science-based "superculture." In this process the character of communication across cultures is of the utmost importance. *The critical question is whether communication is designed to make all cultures one or whether it is designed to preserve their variety.* (Italics added.)[39]

A SUMMING UP

What we confront is a new world: a world that is neither paradise nor purgatory, but simply new. And, because of its newness, frightening. Neither a nostalgia for a past that may never have matched the images we preserve of it nor a bitterness that may obscure our myths about the present is going to serve us well.

The motives that prompt human behavior seem to change very little, though they are diversely expressed at various times and places. "All man's history," writes Norman Cousins, "is an endeavor to overcome his loneliness."[40] If that statement is oversimplified, it reminds us, nevertheless, that our most powerful drives—for nurturance, for expressive outlets, for testing opinions, for expanding experience, for simple affection—can be satisfied only through intimate involvement with our contemporaries. And this is unlikely to change no matter how radically the world is transformed physically. As Herbert Simon conjectured, "For most people, their relations to other people are really the core of their lives, and I see no reason to suppose that the basic nature of human beings will be changed by computers."[41]

Although it is obviously premature to pronounce judgment on the sterility or richness of social life in the twentieth century, these profiles of social life among Japanese and American young adults suggest that our cities are neither barren social wastelands nor ideal human communities. Our cities have not made it impossible for people to become acquainted; the zoning of activities and specialization of work have not prevented them from knowing a diverse set of people; friends share a wide variety of activities together, although they involve more observing than collaborating; companions share far more of their experience than critics claim, although less than they might wish to; there is greater physical as well as verbal intimacy but, again, less than people might want or need; there is limited sharing of possessions and providing of care; while many differences are never explored, those that are tend to be resolved in mutually satisfying ways; involvement with others has expanded the boundaries of the ego to incorporate the needs of others as part of the self. It is also clear that the two cultures have made unique adjustments to the pressures of contemporary life and in so doing afford some alternative ways of coping with an age of transition. The lack of data from other ages and other cultures makes it impossible to know whether the family of man is improving or deteriorating.

So much attention has been given here to commentators who share a questionable cynicism about the present that it might be wise to balance it with an alternative view, that human relationships have rarely held so much promise: that the erosion of class and racial barriers has increased accessibility; that cities offer a wide set of eligible partners; that the diversity of roles, while making for fewer all-encompassing attachments, may provide an equally rich set of partial relationships; that growing respect for differences cultivates communicative empathy; that choosing companions is a far sounder base for true intimacy. The late twentieth-century novelist Lillian Smith found it strange that ours should be viewed as an age of estrangement and made a strong case for the present:

> I believe that future generations will think of our times as the age of wholeness: when the walls began to fall; when the fragments began to be related to each other; when man learned finally to esteem the tenderness and reason and awareness which set him apart from other living creatures; when he learned to realize his brokenness and his great talent for creative ties that bind him together again; when he learned to accept his own childhood and in the acceptance to become capable of maturity; when he began to realize his infinite possibilities even as he sees more clearly his limitations; when he began to see that sameness and normality are not relevant to human beings but to machines and animals.[42]

For the Specialist

A number of conceptual and technical issues raised by this comparative study may be of special interest to behavioral scientists in Japan and the United States. Some of these can be addressed briefly here.

The Barnlund-Campbell Dimensions of Interpersonal Relations instrument consisted of a set of eight related subscales: Stranger Scale, Acquaintance Inventory, Interact Scale, Verbal Communication Scale, Physical Communication Scale, Responsibility Scale, Difference Scale, and Affiliation Scale. The instrument was "forward translated" by a bilingual professional translator and "backward translated" by a second bilingual professional translator, with the final edition evaluated by a third professioal translator. Discrepancies in the Japanese and English forms were resolved by seeking behavioral rather than literal equivalence.

All Japanese and American colleagues were briefed on the instrument, were supplied with a standardized set of instructions for administering it, and were provided with a set of answers to any questions that might arise during the testing period.

There are several ways of estimating the validity and reliability of the Dimensions of Interpersonal Relations instrument. Although behavioral scientists rarely ask respondents to appraise the design of the studies in which they participate, we did so in this instance. That roughly two thirds (60 percent of the Japanese; 70 percent of the Americans) felt they gave "an accurate and fairly complete picture of their behavior with close companions" is reassuring. In the remaining instances respondents felt it may have "overemphasized" or "underemphasized" certain features of their relationships, but there was little consistency in the specific items identified. A more objective assessment is found in the reliability coefficients for the separate scales that make up the questionnaire. The Spearman-Brown coefficients of reliability range from .66 to .81 and the Alpha coefficients are all over .95. In short, all the scales reach or exceed the standards generally accepted for group comparisons in the social and behavioral sciences.

Several features of the Barnlund-Campbell Dimensions of Interpersonal Relations questionnaire have unique value. One of these is the desirability of permitting people to structure their social networks as they experience them rather than according to the categories of associates imposed by investigators. Asking respondents to name the fifteen people closest to them seems better to reflect the seamless circle of companions that actually exists. Also, the extensive background information provided by the Acquaintance Inventory, ranging from age, sex, and nationality to where partners met, how often they spent time together, and the durability of the relationship exposed the immense heterogeneity of companions in real life; this variability clearly contradicts the similarity so consistently reported in studies based on exclusive categories of companions.

Another feature that seems to recommend itself was the combination of extensive coverage (of fifteen partners) with intensive examination of many facets of behavior with a few partners (the two ranked closest, the two most distant, and one occupying the midpoint on the scale of intimacy). The Dimensions of Interpersonal Relations instrument reveals how narrow and highly selective inquiry into interpersonal behavior has been to the present day. Where there has been extensive study of verbal disclosure and of certain features of nonverbal interaction, a surprising number of facets of communicative behavior have been almost totally neglected: Few have studied the activities companions share or the nature of the relationships they promote; few have probed the character of conflicts or how they are managed; few have explored the depth of commitment in terms of possessions shared or sacrifices made; almost nothing is known of the impact of intimate involvement on the ego boundaries of the people involved.

The internal arrangement of the questions within the topics that make up each subscale also appears to be provocative and is a feature to which the designers of the instrument remain committed. The closeness of the five relationships on the horizontal axis when combined with a series of questions of increasingly intimate nature on the vertical axis permit a rich exploration of which behaviors are associated with increasing closeness. In addition, they should promote a more dynamic analysis of the acts that signify increasing or decreasing closeness.

Yet there are clearly some limitations in this initial effort to probe the social networks and interpersonal behavior of people. The most important is found in the length of the instrument, the time it requires to administer it (two hours), and fatigue that may distort the answers given. It is an exhaustive questionnaire incorporating nearly fifteen hundred questions and usually requires two one-hour sessions of testing. There are, fortunately, several ways of correcting or compensating for the length. One possibility that involves no modification of the existing questionnaire is to use each subscale with different, but matched, samples and combine the scores to construct a cultural profile. Each individual would only complete the Acquaintance Inventory and one subscale, a task requiring roughly thirty minutes of testing.

Another possibility is to consider ways of shortening or compressing the instrument to reduce the time required to complete it. One way to do this would be to reduce the size of the social circle included. This is even suggested by the fact that a few participants reported some difficulty differentiating among the people they listed as "thirteenth, fourteenth, or fifteenth" and by the fact that the curves of intimate behavior dropped to very low levels by the time behavior with the two most distant associates was described. It may be of greater importance to know more about subtleties of behavior with closer companions. Reducing the size of the social circle from fifteen to ten partners would shorten the Acquaintance Inventory by one third.

This change could be combined with reducing the number of partners studied intensively from five to four. Instead of reporting details of behavior with five people (one, two, eight, fourteen, fifteen) participants could report their actions with only four partners within this smaller perimeter (for example, those identified as one, three, six, ten or even one, two, three, four). This would reduce the number of answers required by one fifth. The results within some of the subscales also suggest a certain amount of redundancy, and some topics might be omitted without serious loss of information. And a few items (surprisingly few) might be simplified through rephrasing.

The data were processed by computer: Chi-squares were employed to test the significance of the categorical data found in the Stranger Scale and Acquaintance Inventory (as well as on the Instrument Evaluation and Desired Future Relationship questions); ANOVAS were computed for each of the subsequent subscales, and one-way and two-way analyses of variance were calculated to test the reliability of differences in overall scores and topical and target person differences within subscales.

The computations revealed that the cultures resembled and differed from each other with respect to behavior with strangers and on the attributes of the companions in the social circles of respondents. (See details in Chapters 3–9.) Extremely high levels of significance (.001) differentiated the cultures with respect to "interaction patterns," "verbal communicative behavior," and "physical communicative behavior" (all above .001). Significant differences were found with respect to accommodation to the needs of partners and extent of incorporation of the other as part of the self. No reliable cultural difference was found with regard to the management of differences except that the mode of resolution varied from topic to topic (but not from partner to partner). In short, the similarities and differences reported can be viewed with considerable confidence, the statistical tests exceeding not only the .05 and .01 levels of probability but in most cases the .001 level as well.

References

Prologue

1. Robert O. Brain, *Friends and Lovers* (New York: Basic Books, 1976), p. 12.
2. Alfred North Whitehead, *Science and the Modern World* (London: Cambridge University Press, 1932), p. 70.
3. Gregory Stone and Harvey Faberman, eds., *Social Psychology Through Symbolic Interaction* (Waltham, Mass.: Xerox Publishing, 1970), p. 89.
4. Edward Hall, *The Silent Language* (Greenwich, Conn.: Fawcett Publications, 1961), p. 93.
5. The needs of the specialist and generalist need to be equally respected. For this reason the text has been prepared, as far as possible, to provide a readable account of social behavior in Japan and the United States. The data have been subordinated to the issues to which they apply and statistical jargon has been avoided. Accuracy, however, has not been compromised.
6. The physical world places constraints upon meanings; the social world does not. Social reality is, truly, a fiction, a fabrication of its authors who, by their commitment to this fiction, transform it into reality. One does not have freedom in interpreting the physical world; one who defines breathing as unnecessary will not survive long. But the person who defines someone as an enemy, and acts on that interpretation, will probably provoke hostile attitudes and acts from them.
7. George Homans, *Social Behavior: Its Elementary Forms* (New York: Harcourt Brace Jovanovich, 1961), p. 1.
8. Members of Bellagio Consortium, "Reconstituting the Human Community" (New Haven: Hazen Foundation, 1972), p. 12.

Chapter 1

1. Maurice Friedman, *Martin Buber: The Life of Dialogue* (New York: Harper & Row, 1960), p. 122.
2. T. S. Eliot, "The Hollow Men," in *T. S. Eliot: The Complete Poems and Plays* (New York: Harcourt Brace Jovanovich, 1962), p. 83.
3. Eliot, "The Cocktail Party," in *T. S. Eliot*, p. 360.
4. Kaneko Mitsuharu, "Song of Loneliness," in *Contemporary Japanese Literature*, ed. Howard Hibbett (New York: Knopf, 1977), p. 314.
5. Arthur Kimball, *Crisis in Identity in Contemporary Japanese Literature* (Rutland, Vt.: Tuttle, 1973), p. 10.
6. Yamanouchi Hisaaki, *The Search for Authenticity in Modern Japanese Literature* (Cambridge, England: Cambridge University Press, 1978).
7. Mishima Yukio, *The Sailor Who Fell from Grace with the Sea*, trans. John Nathan (New York: Knopf, 1965), p. 51.
8. Edward Albee, *The Zoo Story and Other Plays* (New York: Coward-McCann, 1960), p. 43.
9. Eugène Ionesco, "The Bald Prima Donna," in *Plays* (London: Calder, 1958), p. 115.
10. Samuel Beckett, "Waiting for Godot," in *I Can't Go On, I'll Go On*, ed. Richard Seaver (New York: Grove, 1976), pp. 436–437.
11. Eliot, "Four Quartets," in *T. S. Eliot*, p. 121.

12. Abe Kobo, *Friends*, trans. Donald Keene (New York: Grove, 1969), p. 23.
13. Paul Tillich, *New Images of Man* (New York: Museum of Modern Art, 1959), p. 9.
14. Jacques Dupin, *Joan Miró: Life and Work* (New York: Abrams, 1959), p. 375.
15. Robert Kolker, *A Cinema of Loneliness* (Oxford, England: Oxford University Press, 1980), p. 11.
16. Paul Simon and Arthur Garfunkel, "Dangling Conversations," in *Paul Simon Complete* (New York: Warner, 1978), pp. 83–85.
17. Abraham Kaplan, "The Life of Dialogue," in *Communication*, ed. John Roshansky (Amsterdam: North-Holland, n.d.), p. 95.
18. Martin Buber, *The Way of Man* (London: Routledge and Kegan Paul, 1950), p. 20.
19. Michael McIntyre, *The Shogun Inheritance* (London: Collins, 1981), p. 180.
20. Mita Munesuke, "Patterns of Alienation in Contemporary Japan," *Journal of Social and Political Ideas in Japan* 5 (1967): 139.
21. William Schutz, *FIRO: A Three-Dimensional Theory of Interpersonal Behavior* (New York: Holt, Rinehart and Winston, 1960).
22. Helen Lynd, *On Shame and the Search for Identity* (London: Routledge and Kegan Paul, 1958), p. 46.
23. Franz Boas, "The Ethnological Significance of Esoteric Doctrines," *Science* 15 (1902): 874.

Chapter 2

1. Philip Slater, *The Pursuit of Loneliness* (Boston: Beacon, 1970), p. 7.
2. Nothing exists apart from some context, natural or artificial. It is in the character of interaction with the challenges of the environment, physical and social, that an organism most fully reveals its nature. See, for example, Roger Barker, *Ecological Psychology* (Stanford, Calif.: Stanford University Press, 1968).
3. John Pfeiffer, *The Emergence of Society* (New York: McGraw-Hill, 1977), p. 41.
4. Pfeiffer, *Emergence of Society*, p. 28.
5. Eric Hoffer, *The Temper of Our Time* (New York: Harper & Row, 1967), pp. 14–16.
6. See Pietro Tapinos, *Six Billion People* (New York: McGraw-Hill, 1978) and Colin McEvedy and Richard Jones, *Atlas of World Population History* (New York: Penguin, 1978).
7. Jonas Salk and Jonathan Salk, *World Population and Human Values* (New York: Harper & Row, 1981), p. 29.
8. Quentin Stanford, *The World's Population* (New York: Oxford University, 1972), p. 35.
9. Statistics Bureau, Prime Minister's Office, *Statistical Handbook of Japan*. (Tokyo: Kogei, 1982); *Statistical Abstract of the United States* (Washington, D.C.: Superintendent of Documents, 1982).
10. Salk and Salk, *World Population*, pp. 102–104.
11. Desmond Morris, *The Naked Ape* (London: Cape, 1967), p. 185.
12. Arnold Toynbee, "Has Man's Metropolitan Environment Any Precedent?" in *Human Identity in the Urban Environment*, ed. Gwen Bell and Jacqueline Tyrwhitt (New York: Penguin, 1972), p. 84.
13. Christopher Alexander, "The City as a Mechanism for Sustaining Human

Contact," in *Environment for Man: The Next Fifty Years,* ed. William Ewald (Bloomington: Indiana University Press, 1967), pp. 60–120.

14. Robert Brain, *Friends and Lovers* (New York: Basic Books, 1976), p. 257.

15. Ernest van der Haag, "Of Happiness and Despair We Have No Measure," in *Man Alone,* ed. E. and M. Josephson (New York: Dell, 1962), p. 184.

16. Alexander, "The City as a Mechanism," *Environment for Man,* p. 60.

17. Lyn H. Lofland, *A World of Strangers* (New York: Basic Books, 1973), p. 176.

18. Stanley Milgram, "The Experience of Living in Cities," *Science* 5, January–March, 1970, p. 1461.

19. Lofland, *World of Strangers,* p. 83.

20. Lee McEvoy, as quoted in *The Gater,* San Francisco State University, 5 January 1968, p. 3.

21. Vance Packard, *A Nation of Strangers* (New York: McKay, 1972), p. 198.

22. Warren Bennis and Philip Slater, *The Temporary Society* (New York: Harper & Row, 1968).

23. Delos Three, "Living in High Densities," in Bell and Tyrwhitt, *Human Identity,* p. 212.

24. Charles Peguy and Robert Hughes, *Shock of the New* (New York: Knopf, 1981), p. 9.

25. Kenneth Kenniston, *The Uncommitted* (New York: Delta, 1965), p. 212.

26. Margaret Mead, *Culture and Commitment* (New York: Doubleday, 1970).

27. Edwin Reischauer, *The Japanese* (Cambridge, Mass.: Harvard University Press, 1982), p. 231.

28. Frieda Fromm-Reichman in L. and N. Zunin, *Contact: The First Four Minutes* (New York: Ballantine, 1974), p. 8.

29. Packard, *Nation of Strangers,* p. 198.

30. Slater, *Pursuit of Loneliness.*

31. Ronald Laing, *The Politics of Experience* (New York: Ballantine, 1967), p. 53.

32. Herman Lantz, "Number of Childhood Friends as Reported in the Life Histories of a Psychiatrically Diagnosed Group of 1,000," *Marriage and Family Living* 18 (1956): 107–108.

33. Nishiyama Kazuo, "Images as Barriers to Intercultural Communication" (Paper presented at the Communication Association of the Pacific, June 1981).

34. Dean Barnlund, *Public and Private Self in Japan and United States* (Tokyo: Simul Press, 1973).

35. Roland Penrose, *Scrapbook* (New York: Rizzoli, 1981), p. 290.

Chapter 3

1. Harry F. Harlow, *Learning to Love* (San Francisco: Albion, 1971).

2. For a more complete résumé of the facts that support these generalizations, see the *U.S. Statistical Abstracts* and *White Papers of Japan: Annual Abstract of Official Reports and Statistics of the Japanese Government* (Tokyo: Institute of International Affairs, 1982).

3. William Caudill, "The Influence of Social Structure and Culture on Human Behavior in Modern Japan," *Journal of Nervous and Mental Disorders* 157 (1973): 255.

4. Ralph Waldo Emerson, "Self Reliance," in *Selected Writings of R. W. Emerson,* ed. Brooks Atkinson (New York: Random House, 1950), p. 148.

5. Nakane Chie, *Japanese Society* (Berkeley: University of California Press, 1970).

6. Student paper, intercultural communication class, San Francisco State University, 1978.

7. Edwin O. Reischauer, *The Japanese* (Cambridge, Mass.: Harvard University Press, 1981), p. 163.

8. Nakane Chie, "You and Me," in *Introducing Japan*, ed. Paul Norbury (New York: St. Martin's Press, 1977).

9. Nakane, *Japanese Society*, p. 10.

10. Urie Bronfenbrenner, "Alienation and the American Psychologist," *American Psychological Association Monitor* 5 (1975): 2.

11. Fritz Perls, *Gestalt Therapy Verbatim* (San Francisco: Real People Press, 1980), p. 4.

12. Doi Takeo, *The Anatomy of Dependence*, trans. John Bester (Tokyo: Kodansha, 1973).

13. Robert Ozaki, *The Japanese: A Cultural Portrait* (Tokyo: Tuttle, 1978), pp. 182, 195.

14. Student paper, 1978.

15. Dean C. Barnlund, *Public and Private Self in Japan and United States* (Tokyo: Simul Press, 1975), p. 130.

16. Kurt Singer, *Mirror, Sword and Jewel* (Tokyo: Kodansha, 1973), p. 63.

17. Barnlund, *Public and Private Self*, p. 129.

18. Harumi Befu, "Japan and America: How We See Each Other," United States–Japan Trade Council, 1973, p. 6.

19. Jack Seward, *The Japanese* (New York: Morrow, 1972), p. 31.

20. Ozaki, *Japanese: A Cultural Portrait*, p. 189.

21. Emory Bogardus, "A Social Distance Scale," *Sociology and Social Research* 17 (1925): 299–308.

22. Paul Wright, "The Delineation and Measurement of Some Key Variables in the Study of Friendship," *Representative Research in Social Psychology* 5 (1974): 93–96.

23. Clifford Swenson, "Love: A Self-Report Analysis with College Students," *Journal of Individual Psychology* 17 (1961): 167–171.

24. Irwin Altman and Dalmas Taylor, *Social Penetration: The Development of Interpersonal Relationships* (New York: Holt, Rinehart and Winston, 1973).

25. N. A. Polansky, E. Weiss, and A. Blum, "Verbal Accessibility in Maladjustment and Wellness" (Paper presented at American Psychological Association Convention, Philadelphia, 1961).

26. Mary Parlee, "The Friendship Bond," *Psychology Today* 12, no. 4 (1979): 43–114.

27. See Charles Frake, *Language and Description* (Stanford, Calif.: Stanford University Press, 1982); Nomura Naoki and Dean C. Barnlund, "Patterns of Interpersonal Criticism in Japan and United States," *International Journal of Intercultural Communication* 7 (1983): 1–18; Dean C. Barnlund and Shoko Araki, "Intercultural Encounters: The Management of Compliments by Japanese and Americans," *Journal of Cross-Cultural Psychology* 16 (1985): 9–26.

Chapter 4

1. Abe Kobo, *Friends* (New York: Grove, 1969), p. 55.

2. Lyn Lofland, *A World of Strangers* (New York: Basic Books, 1973), p. 12.

3. Arnold Toynbee, "Has Man's Metropolitan Environment Any Precedent?" in *Human Identity in the Urban Environment*, ed. Gwen Bell and Jacqueline Tyrwhitt (London: Penguin, 1972), p. 15.

4. Lofland, *World of Strangers*, p. ix.

5. Margaret Wood, *The Stranger* (New York: Columbia University Press, 1934), p. 221.

6. Wood, *The Stranger*, p. 231.

7. Elaine Walster and William Walster, *A New Look at Love* (Menlo Park: Addison-Wesley, 1978), p. 128.

8. Erving Goffman, *Behavior in Public Places* (New York: Free Press, 1963), p. 24.

9. Goffman, *Behavior*, p. 140.

10. Leonard Doob, *Pathways to People* (New Haven, Conn.: Yale University Press, 1975), p. 211.

11. Abraham S. Luchins and Edith Luchins, "Effects of Preconceptions and Communications on Impressions of a Person," *Journal of Social Psychology* 81 (1970): 243–252.

12. The term "stereotype" is much abused, often employed to derogate someone else's image that differs from our own. Images are tentative, stereotypes are not; they are images that have congealed to the extent that they resist alteration in the face of evidence that they are incorrect. An image of the other person, subject to continuing refinement, is essential for any effort to communicate.

13. Fosco Maraini, *Tokyo* (Amsterdam: Time-Life Books, 1976), p. 137.

14. Myron Brenton, *Friendship* (New York: Stein and Day, 1974), p. 116.

15. Lofland, *World of Strangers*, p. 176.

16. Lofland, *World of Strangers*, p. 82.

17. Alexis de Tocqueville, *Democracy in America* (New York: Mentor, 1956), p. 222. (Originally published 1835.)

18. Kurt Lewin, *Resolving Social Conflicts* (New York: Harper & Row, 1948), p. 18.

19. Robert Ozaki, *The Japanese* (Tokyo: Tuttle, 1978), pp. 186–187.

20. Nakane Chie, "You and Me," in *Introducing Japan*, ed. Paul Norbury (New York: St. Martin's Press, 1977), p. 57.

21. Morita Shoma, as quoted in Herbert Passin, *Japan and the Japanese* (Tokyo: Kinseido, 1980), p. 115.

22. Kano Tsutomu, ed., *The Silent Power* (Tokyo: Simul, 1976), p. 8.

23. Ozaki, *The Japanese*, p. 209.

24. Edward Seidensticker, as quoted in Martin Hurlimann and Francis Kind, *Japan* (New York: Viking, 1970), p. 11.

25. From the Stranger Scale in Barnlund-Campbell's Dimensions of Interpersonal Relations, 1975.

26. Barnlund-Campbell's Dimensions of Interpersonal Relations.

27. Emil Durkheim, *Sociology and Philosophy* (Glencoe, Ill.: Free Press, 1953), p. 37.

28. Wood, *The Stranger*, p. 224.

29. Abraham Kaplan, "The Life of Dialogue," in *Communication*, ed. John Roslansky (Amsterdam: North Holland, n.d.), p. 102.

30. Abe, *Friends*, p. 18.

Chapter 5

1. Tony Jones, "Friends: Making the Connection," *Harper's*, August 1973, p. 3.

2. Roger Barker, *Ecological Psychology* (Stanford, Calif.: Stanford University Press, 1968), p. 145.

3. Mary Parlee, "The Friendship Bond," *Psychology Today* 12, no. 4 (1979): 113.

4. Myron Brenton, *Friendship* (New York: Stein and Day, 1974), p. 130.

5. Graham Allan, A *Sociology of Friendship and Kinship* (London: Allen and Unwin, 1979), p. 139.

6. Erving Goffman, *Relations in Public* (New York: Harper & Row, 1971), p. 193.

7. From the Acquaintance Inventory in Barnlund-Campbell's Dimensions of Interpersonal Relations, 1975.

8. Blaise Pascal, as quoted in W. Barrett, *Irrational Man: A Study in Existential Philosophy* (New York: Doubleday, 1962).

9. Allan, *Sociology of Friendship*, p. 43.

10. Mary Parlee, "The Friendship Bond," p. 113.

11. Jane Howard, "All Happy Clans are Alike," *Atlantic Monthly*, May 1978, p. 37.

12. Joel Block, *Friendship* (New York: Macmillan, 1980), p. 220.

13. George Homans, *Social Behavior: Its Elementary Forms* (New York: Harcourt Brace Jovanovich, 1961).

14. Parlee, "The Friendship Bond," p. 49.

15. Carol Werner and Pat Parmelee, "Similarity of Activity Preferences Among Friends: Those Who Play Together Stay Together," *Social Psychology Quarterly* 42 (1979): 62–66.

16. Derek Phillips, "Social Participation and Happiness," *The American Journal of Sociology* 72 (1967): 479–488.

17. From the Interact Scale in Barnlund-Campbell's Dimensions of Interpersonal Relations, 1975.

18. Allan, *Sociology of Friendship*.

19. Brenton, *Friendship*, p.14.

Chapter 6

1. Ashley Montagu and Floyd Matson, *The Human Connection* (New York: McGraw-Hill, 1979), p. ix.

2. Eduard Lindeman and T. V. Smith, *The Democratic Way of Life* (New York: Mentor, 1951), pp. 105–106.

3. Paul Goodman, "On Not Speaking," New York Review. *New York Times Book Review*, 20 May 1971, p. 41.

4. Michel Montaigne, "On Conversation," in *Selected Essays*, ed. Blanchard Bates (New York: Modern Library, 1949), p. 412.

5. Edward Albee, *The Zoo Story and Other Plays* (New York: Coward-McCann, 1960), p. 19.

6. Paul Watzlawick, Janet Beavin, and Don Jackson, *Pragmatics of Human Communication* (New York: Norton, 1967).

7. Goodman, "On Not Speaking," p. 42.

8. Gregory Bateson, *Steps to an Ecology of Mind* (New York: Ballantine, 1972), pp. 9–13.

9. Charles Cooley, *Human Nature and the Social Order* (New York: Scribner's, 1902).

10. George Herbert Mead, *Mind, Self and Society* (Chicago: University of Chicago Press, 1934).

11. Georg Simmel, *The Sociology of Georg Simmel* (New York: Free Press, 1950). (Originally published in 1908.)

12. Irwin Altman and Dalmas Taylor, *Social Penetration* (New York: Holt, Rinehart and Winston, 1973), p. 7.

13. Dean Barnlund, *Public and Private Self in Japan and United States* (Tokyo: Simul Press, 1975).

14. Sidney Jourard, *The Transparent Personality* (New York: Van Nostrand, 1964), p. 25.

15. Jourard, *Transparent Personality*, p. 103.

16. Maria A. Rickers-Ovsiankina and Arnold A. Kusmin, "Individual Differences in Social Accessibility," *Psychological Reports* 4 (1958): 403.

17. Michael Argyle, *The Psychology of Interpersonal Behaviour* (London: Penguin, 1967), p. 60.

18. Altman and Taylor, *Social Penetration*, pp. 41–42.

19. Dalmas Taylor and Irwin Altman, "Intimacy Scaled Stimuli for Use in Studies of Interpersonal Relationships" (Mimeographed research report no. 9, Naval Medical Research Institute, Bethesda, Maryland, 1960).

20. Shirley J. Gilbert, "Empirical and Theoretical Extensions of Self Disclosure," in *Explorations in Interpersonal Communication*, ed. Gerald Miller (Beverly Hills, Calif.: Sage, 1976), p. 205.

21. Charles Berger, Royce Gardner, Glen Clatterbuck, and Linda Schulman, "Perceptions of Information Sequencing in Relationship Development" (Mimeographed report, Northwestern University, Department of Communication Studies, n.d.).

22. Charles Berger, "The Acquaintance Process Revisited: Explorations in Interaction" (Paper presented at Speech Communication Association Convention, New York, December 1973).

23. Joseph Luft, *Of Human Interaction* (Palo Alto, Calif.: National Press, 1969), p. 126.

24. Peter Kelvin, "Predictability, Power and Vulnerability in Interpersonal Attraction," in *Theory and Practice in Interpersonal Attraction*, ed. Steve Duck (New York: Academic Press, 1977), p. 363.

25. Kelvin, "Predictability," p. 369.

26. Kelvin, "Predictability," p. 373.

27. Barnlund, *Public and Private Self*.

28. Maureen D'Honnau, "Question of the Week: Do You Have Many Japanese Friends?" *Japan Times*, 30 September 1979, p. 8.

29. From the Verbal Communication Scale in Barnlund-Campbell's Dimensions of Interpersonal Relations, 1975.

30. Pablo Picasso, as quoted in Alexander Liberman, *The Artist in His Studio* (New York: Viking, 1968), p. 115.

31. Luft, *Of Human Interaction*, p. 219.

32. Takie Lebra, "Shame and Guilt: A Psychocultural View of the Japanese Self," *Ethos* 11 (Fall 1983): 193.

33. Robert Guillain, *The Japan I Love* (New York: Tudor, n.d.), p. 11.

34. Edward Seidensticker, "Review of the Japanese Language in Contemporary Japan," *Journal of the Association of Teachers of Japanese* 13 (1978): 202.

35. Ishii Satoshi and Donald Klopf, "A Comparison of Communication Activities of Japanese and American Adults" (Paper presented at the Communication Association of the Pacific, Tokyo, 1975).

36. Robert Ozaki, *The Japanese: A Cultural Portrait* (Tokyo: Tuttle, 1978), p. 229.

37. Eto Jun, "Japanese Shyness with Foreigners," in *Introducing Japan*, ed. Paul Norbury (New York: St. Martin's Press, 1977), p. 75.

38. Kurt Singer, *Mirror, Sword and Jewel* (Tokyo: Kodansha, 1973), p. 46.

39. Doi Takeo, "The Mind and Secrets," in *The Anatomy of Self* (Tokyo: Kodansha, 1985).

40. Edith Ching Hayama, "Getting to Know You," *Japan Times*, 5 July 1984, p. 12.
41. Albee, *Zoo Story*, p. 43.
42. Barnlund, *Public and Private Self*, p. 155.

Chapter 7

1. Ashley Montagu and Floyd Matson, *The Human Connection* (New York: McGraw-Hill, 1979), pp. 87–88.
2. Julius Fast, *Body Language* (New York: Pocket Books, 1971), p. 6.
3. Albert Mehrabian, *Silent Messages* (Belmont, Calif.: Wadsworth, 1971), p. 44.
4. See Jurgen Ruesch and Weldon Kees, *Nonverbal Communication* (Berkeley: University of California Press, 1956).
5. Desmond Morris, *Manwatching: A Field Guide to Human Behavior* (New York: Abrams, 1977), p. 24.
6. Frank Trippet, "Why So Much Is Beyond Words," *Time*, 13 July 1981, p. 71.
7. Arnold Shapiro and Clifford Swenson, "Patterns of Self-Disclosure Among Married Couples," *Journal of Counseling Psychology* 16 (1969): 179.
8. John Bardeen, "Interpersonal Perception Through the Tactile, Verbal and Visual Modes" (M.A. thesis, San Francisco State University, 1970).
9. Ruesch and Kees, *Nonverbal Communication*.
10. Miles Patterson, "Stability of Nonverbal Immediacy Behaviors," *Journal of Experimental Social Psychology* 9 (1973): 97–109.
11. Erving Goffman, *Relations in Public* (New York: Colophon, 1971), p. 248.
12. Edwin O. Reischauer, *The Japanese* (Cambridge, Mass.: Harvard University Press, 1981), pp. 34–35.
13. Reischauer, *The Japanese*, p. 137.
14. Roy Miller, *Japan's Modern Myth* (Tokyo: Weatherhill, 1982), p. 85.
15. Thomas Muller, as quoted in Colleen Cordes, "Immigration: Mix of Cultures Stirs Old Fears," *American Psychological Association Monitor* 15 (1984): 1.
16. Erving Goffman, *Presentation of Self in Everyday Life* (New York: Doubleday/Anchor, 1959), p. 2.
17. From the Physical Communication Scale in Barnlund-Campbell's Dimensions of Interpersonal Relations, 1975.
18. Edward T. Hall, *The Silent Language* (New York: Fawcett, 1966), p. 15.
19. Ralph Waldo Emerson, "On Gifts and Presents," in *Emerson's Essays* (Philadelphia: Spencer, 1936).
20. Marcel Mauss, *The Gift* (New York: Free Press, 1954), p. 18.
21. Robert Brain, *Friends and Lovers* (New York: Basic Books, 1976), p. 147.
22. Erving Goffman, *Behavior in Public Places* (New York: Free Press, 1963), p. 124.
23. Morris, *Manwatching*, p. 131.
24. Edward T. Hall, *The Hidden Dimension* (New York: Doubleday, 1969).
25. Nan Sussman and Howard Rosenfeld, "Influence of Culture, Language and Sex on Conversational Distance," *Journal of Personality and Social Psychology* 42 (1982): 67–74.
26. Sussman and Rosenfeld, "Conversational Distance," p. 73.
27. Mark Knapp, *Nonverbal Communication in Human Interaction* (New York: Holt, Rinehart and Winston, 1972), pp. 107–108.
28. J. L. Taylor, as quoted in Montagu and Matson, *Human Connection*, pp. 88–89.
29. Nancy Henley, "Power, Sex and Nonverbal Communication," *Berkeley Journal of Sociology* 18 (1932): 1–26.

30. See William Caudill and Helen Weinstein, "Maternal Care and Infant Behavior in Japan and America," *Psychiatry* 32 (1969): 12–43; William Caudill and C. Schroeder, "Child Behavior and Child Rearing in Japan and United States: An Interim Report," *Journal of Nervous and Mental Diseases* 157 (1973): 240–241; William Caudill and David Plath, "Who Sleeps with Whom? Parent-Child Involvement in Urban Japanese Families," *Psychiatry* 29 (1966): 344–366.

31. Michael O. Watson, *Proxemic Behavior: A Cross-Cultural Study* (The Hague: Mouton, 1970).

32. Sidney Jourard, "An Exploratory Study of Body Accessibility," *British Journal of Social and Clinical Psychology* 5 (1966): 221–231.

33. Dean Barnlund, *Public and Private Self in Japan and United States* (Tokyo: Simul Press, 1975).

34. Rob Elzinga, "Nonverbal Communication: Body Accessibility Among Japanese," *Psychologia* 18 (1975): 205–211.

35. Darhl Pedersen, "Self-Disclosure, Body-Accessibility and Personal Space," *Psychological Reports* 33 (1973): 975–980.

36. Peter Kelvin, "Predictability, Power and Vulnerability in Interpersonal Attraction," in *Theory and Practice in Interpersonal Attraction*, ed. Steve Duck (New York: Academic Press, 1977), p. 374.

37. J. LaPlanche and J. Pontanlis, *The Language of Psychoanalysis* (New York: Norton, 1974), p. 418.

38. Harry Harlow, *Learning to Love* (San Francisco: Albion, 1971), p. 45.

39. Harlow, *Learning to Love*, p. 35.

40. Milton J. Wayne, "An Experimental Study of the Meaning of Silence in Three Cultures" (M.A. thesis, International Christian University, 1973).

41. Edward Seidensticker, *Japanese and Americans* (Tokyo: Asahi Press, 1977), p. 54.

42. Miller, *Japan's Modern Myth*.

43. Hall, *Silent Language*, p. 139.

44. Thomas Bruneau, "Communicative Silences: Forms and Functions," *Journal of Communication* 23 (1973): 17–46.

45. Richard L. Johannsen, "The Functions of Silence: A Plea for Communication Research," *Western Speech* 38 (1974): 25–35.

Chapter 8

1. Ronald Laing, *The Self and Others* (London: Tavistock, 1961), p. 127.

2. Richard Sutherland, "An Anatomy of Loving," *Journal of Religion and Health* 11 (1972): 167–174.

3. John J. LaGaipa, "Testing a Multidimensional Approach," in *Theory and Practice in Interpersonal Attraction*, ed. Steve Duck (New York: Academic Press, 1977).

4. Vance Packard, *A Nation of Strangers* (New York: McKay, 1972).

5. Irwin Altman and Dalmas Taylor, *Social Penetration* (New York: Holt, Rinehart and Winston, 1973).

6. O'Hara, "What Would You Refuse to Lend?" *San Francisco Chronicle*, 17 July 1977, p. 8.

7. Arthur Miller, "Arthur Miller Ponders 'The Price'," *New York Times*, 28 January 1968, p. D5.

8. John J. LaGaipa, "Interpersonal Attraction and Social Exchange," in Duck, *Interpersonal Attraction*.

9. Alan Gross and Julie Latané, "Receiving Help, Reciprocation, and Interpersonal Attraction," *Journal of Applied Social Psychology* 4 (1974): 220.

10. U. G. Foa, "Interpersonal and Economic Resources," *Science* 171 (1971): 345–351.

11. Lee Beach and William Carter, "Appropriate and Equitable Repayment of Social Debts," *Organizational Behavior and Human Performance* 16 (1976): 280–293.

12. Gerald Chasin, "A Study of the Determinants of Friendship Choice and the Content of the Friendship Relationship," *Dissertation Abstracts* 29 (1968): 681.

13. Ruth Benedict, *The Chrysanthemum and the Sword* (Boston: Houghton Mifflin, 1946), p. 104.

14. Michael Argyle, *The Psychology of Interpersonal Relations* (New York: Penguin, 1967), p. 118.

15. Leslie Miller, "Intimacy," in *Friends, Enemies and Strangers*, ed. Alan Blum and Peter McHugh (Norwood, Mass.: Ablex, 1979), p. 169.

16. Michael Roloff, "Communication Strategies, Relationals, and Relational Change," in *Explorations in Interpersonal Communication*, ed. Gerald Miller (Beverly Hills, Calif.: Sage, 1976), p. 193.

17. Leslie A. Baxter and Tara L. Shepherd, "Sex Role Identity, Sex of Other, and Affective Relationship as Determinants of Interpersonal Conflict Rules" (Paper presented at the Western Speech Communication Association Convention, 1976), p. 4.

18. Fred N. Kerlinger, "Decision-Making in Japan," *Social Forces* 30 (1951): 36.

19. Robert Ozaki, *The Japanese: A Cultural Portrait* (Tokyo: Tuttle, 1978), p. 232.

20. Richard Halloran, *Japan: Images and Realities* (New York: Knopf, 1969), p. 231.

21. Harumi Befu, "Japan and America: How We See Each Other," *United States–Japan Trade Council* (Washington, D.C.: 1973), p. 6.

22. Ozaki, *The Japanese*, p. 228.

23. Nakane Chie, *Human Relations in Japanese Society* (Tokyo: Ministry of Foreign Affairs, 1972), p. 84.

24. Shirono Itsuo, "Decision-Making: A Cross-Cultural Perspective," *Communication* 7 (1982): 196–212.

25. Robert E. Kaplan, "Maintaining Interpersonal Relationships," *Interpersonal Development* 6 (1975): 106.

26. William James, "The Social Self," in *Psychology* (New York: Holt, Rinehart and Winston, 1892), p. 190.

27. Carson McCullers, *Member of the Wedding* (New York: New Directions, 1951): 51.

28. George Santayana, as quoted in Joel Block, *Friendship* (New York: Macmillan, 1980), p. 198.

29. Wilson Van Dusen, in Carl Rogers, Barry Peterson, et al., *Person to Person: The Problem of Being Human* (Walnut Creek, Calif.: Real People Press, 1967), p. 229.

30. Robert H. Katz, *Empathy: Its Nature and Uses* (New York: Free Press, 1963), pp. 41–47.

31. Rosalind Dymond, "A Scale for the Measurement of Empathic Ability," *Journal of Consulting Psychology* 13 (1949): 127–133.

32. Milton J. Bennett, "Overcoming the Golden Rule: Sympathy and Empathy," in *Communication Yearbook*, ed. Dan Nimmo (International Communication Association, 1979), p. 422.

33. Harry Stack Sullivan, *Concepts of Modern Psychiatry* (Washington, D.C.: William Alanson White Psychiatric Foundation, 1947), p. 20.

34. Carrie Snodgrass, in Bart Mills, "Whatever Happened to Carrie Snodgrass?" Datebook, *San Francisco Sunday Chronicle and Examiner*, 7 May 1978, p. 17.

35. Irwin Mahler, "What Is the Self-Concept in Japan?" *Psychologia* 19 (1976): 132.

36. Edwin O. Reischauer, *The Japanese* (Cambridge, Mass.: Harvard University Press, 1982), p. 146.

37. Ozaki, *The Japanese*, p. 184.

38. From the Affiliation Scale in Barnlund-Campbell's Dimensions of Interpersonal Relations, 1975.

Chapter 9

1. John Pfeiffer, *The Emergence of Society* (New York: McGraw-Hill, 1977), p. 86.

2. William Barrett, "The Decline of Religion," in E. and M. Josephson, *Man Alone* (New York: Dell, 1962), p. 169.

3. Abraham Kaplan, "The Life of Dialogue," in *Communication*, ed. John Roslansky (Amsterdam: North-Holland, n.d.), p. 102.

4. Paul Goodman, *Utopian Essays and Practical Proposals* (New York: Vintage, 1962), p. 257.

5. John Gardner, *No Easy Victories* (New York: Harper & Row, 1968), p. 26.

6. Hannah Arendt, *The Human Condition* (New York: Doubleday, 1958), p. 48.

7. Christopher Alexander, "The City as a Mechanism for Sustaining Human Contact," in *Environment for Man: The Next 50 Years*, ed. W. R. Ewald (Bloomington: Indiana University Press, 1967), p. 62.

8. Edgar Friedenberg, *Coming of Age in America* (New York: Vintage, 1965), p. 240.

9. Alexander, "City as a Mechanism," p. 61.

10. Frieda Fromm-Reichman, "Loneliness," *Psychiatry* 22 (1959): 3.

11. Robert Brain, *Friends and Lovers* (New York: Basic Books, 1976), p. 209.

12. Arendt, *Human Condition*, p. 4.

13. Plato, *The Republic*, transl. B. Jowett (New York: Heritage Press, 1944), Book 7, p. 363.

14. Gregory Bateson, *Mind and Nature* (New York: Bantam, 1979), p. 33.

15. Mary Parlee, "The Friendship Bond," *Psychology Today* 12, no. 4 (1979): 43.

16. George Homans, *Social Behavior: Its Elementary Forms* (New York: Harcourt Brace Jovanovich, 1961).

17. Edward Norbeck and George DeVos, "Culture and Personality: The Japanese," in *Psychological Anthropology*, ed. Francis Hsu (Cambridge: Schenkman, 1972), p. 52.

18. Nakane Chie, *Japanese Society* (Berkeley: University of California Press, 1970), p. 20.

19. Doi Takeo, "Amae: A Key Concept for Understanding Japanese Personality Structure," in *Japanese Culture: Its Development and Characteristics*, ed. Robert Smith and Richard Beardsley (Chicago: Aldine, 1962), p. 133.

20. Robert Ozaki, *The Japanese: A Cultural Portrait* (Tokyo: Tuttle, 1978), p. 189.

21. Edwin Reischauer, *The Japanese* (Cambridge, Mass.: Harvard University Press, 1981), p. 231.

22. Roger Rosenblatt, "The Rugged Individual Rides Again," *Time*, 15 October 1984, p. 116.

23. Doi Takeo, *The Anatomy of Dependence* (Tokyo: Kodansha International, 1973).

24. Matsuyama Yukio, "A Candid Letter from Japan to America," This World, *San Francisco Sunday Chronicle and Examiner*, 26 October 1980, p. 35.

25. Henry Grunwald, "Loving America," *Time*, 5 July 1976, p. 36.

26. David MacEachron, "What Can Americans Learn from Japan?" *International House Bulletin* (Summer 1983): 2.

27. Alexis de Tocqueville, *Democracy in America* (New York: Mentor, 1956), p. 221. (Originally published 1835.) In an earlier comparative study, *Public and Private Self in Japan and United States*, some Japanese felt descriptions of the United States were unfair to Americans, and some Americans felt that descriptions of the Japanese were unfair to Japanese. This is an understandable reaction when one realizes that Japanese readers were evaluating American culture on the basis of Japanese values, and Americans were evaluating Japanese culture on the basis of American values. Both saw the other as deficient in at least some of their own most valued attributes.

28. Hermann Hesse, *Steppenwolf* (New York: Holt, Rinehart and Winston, 1957), p. 24.

29. Ernest Becker, *The Birth and Death of Meaning* (New York: Free Press, 1962), p. 82.

30. Milton J. Bennett, "Overcoming the Golden Rule: Sympathy and Empathy," in *Communication Yearbook*, ed. Dan Nimmo (International Communication Association, 1979), p. 408.

31. George Packard, "A Crisis in Understanding," in *Discord in the Pacific*, ed. Henry Rosovsky (Washington, D.C.: Columbia, 1972), p. 130.

32. Charles Krauthammer, "Deep Down, We're All Alike, Right? Wrong," *Time*, 15 August 1983, p. 32.

33. Hermann Hesse, *Demian* (New York: Bantam Books, 1965), p. 122.

34. Sheila Ramsey, "Double Vision: Nonverbal Behavior East and West" (Paper presented at Second International Conference on Nonverbal Behavior, Toronto, Canada, 1983, Conference on Nonverbal Behavior), p. 33.

35. William Caudill, "The Influence of Social Structure and Culture on Human Behavior in Modern Japan," *The Journal of Nervous and Mental Diseases* 157 (1973): 255.

36. Philip Slater, *The Pursuit of Loneliness* (Boston: Beacon, 1970), p. 118.

37. S. N. Eisenstadt, "Modernization and the Dynamics of Civilization," *International House Bulletin* 5 (1985): 2.

38. Kenneth Boulding, "Foreword," in *Communicating Across Cultures for What?*, ed. John Condon and Saito Mitsuko (Tokyo: Simul Press, 1976), p. 1.

39. Boulding, "Foreword," p. 2.

40. Norman Cousins, "Modern Man Is Obsolete," in *Man's Search for Himself*, ed. Rollo May (New York: Norton, 1953), p. 27.

41. Herbert Simon, as quoted in "Herbert Simon: A Software Psychologist Who Isn't," *American Psychological Association Monitor*, April 1981, p. 15.

42. Lillian Smith, as quoted in George P. Brockway, "You Do It Because You Love Somebody," *Saturday Review*, 22 October 1966, pp. 53–54.

Index

Abe Kobo, 4, 6, 53, 71
Abstract art, 7
Accommodation Scale, 48, 151, 153
Acquaintance Description Form, 44
Acquaintance Inventory, 47, 76–77
  and demographic similarity, 78
Action language, 125
Activities profiles, 92
Adopted children, 75
Adventures of Augie March, The (Bellow),
  95
Aestheticism, 115
Affiliation, 183–184
Affiliation Scale, 164–166
Age of companions, 80
Albee, Edward, 4, 5, 99
Alexander, Christopher, 21, 173–174
"Alienation of Labor, The" (Marx), 3
Allan, Graham, 76, 80, 94
Allen, Woody, 8
Altman, Irwin, 45, 101, 103–104, 105,
  148–149
Altruism, 161
Amae theory, 41, 186
Amazonian Cosmos, The (Reichel-
  Dolmatoff), 46
Analogic symbolization, 123
Anatomy of Dependence (Doi), 150
"Anatomy of Loving, The" (Sutherland),
  147
And Yet We Live, 8
Anti-contact strategies, 20
Antonioni, Michelangelo, 8
Appendix material, 195–197
Arendt, Hannah, 172

Argyle, Michael, 104–105, 153
Aristotle, 11
Assistance, providing, 149–150
Attachment, forms of, 74–76
Attractive strangers, 65–66
Attributes of friends, 40
Auden, W. H., 74
Awareness, 164

Bald Soprano, The (Ionesco), 5
Bacon, Francis, 7
Bardeen, John, 125
Barker, Roger, 74
Barnlund-Campbell Dimensions of
  Interpersonal Relations questionnaire,
  46–51, 195–197
Barrett, William, 169–170
Bateson, Gregory, 100, 176
Baxter, Leslie, 154
Beavin, Janet, 100
Becker, Ernest, 189
Beckett, Samuel, 4, 5
Beech, Lee, 150
Befu, Harumi, 42, 156
Behavioral sciences, 11–12
Bellow, Saul, 95
Benedict, Ruth, 46, 150
Bennett, Milton, 162, 189
Bennis, Warren, 25
Berger, Charles, 105
Bergman, Ingmar, 8
Block, Joel, 86
Blow-up, 9
Boas, Franz, 13

Body Accessibility questionnaire, 140
Body language, 100
Bogardus, Emory, 44
Boulding, Kenneth, 193
Box Man, The (Abe), 4
Boy, 8
Brian, Robert, 22, 136
Brainwashing, 101
Brenton, Myron, 59, 75
Broken Heart: The Medical Consequences of
    Loneliness, The (Lynch), 30
Bronfenbrenner, Urie, 41
Bruneau, Thomas, 143
Buber, Martin, 10, 74
Buddhism, 38
Building design, 22
Buñuel, Luis, 8
Bureaucracies, 23-24

Cahokia, 17
Camus, Albert, 3
"Candid Letter from Japan to America"
    (Matsuyama), 186-187
Carter, William, 150
Casablanca, population growth of, 18
Cassatt, Mary, 7
Casual friendships, 151
Catcher in the Rye (Salinger), 3
Caudill, William, 37, 139-140, 192
Chang-Chou, 17
Chaplin, Charlie, 8
Chasin, Gerald, 150
Chrome Yellow (Huxley), 4
Chrysanthemum and the Sword (Benedict),
    150
Cinema of Loneliness, A (Kolker), 8
Cities
    adaptation to, 27-28
    first cities, 17-18
    interpersonal challenge of, 172-174
    social order of, 22-27
    supercities, 18-20
Class relationships, 94
Collaboration, 157
Collaborative relationships, 89-91
Collective myth, 13
Commitment, 147-153
    conclusions on, 183
    and culture, 150-151
Commuting, 26
Companions. See Friends
Competitive relationships, 89
Conflict, 39, 153-160
    Americans and, 157
    conclusions on, 183
    and friendship, 43
    Japanese and, 155-157
Confucianism, 38

Context-cracking, 191
Context specific relationships, 94
Contextualized self, 116
Continuity, lack of, 25-26
Contracts, 30
Conversation, 42. See also Language
    small talk, 99-100
    with strangers, 67-68
Cooley, Charles, 101
Coping strategies, 154-155
Co-presence, 89
Cousins, Norman, 193
Critical companions, 91-92
Crossroads, 8
Cultural profile
    of Japan, 38-39
    of United States, 37-38
Culture and Commitment (Mead), 25-26

Darwin, Charles, 125
Decision making, 158-160
Dehumanizing relationships, 29-30
De Kooning, Willem, 7, 8
Delicate Balance, A (Albee), 5
Democracy, 187-188
Dependence, 41
Determinism, 10
De Tocqueville, Alexis, 31, 60, 143,
    187-188
DeVos, George, 179
D'Honnau, Maureen, 108
Differences, 190
Difference Scale, 158-160
Digital symbolization, 123
Dimensions of Interpersonal Relations
    questionnaire. See Barnlund-Campbell
    Dimensions of Interpersonal Relations
    questionnaire
Disciplining children, 112, 114
Disclosure
    American style, 112-114
    Japanese style, 114-118
    pacing of, 106-107
    of self, 102-104
    verbal, 104-108
    and vulnerability, 107-108
Discrete Charm of the Bourgeoisie, The, 8
Distancing tactics, 20
Diversity of cultures, 193
Divorce, 29
Doi Takeo, 41, 117-118, 150, 185, 186
Dolce Vita, La, 8
Doob, Leonard, 57
Dostoyevski, F., 3
Dropping-in, 21-22
Dubuffet, Jean, 7
Dupin, Jacques, 7
Durability of relationships, 82-83

Durkheim, Emil, 70
Dymond, Rosalind, 162

Ecology, 15–16, 171
Education, 36–37
Efron, David, 125
Ego incorporation, 160–164
Egoism, 9
Eliot, T. S., 2, 4, 6
Elzinga, Rob, 140
Emerson, Ralph Waldo, 37, 136
Emotional disturbances, 30
Empathy, 162
Entertaining, 135–136
Environment for companions, 82
Equality, 37
  ideal of, 60
Equity principle, 149
Ethnology, 13
Eto Jun, 116
Existentialism, 9–10
*Expression of Emotions in Man and Animals,
  The* (Darwin), 125

Face of Another (Abe), 4, 8
Fads, 13, 15
Family
  as close companions, 85–86, 178
  in Japan, 38–39
  nuclear, 37
  relations with, 78–79
  strength of ties to, 84
Fast, Julius, 122
Fellini, Federico, 8
Film, as popular art, 8–9
Fine arts, 6–8
First impressions, 58–59, 125. *See also*
  Strangers
Foa, U. G., 150
Focused interactions, 56
Forced mobility, 24–25
Frake, Charles, 46
Frankness, 41
Freud, Sigmund, 125
Friedenberg, Edgar, 173
Friedman, Maurice, 1, 9
Friends
  comparisons of, 43–44
  conclusions on, 180–181
  and egoism, 9
  inaccessibility of, 21–22
  inquiries about, 44–46
  instant, 130
  relations with, 40–41
  time for, 79, 83, 134–135
Friends (Abe), 6, 71
Fromm-Reichman, Frieda, 174

Functions of communication, 174–176
Future, view of, 193

Gardner, John, 170–171
Generation gap, 25–26
Genet, Jean, 4
Genovese case, 55
Gesture and Environment (Efron), 125
Giacometti, Alberto, 7
Gift giving, 136
"Gifts and Presents" (Emerson), 136
Gilbert, Shirley, 105
Go-between in marriage, 138
Goffman, Erving, 56, 76, 126, 132, 137,
  176
Golden Rule, 162
Golding, William, 3
Goodbye ritual, 137
Goodman, Paul, 98–99, 100, 170
Gorky, Arshile, 7
Gosho Heinosuke, 8
Grass, Günter, 3
Greetings, 55–57, 104–106
  nonverbal communication by, 137
Gross, Alan, 149–150
Grunwald, Henry, 187
Guillain, Robert, 115

Hall, Edward, 138, 143
Halloran, Richard, 156
Harappa, 17
Harlow, Harry F., 35, 141
Have I Told You Lately That I Love You?,
  29
Hayama, Edith Ching, 118–119
Help, giving and receiving, 149–150
Helping Scale, 148
Henley, Nancy, 139
Hesse, Hermann, 3, 189
Hierarchical relationship, 89
History, 11–12, 169–170
Hoffer, Eric, 18
Homans, George, 87, 179
Homecoming, The (Osaragi), 4
Homicide, 31
Hopper, Edward, 7
Howard, Jane, 83–84
"How to Enter a Hakan House" (Frake),
  46
Husbands and wives, 75
Huxley, Aldous, 3, 4
Hypocrisy, 113

Ichikawa Kon, 8
Identity clues, 59
Ikiru, 8

Imai Tadashi, 8
Inaccessibility to people, 21
Inadequacy, symptoms of, 185–188
Incline hypothesis, 94
Independence, 41, 164
Independent relationships, 88–89
Indifference to strangers, 54, 55
Individualism, 37, 186
Industrialization, 36–37
Infant communication, 101
Instant friendships, 130
Intensity of involvement, 93
Interaction frequency, 83
Interact Scale, 47, 96–92
Intercultural encounters, 189–192
Interpersonal challenge, 172–174
Interpersonal profiles, 39–44, 92–93
Intimacy Scale, 45
  and disclosure, 105
Intimate distance, 138
Ionesco, Eugène, 4, 5
Ishii Satoshi, 115–116
Isolation in cities, 27–29
I-thou relationships, 10, 74

Jackson, Don, 100
James, William, 160
Japanese Society (Nakane), 150
Japan's Modern Myth (Miller), 142
Jargon of bureaucracies, 24
Jericho, 17
Johannsen, R., 143
Jones, Tony, 73
Jourard, Sidney, 102, 103, 140
Jourard-Lasakow Self-Disclosure
  questionnaire, 103

Kafka, Franz, 3
Kaneko Mitshuharu, 2–3
Kano Tsutomu, 61
Kaplan, Abraham, 9, 71, 170
Kaplan, Robert, 160
Kaseki, 8
Kawara On, 7
Kees, Weldon, 125
Kelvin, Peter, 107–108, 141
Keniston, Kenneth, 25
Kimball, Arthur, 4
Kin. *See* Family
Kinugasa Teinosuke, 8
Kitano, 61
Kleenex friendships, 29
Klopf, Donald, 115–116
Kolker, Robert, 8
Krapp's Last Tape (Beckett), 5
Krauthammer, Charles, 190
Kudo Tetsumi, 7

Kuh, Katherine, 7
Kurosawa Akira, 8
Kusmin, Arnold, 104

LaGaipa, John, 148, 149
Laing, Ronald, 29, 147
Language. *See also* Conversation
  and intimacy, 97–121
  limits of, 122–123
  use of, 42
Lantz, Herman, 30
LaPlanche, J., 141
Laski, Harold, 116
Latané, Julie, 149–150
Lawrence, D. H., 3
Lebra, Takie, 114
LaBrun, Rico, 7
Lewin, Kurt, 60, 102
Life-styles, 25–26
Lindeman, Eduard, 98
Locale
  and acquaintances, 77–78
  power of, 23
  and strangers, 59–60
Lofland, Lyn, 22, 23, 53, 54, 59
Loneliness
  in cities, 27–29
  and disclosure, 106–107
  in Japan, 62
  pathology of, 30–31
Looking-glass self, 101
Love Scale, 44–45
Luft, Joseph, 107, 114
Lynch, James, 30
Lynd, Helen, 12

MacEachron, David, 187
McIntyre, Michael, 10
Macroacts, 132–133
Mahler, Irwin, 163
Malaise, symptoms of, 184–185
Manet, Edouard, 7
Man Vanishes, A, 8
Maraini, Fosco, 58
Marini, Marino, 7
Marriage, 158–159
Marx, Karl, 3, 74
Matisse, Henri, 7
Matson, Floyd, 97
Matsuyama Yukio, 186–187
Maugham, Somerset, 3
Mauss, Marcel, 136
Mead, George Herbert, 101, 161
Mead, Margaret, 25–26, 46
Mechanization, 29–30
Mehrabian, Albert, 122
Member of the Wedding (McCullers), 161

Microacts, 132–133
Middletown studies, 28
Miki Tomio, 8
Milgram, Stanley, 22
Miller, Arthur, 4, 149
Miller, Leslie, 154
Miller, Roy, 129–130, 142
Miró, Joan, 7
Mishima Yukio, 4
Mistrust of strangers, 54
Mita Munesuke, 11
Mizoguchi Kenji, 8
Mobility, 24–25
Modernization, 36–37
Modern Times, 8
Mohenjo-Daro, 17
Mono no aware, 8
Montagu, Ashley, 97, 121
Montaigne, Michel, 99
Monte Alban, 17
Moon and Sixpence, The (Maugham), 3
Morita Shoma, 61
Morris, Desmond, 20, 21, 124, 137
Motherwell, Robert, 8
Multiple-strand relations, 172
Music, popular, 8–9
Mutuality, 164

Nakane Chie, 31, 40, 61, 150, 185
Nakanishi Natsuyuki, 7
Naruse Mikio, 8
Nationality of companions, 80–81
Natsume Soseki, 4
New Images of Man (Tillich), 6–7
Nishiyama Kazuo, 32
No Exit (Sartre), 4
Nomura Naoki, 47
Noninvolvement, 29
Nonmeeting, tactics of, 29
Nonpersons, 40
Nonverbal communication, 42, 121–145
  conclusions on, 182–183
  in greetings, 137
  in Japan, 127–130
  in United States, 130–132
Nonverbal Communication (Ruesch &
  Kees), 125
Norbeck, Edward, 179
Nostalgia, 13
Notes from Underground (Dostoyevski), 3
Notte, La, 8
Novelists, 3–4
Nuclear family, 37
Nutritional density, 19

Object language, 125
Oe Kenzaburo, 4

Okamoto Shinjiro, 7
O'Neill, Eugene, 4
One-night stands, 29
Osaraji Jiro, 4
Outsiders, 40
Ozaki, Robert, 41, 43, 61, 116, 155, 156,
  163, 185
Ozu Yasujiro, 8

Packard, George, 190
Packard, Vance, 24, 28, 148
Painters, 6–8
Paolozzi, Eduardo, 7
Parlee, Mary, 45, 75, 177
Parmalee, Pat, 87
Pascal, Blaise, 79
Pathology
  of cities, 30–31
  social, 184–185
"Pattern of Criticism in Japan and United
  States" (Nomura & Barnlund), 46–47
Patterns of Culture (Benedict), 46
Patterson, Miles, 126
Paul, St., 99
Pedersen, Darhl, 140
Peers, 181
Peguy, Charles, 25
Penrose, Roland, 33
People-phobia, 61
Personal crisis, 106–107
Personal disclosure, 41–42
Personal distance, 138
Personality. See Self
Personal Matter, A (Oe), 4
Personal relations, 32–33
Personal space, 137–139
Person-specific relationships, 94
Pessimism, 1–2
Pfeiffer, John, 16, 18, 169
Phillips, Derek, 87
Philosophy, twentieth-century, 9–10
Physical accessibility to companions,
  81–82
Physical aggression, 30–31, 154
Physical communication. See Nonverbal
  communication
Physical Communication Scale, 48,
  132–133
Picasso, Pablo, 7, 113
Pinter, Harold, 4
Plato, 176
Play, as expression of affection, 141
Playwrights, 4–6
Poets, 2–3
Polansky, N. A., 45
Pontanlis, J., 141
Popular artists, 8–9

Population
  density. 19-20
  and urbanization, 18-20
Possessions, sharing of, 148-149
Potlatch ceremonies, 136
Privacy, 28
  and self, 101
  and strangers, 70
Propinquity of companions, 81-82
Prosocial efforts, 154-155
Proxemics, 138
Psychic challenge, 171-172
Public and Private Self in Japan and United States, 112, 140
Public distance, 138

Ramsey, Sheila, 191
Rashomon, 8
Reconciliation process, 43-44
Regression, 154
Reichel-Dolmatoff, Gerardo, 46
Reischauer, Edwin, 26, 40, 127, 129, 163, 185, 186
Relatives. *See* Family
Religion
  inspirational activities, 93-94
  of Japan, 38
Renoir, Jean, 8
Renoir, Pierre-Auguste, 7
Republic, The (Plato), 176
Resnais, Alain, 8
Resolving Social Conflicts (Lewin), 102
Revenge, 154
Rhetoric (Aristotle), 11
Richier, Germaine, 7
Rickers-Ovsiankina, Maria, 104
Riesman, David, 22
Rites of passage, 57-58
Roloff, Michael, 154
Roper organization, 59
Rosenberg, Harold, 113
Rosenblatt, Roger, 186
Rosenfeld, Howard, 138
Ruesch, Jurgen, 125
Ruined Map, The, 8
Rules of the Game, 8

Sacrifice and intimacy, 150
Saito Yoshishige, 7
Salinger, J. D., 3
Salk, Jonas and Jonathan, 20
Samurai tradition, 115, 131
Santayana, George, 161
Sartre, Jean-Paul, 3, 4
Satiation effect, 149
Scenes from a Marriage, 8
Schutz, William, 11-12

Sculptors, 7
Segal, George, 7
Segregation and avoidance, 153
Seidensticker, Edward, 62, 115, 142
Selden Hay study, 94
Self
  and communication, 101-104
  concepts of, 163-164
  disclosure of, 102
  ego incorporation, 160-164
Self-Disclosure Inventory, 109
Sensual expression, 141
Serial monogamy, 29
Seward, Jack, 43
Sex of companions, 81
Sexual expression, 141
Shannon, Claude, 11
Shapiro, Arnold, 124
Shared activities, 87-88, 181
Sharing possessions, 148-149
Shaw, G. B., 4
Shepherd, Tara, 154
Shintoism, 38
Shirono Itsuo, 156
Sian, 17
Significant others, 161
Sign language, 125
Silence, 100, 141-143
  Japanese and, 129
Silence, The, 8
Similarity and strangers, 66-67
Simmel, Georg, 101
Simon, Herbert, 193
Simon and Garfunkel, 8-9
Singer, Kurt, 42, 117
Single-strand relations, 172
Slater, Philip, 15, 25, 28, 192
Small talk, 99-100
Smith, Lillian, 194
Smith, T. V., 96
Snodgrass, Carrie, 162
Social activity
  and companions, 87
  in Japan, 185-186
Social distance, 138
Social Distance Scale, 44
Social exchange theory, 87
Social function of communication, 174
Social mobility, 25
Social order of cities, 22-27
Social Organization of the Manu'a (Mead), 46
Socrates, 12
"Song of Loneliness" (Kaneko Mitsuharu), 2-3
Spatial norms, 137-139
Spiritual crises, 3
Status and mobility, 25
Step hypothesis, 94

Steppenwolf (Hesse), 189
Still, Clyfford, 8
Stranger, The (Camus), 3
Strangers, 29. See also First impressions
    American attitudes about, 60
    attractive strangers, 65–66
    consequences of talking to, 67–68
    cultural contexts of, 180
    engagements with, 56–62
    evaluation of, 57–58
    initial encounters with, 64–65
    and intimacy, 70–71
    Japanese attitudes about, 61–62
    motive to communicate with, 64
    relations with, 39–40
Stranger Scale, 47, 63–64
Strangership, 62–68
Submission, 164
Suicide, 31
Sullivan, Harry Stack, 162
Supercities, 18–20
Sussman, Nan, 138
Sutherland, Richard, 147–148
Swenson, Clifford, 44–45, 124
Symbols, interaction of, 101
Sympathy, 161

Tanin, 61
Tanizaki, 4
Tapies, Antoni, 8
Target persons, 91
Tatara, 163
Taylor, Dalmas, 45, 101, 103–104, 105, 148–149
Temporary society, 25
Territoriality, 138
Teshigahara Hiroshi, 8
Theoretical density, 19
Three, Delos, 25
Tikal, 17
Tillich, Paul, 6–7
Time
    as commodity, 26–27
    for friends, 79, 83, 134–135
    and nonverbal communication, 134–135
Tokyo Story, 8
Touch, 139–140

Toynbee, Arnold, 21, 26, 54
Transcience, age of, 28
Transportation, 26
Trippet, Frank, 124

Unfocused interaction, 56
Urbanization, 18–20
    social consequences of, 20–22
Uruk, 17

Vandalism, 30–31
Van der Hag, 22
Van Dusen, Wilson, 161
Verbal aggression, 154
Verbal Communication Scale, 48, 109–110
    results of, 110–118
Verbal intimacy, 182
Vertical society, 31
Vulnerability, 107–108

Waiting for Godot (Beckett), 5
Wakabayashi Tsutomu, 7
Walster, Elaine and William, 55
Watson, Michael, 140
Watzlawick, Paul, 100
Wayne, Milton, 142
Weaver, Warren, 11
Werner, Carol, 87
We-they problem, 185
"Why Do Frenchmen?" (Bateson), 100
Women in the Dunes, The (Abe), 4
Wood, Margaret, 55, 70
Woolf, Virginia, 3
Words. See Language
Wright, Paul, 44

Yamanouchi Hisaaki, 4
Yoshihara Hideo, 7

Zen Buddhism, 142
Zoo Story (Albee), 5, 99